W9-AUE-528

DON GIOVANNI
Vocal Score

DON GIOVANNI
Vocal Score

Wolfgang Amadeus
MOZART

DOVER PUBLICATIONS, INC.
Mineola, New York

Don Giovanni in Full Score
is available in Dover edition 0-486-23026-0.

Bibliographical Note

This Dover edition, first published in 2004, is a republication of the edition originally published by G. Schirmer, New York, 1900. An introductory essay has been omitted.

International Standard Book Number: 0-486-43155-X

Manufactured in the United States of America
Dover Publications, Inc., 31 East 2nd Street, Mineola, N.Y. 11501

Il Dissoluto Punito

ossia

DON GIOVANNI

('The Libertine Punished, or Don Juan')

Opera buffa in two acts

K. 527 (1787)

Music by

WOLFGANG AMADEUS MOZART

Libretto by Lorenzo da Ponte

English Version by Natalie Macfarren

First performance

29 October, 1787, National Theatre, Prague

CHARACTERS

Don Giovanni, *a young and extremely licentious nobleman* .... baritone

Donna Anna, *a lady betrothed to Don Ottavio* .... soprano

Don Ottavio .... tenor

Il Commendatore .... bass

Donna Elvira, *a lady of Burgos, abandoned by Don Giovanni* .... soprano

Leporello, *servant of Don Giovanni* .... bass

Masetto, *lover of Zerlina* .... bass

Zerlina, *a peasant girl* .... soprano

Peasants, Musicians, Servants, Demons

Setting: A city in Spain (traditionally Seville)

ACT I

ACT II

* Numbers marked with an asterisk were added in 1788 for the Vienna production.

DON GIOVANNI

Vocal Score

Don Giovanni.

Overture.

Andante.

W. A. MOZART.

Tutti
Piano.
f
Strings
Fl.
Cl.
p
Ob.
Cl.
Fag.
Ob.
Fag.
Cor.
Tymp &c.
Vl.
p
sf
3
Strs
Tutti
sf
Strs.
Tutti
Ob.
Fag.
Fl.
Vl.
cresc.
p
f

Moderato.

Wind
Vln.
Fl.
Fag.
Vlns.
Vlns.
Wind
cresc.
Tutti

Tutti
Vlns
sf
p
Tutti
Vlns.
sf
p
Wind
Strs.
f
p
f
p
f
p
f
p
f
p
p
f

Ob.
Fl.
Ob.
Fl.
Str.
Fl.
Str.
Wind.

Vln.

cresc.
Wind.
Str.

Tutti.
f
Vln.
p
Vln.
Fag.

Act I.

Nº 1. Introduction.

Scene — A Garden, Night.

Leporello, in a cloak, discovered watching before the house of Donna Anna; then Donna Anna and Don Giovanni, afterwards the Commandant.

Molto allegro.
Piano.
Ob.
p
f
Strings & Fag.
Vlns.
(wrapt in a dark mantle, impatiently pacing to and fro before the steps to the palace).
Leporello.
L.
Not-te e gior-no fa - ti - car, per chi nul-la sa gra - dir; pio-va e
Rest I've none by night or day, Scant-y fare and doubtful pay, Ev-'ry
ven - to sop-por-tar, mangiar ma-le, e mal dor - mir!
whim I must ful - fil; Take my place who-ev-er will!
Vo - glio far il gen-til - uo - mo, e non
I my - self will go a - court-ing, I the
fp
Oh.
Fag.
tr

L.
vo-glio più ser - vir, e non vo-glio più ser - vir, no, no, no,
gen-tle-man will play, But with him no more I'll stay, No, no, no,
(facing the palace)
no, no, no, non vo-glio più ser-vir. Oh che ca-ro galant-
no, no, but with him no more I'll stay. Gaily he with-in is
uo-mo! Voi star den-tro col-la bel-la, ed io far la sen-ti-
sporting, I must keep off all in-trusion, For his lordship needs se-
nel-la, la sen-ti-nel-la, la sen-ti-nel-la! Vo - glio
clu-sion, he needs se clu-sion, he needs se-clu-sion. I my-
far il gen-til - uo-mo, e non vo-glio più ser-
self will go a-court-ing, I the gen-tle-man will
vir, e non vo-glio più ser-vir, No, no, no, no, no, no, non vo-glio
play, But with him no more I'll stay, No, no, no, no, no, but with him no
p
sf p
fp
f
tr

L.
più ser-vir. Ma mi par, che ven-ga gen-te; ma mi par, che venga
more I'll stay. Hark, I think I hear him coming, I'll keep safe out of his
L.
gen-te; non mi vo-glio far sen-tir, ah non mi vo-glio far sen-tir, non mi
way, here I'll keep safe out of his way, here I'll keep safe out of his way, But with
cresc.
f
p
L.
vo-glio far sen-tir, No, no, no, no, no, non mi vo-glio far sen-
him no more I'll stay, No, no, no, no, no, but with him no more I'll
L.
tir.
stay.
(Hides himself.)
Tutti.
cresc.
f
Donna Anna. (Holding Don Giovanni firmly by the arm.)
A.
(her voice sti-fled by agita-tion.)
Non spe-rar, se non m'uc-ci-di, ch'io ti la-sci fug-gir mai.
I will know, unless thou slay me, vile in-tru-der, who thou art.
Strings.
Tutti.
fp
fp
fp
f
p
f

Donna Anna. (her
Non spe-
I will
Don Giovanni. (Trying to conceal his features.)
Don-na fol-le! indar-no gri-di, chi son io, tu non sa-prai.
Stay me not, fair maid, I pray thee, I this in-stant must de-part.
Leporello.
Che tu-
'Tis my
Str.
voice gaining strength)
rar, se non m'uc-ci-di, ch'io ti la-sci fug-gir mai, non spe-
know, un-less thou slay me, vile in-tru-der, who thou art, I will
Don-na fol-le! in-dar-no gri-di, chi son io tu non sa-
Stay me not, fair maid I pray thee, I this instant must de-
mul-to! o ciel! che gri-di! Il pa-
mas-ter! these eyes be-tray me, Or to
(with full strength.)
rar, ch'io ti la-sci fug-gir mai. Gen-te! ser-vi al tra-di-to-re!
know, vile in-tru-der, who thou art! Help, oh heav'n! will none befriend me? (almost
prai, no, tu non sa-prai. Ta-ci, e
part, yes, I must de-part. May the
dron in nuo-vi guai.
fly he has at heart.
cresc.

(freeing herself)
A.
hissing; tries to cover her mouth)
Sce - le - ra - to!
Vile be-tray-er!
Sce - le - ra - to!
Vile be-tray-er!
G.
tre-ma al mio fu-ro - re!
fu-ries all at-tend thee!
Scon - si-glia-ta!
Fair en-slav-er!
Scon - si-glia-ta!
Fair en-slav-er!
L.
p
Sta a ve -
'Tis my
Str. & Cor.
f
p
cresc.
fp
p
(turning to the palace)
Gen - te! ser - vi!
Help, as-sistance!
(seizing her roughly)
f
Co-me fu-ria di - spe - ra - ta ti sa -
Heaven, come to my as - sistance, I'll pur -
Ta - ci, e tre-ma!
Hush, or tremble!
f
Que-sta fu-ria di-spe -
Thou shalt rue thy mad re -
f
der che il li - ber - ti - no mi fa - rà pre - ci - pi - tar.
master makes re-sistance, Hush, I'll list to what he saith.
Che tu -
'Tis my
Tutti.
f
prò per - se - gui - tar.
sue thee un - to death.
Co-me fu-ria di - spe - ra - ta, di - spe -
Heaven, oh, in mer-cy come to my as -
ra - ta mi vuol far pre - ci - pi - tar,
sistance, Silence, speak not 'bove thy breath!
Que-sta fu - ria di - spe -
Thou shalt rue thy mad re -
mul - to!
mas - ter!
oh ciel, che gri - di!
it is my mas - ter!
3

A.
ra - ta, ti sa - prò per -
sistance, I'll pur - sue thee
G.
ra - ta mi vuol far pre -
sistance, Hush, nor speak a -
L.
Sta a veder che il li - ber - ti - no mi fa - rà pre - ci - pi - tar, sta a veder che il li - ber -
'Tis my master makes resistance, Hush, I'll list to what he saith, 'Tis my master makes re -
A.
se - - gui - tar. Sce - le - ra - to! Sce - le -
un - - to death. Help, as - sistance! Help, as -
G.
ci - - pi - tar. Scon - si - gliata! Scon - si -
bove thy breath. Hush, or tremble! Hush, or
L.
ti - no mi fa - rà preci - pi - tar.
sistance, hush, I'll list to what he saith.
A.
ra - to! Gen - te! ser - vi! Co - me fu - ria di - spe -
sistance! Help, assistance! Heaven, come to my as -
G.
glia - ta! Ta - ci, e tre - ma! Que - sta
tremble! Hush or tremble! Thou shalt
L.
Sta a ve - der che il li - ber - ti - no mi fa - rà pre - ci - pi - tar.
'Tis my mas - ter makes re - sistance, I will list to what he saith.

A.
ra - ta, ti sa - prò per - se - gui - tar, co - me fu - ria di - spe -
sistance, I'll pur - sue thee un - to death. Heaven, oh in mer - cy
G.
fu - ria di - spe - ra - ta mi vuol far pre - ci - pi - tar, que - sta
rue thy mad re - sistance, Si - lence, speak not 'bove thy breath, thou shalt
L.
f
Che tu - mul - to, oh ciel, che gri - di!
'Tis my mas - ter, it is my mas - ter!
f
3
A.
ra - ta, di - spe - ra - ta, ti sa -
come to my as - sistance. I'll pur -
p
G.
fu - ria di - spe - ra - ta mi vuol
rue thy mad re - sistance. Hush, nor
p
L.
p
Sta a veder che il li - ber - ti - no mi fa - rà pre - ci - pi -
'Tis my master makes re - sistance, I will list to what he
Ob. Fag. & Str.
p
A.
prò per - se - gui - tar.
sue thee un - to death.
G.
far pre - ci - pi - tar.
speak a - bove thy breath,
L.
tar, sta a veder che il li - ber - ti - no mi fa - rà pre - ci - pi - tar, sta a veder che il li - ber -
saith, 'tis my master makes resistance, I will list to what he saith, 'tis my master makes re -

A.
ti sa-prò per - se - gui -
I'll pur - sue thee un - to
G.
mi vuol far pre - ci - pi -
hush, nor speak a - bove thy
L.
ti-no mi fa-rà pre-ci-pi-tar, sta a veder che il li-ber-ti-no mi fa-rà pre-ci-pi-
sistance, I will list to what he saith,'tis my master makes re-sistance, I will list to what he
(Seeing the Commandant approach, she runs into the house.)
tar.
death.
(Don Giovanni haughtily confronts the Commandant.)
tar.
breath.
(The Commandant enters hastily, a torch in his left hand, a sword in his right.)
tar.
saith.
Tutti.
ff
ff
The Commandant. (with agitation, but energetically)
C.
Lascia-la, in-de-gno, ba - ti - ti me-co!
Miscreant, unhand her, draw, and de-fend thee!
p
cresc.
Don Giovanni. (slightingly)
G.
Va, non mi de-gno di pu-gnar te-co.
Fly, or I warn thee, to death I'll send thee.
C.
Co-sì pre - ten - di
Cai-tiff, and cow - ard,
f
p
f

G.
C.
L.
Va, non mi de - gno, no!
Beware my an - ger, fly!
da me fug-gir?
thus wouldst thou fly?
Co-sì pre-ten-di da
Caitiff and cow-ard, thus
Leporello.
(Po-tessi al-me - no di quà par-tir!
(How can I safe - ly from hither fly?
mezza voce
più voce
(draws)
Mi - se-ro!
(Die he must!)
Mi - se-ro!
Die thou must!
Mi-
Grey-
me fug-gir?
wouldst thou fly?
Ba - ti - ti!
Guard thyself!
po-tessi al - me - no di quà par-tir!)
How can I safe - ly from hith - er fly?)
(He strikes the torch out of the Commandant's hand.)
(First bout; the Commandant attacks.)
se - ro! at - ten - di se vuoi mo - rir!
beard, come on then, if thou wilt die!
(They fight.)
(2nd bout: Don G. attacks.)
(3rd bout.)
(The Commandant falls mortally wounded.)

(The moon rises slowly;
Andante.
Don Giovanni. sotto voce.
G.
Ah! già ca - de il scia - gu -
Rash old man, I — have un -
The Commandant. (sinking slowly, leaning on his sword)
C.
Ah! soc - cor - so! son tra - di - to! l'as - sas -
Help! as - sistance! all is end - ed! Oh! to
Leporello.
L.
Qual mi - sfat - to!
Oh my mas - ter!
Andante.
Vls. Ob. & Cor.
pp
lights appear in the palace-windows: great excitement within: servants hasten with torches across the background behind the closed gate)
ra - to, af - fan - no - so e a - go - niz - zan - te già dal
done thee! In the pangs of — death thou'rt ly - ing! Mine's the
si - no m'ha fe - ri - to, e dal
die a - lone un - friended, Vile as -
Qual ec - ces - so! En - tro il sen dal - lo spa -
naught will mend thee! Thou wilt rue this woe - ful
se - no pal - pi - tan - te veg - go l'a - ni - ma par -
deed, there's no de - ny - ing, Why to fight was I be -
se - no pal - pi - tan - te
sas - sin, Thoust un - done me!
ven - to pal - pi - tar il cor mi sen - to!
er - ror, Deed of dark - ness, deed of ter - ror!

(Servants return with Don Octavio, and hasten with him from the street into the palace)
G.
tir, veg - go l'a - ni - ma par - tir, già dal
guil'd? why to fight was I be - guil'd? Mine's the
C.
sen - to l'a - ni - ma par - tir,
Heav'n pro - tect and guard my child!
L.
Io non sò che far, che dir, io non sò che far, che dir, en - tro il sen dal - lo spa-
Why to stay was I beguil'd? why to stay was I beguil'd? He will rue this wo - ful
G.
se - no pal - pi - tan - te veg - go l'a - ni - ma par -
deed, there's no de - nying, Why to fight was I be -
C.
sen - to l'a - ni - ma par -
Heav'n pro - tect and guard my
L.
ven - to pal - pi - tar il cor mi sen - to, io non sò che far, che dir, io non sò che far, che
er - ror, Deed of darknees, deed of ter - ror, Why to stay was I be - guil'd? Why to stay was I be -
G.
tir.
guil'd?
(Dies.)
C.
tir.
child!
L.
dir!
guil'd?
Ob.
Vln.
p
Fl.
Fag.

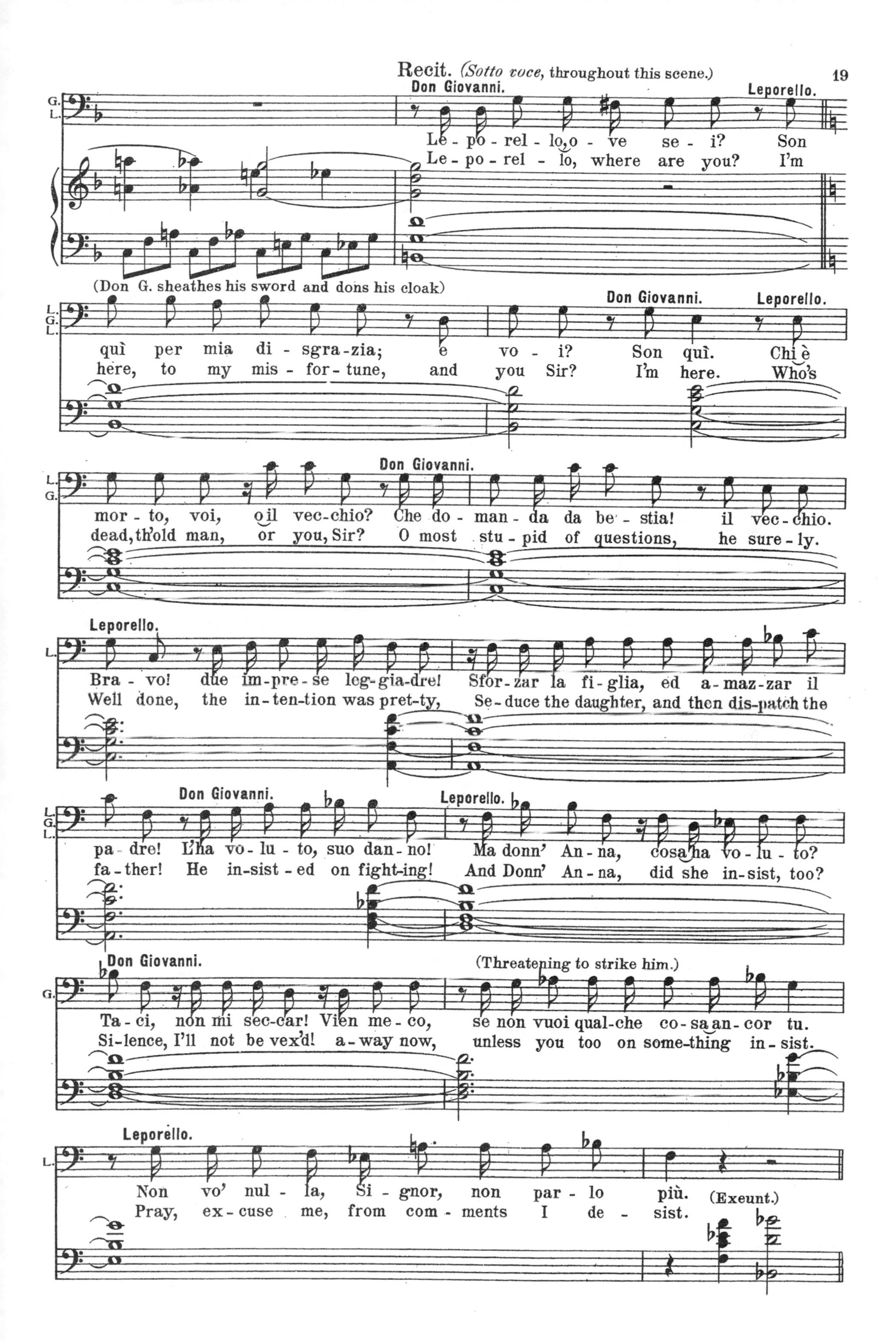
Recit. (Sotto voce, throughout this scene.)
G.
L.
Don Giovanni.
Le-po-rel-lo, o-ve se-i?
Le-po-rel-lo, where are you?
Leporello.
Son
I'm
(Don G. sheathes his sword and dons his cloak)
L.
G.
L.
quì per mia di-sgra-zia; e vo-i?
here, to my mis-for-tune, and you Sir?
Don Giovanni.
Son quì.
I'm here.
Leporello.
Chi è
Who's
L.
G.
mor-to, voi, o il vec-chio?
dead, th'old man, or you, Sir?
Don Giovanni.
Che do-man-da da be-stia! il vec-chio.
O most stu-pid of questions, he sure-ly.
Leporello.
L.
Bra-vo! due im-pre-se leg-gia-dre! Sfor-zar la fi-glia, ed a-maz-zar il
Well done, the in-ten-tion was pret-ty, Se-duce the daughter, and then dis-patch the
L.
G.
L.
pa-dre!
fa-ther!
Don Giovanni.
L'ha vo-lu-to, suo dan-no!
He in-sist-ed on fight-ing!
Leporello.
Ma donn' An-na, cosa ha vo-lu-to?
And Donn' An-na, did she in-sist, too?
Don Giovanni.
G.
Ta-ci, non mi sec-car! Vien me-co,
Si-lence, I'll not be vex'd! a-way now,
(Threatening to strike him.)
se non vuoi qual-che co-sa an-cor tu.
unless you too on some-thing in-sist.
Leporello.
L.
Non vo' nul-la, Si-gnor, non par-lo più.
Pray, excuse me, from com-ments I de-sist.
(Exeunt.)

20
Donna Anna. (agitatedly descending the steps with D. Octavio, and servants bearing torches)
Don Octavio. (Raising his drawn sword.)
Ah! del padre in pe-ri-glio in soc-cor-so vo-liam! Tut-to il mio san-gue
Ah! my fa-ther's in dan-ger, let us haste to his aid! I will de-fend him
ver-se-rò, se bi-so-gna: ma dov'è il sce-le-ra-to?
Donna Anna.
In que-sto lo-co.
with this sword, with my life-blood! But where is the as-sas-sin? 'Twas here I left him.
Attacca.
Nº 2. "Ma qual mai s'offre, oh Dei."
Recit. and Duet.
Allegro assai.
Fl. Ob. Vln.
Viol. Fag. Cor.
(Seeing the corpse) Donna Anna.
Ma qual mai s'of-fre, oh Dei, spet-ta-co-lo fu-ne-sto agli oc-chi mie-i!
What is this I be-hold? Can I believe my senses? Ah me un-happy!
(sinks down beside the body)
Il
My

(throws herself upon the corpse)
D. Octavio.
D. Anna.
A.
O.
A.
Padre, padre mi-o! mio ca-ro padre! Si-gnore! Ah, l'assas-si-no mel tru-ci-
Father, oh my father, look but upon me! Oh ter-ror! Ah, by th'as-sas-sin art thou un-
(examining the corpse more carefully)
dò. Quel san-gue quel-la pia-ga
done! Thou'rt wounded blood is flowing
Cl. Ob. Fag.
f
p
quel volto tin-to e co-per-to del co-lor di mor-te.
this pallor! Si-lent and pale, thou heed-est not my cry-ing!
(D. Octavio offers to raise her; she refuses)
Ei non re-spi-ra più! fred-de le
I cannot hear him breathe! Cold, cold as
(she rises)
(she reels)
membra! Pa-dre mi-o! ca-ro padre! pa-dre a-mato!
marble! Oh my father, best of fathers! an-swer me, father!
Strgs. f
Vln.
Wind.

(D. Octavio supports her, and leads her to the stone seat)
A.
O.
io manco!
oh help me!
Vln.
Wind.
io moro!
I die!
Don Octavio. (to the servants)
Ah! soccor-re-te, a-mi-ci, il mio te-
Oh, by this dire af-fliction her mind's dis-
Maestoso.
O.
so-ro! cer-ca-te-mi, re-ca-te-mi qualche o-
tract-ed! As-sist me, friends, oh leave us not, Give me
Strgs.
maestoso
(A maid-servant hurries into the palace, and returns immediately with a smelling-bottle, which she offers to D. Anna)
Andante.
O.
dor, qual-che spirto! ah non tar-da-te! Donn' Anna! sposa!
aid_ bring some wa-ter, oh bring it quickly! Donn' Anna! dearest!
p
O.
a-mi-ca! il duolo e-stre-mo la meschi-nella uc-ci-de!
oh hear me! Her grief ex-treme hath cru-el-ly o-verwhelm'd her.
f
sfp
p
D. Ann.
Don Octavio.
A.
O.
A.
Ahi! Già rin-vie-ne! da-te-le nuo-vi a-ju-ti.
Ah! She a-wakens, New-ly re-vives her sorrow.
Donna Anna. (with a deep sigh)
Pa-dre mi-o!
Oh my father!
Don Octavio. (to servants)
O.
Ce-la-te, al-lon-ta-na-te agli oc-chi suo-i quel-l'og-get-to d'or-
Oh hasten, and bear a-way, ere she per-ceive it, this me-mo-rial of

(Serving-men raise the Commandant, and bear him into the palace)
rore! A - ni-ma mi-a, con-so-la-ti!
terror! Look up, my dearest, oh, turn to me!
Allegro.
Donna Anna. (springing up and repulsing Don Octavio as if insane)
fa co - re! Fug - gi, cru - de - le, fug - gi! la - scia, che mora anch'i-o!
I'm near thee! Cru - el, why art thou near me? Leave me a - lone to perish!
Strgs.
O - ra ch'è morte, o Di - o! chi a me la vi - - ta diè.
Since he I most did cher-ish Is lost for ev- - er - more!
Don Octavio.
Sen-ti, cor mio, deh sen - ti, guar - da-mi un so - - lo i -
Listen to me, oh, list - en, Turn but thine eyes up -
stante, ti par - la il ca - ro a-mante, che vi - - ve sol per
on me, I know thou'lt not dis-own me, Who love thee ev- - er -

Donna Anna. (perceiving her error, and giving Don Octavio her hand)
O.
A.
te. Tu sei_ per-don, mio be - ne, l'af - fan - no mi - o, le
more. 'Tis thou_ for-give, oh, dear - est, Of all now left me the
fp
p
(approaching the spot where the Commandant fell)
Don Octavio.
A.
O.
pe - ne. Ah, il pa-dre mio dov' è? Il padre?
nearest, My fa-ther I would see! Your father?
Vln.
cresc.
O.
Lascia, o ca-ra, la ri-membran-za a-ma-ra!
Hush, oh, dearest, Breathe not the word thou fearest,
Strgs.
Ob. Fag.
f
fp
mf
p
Donna Anna.
O.
A.
hai_ spo-so e pa-dre in me. Ah! il
Thou'st hus-band and fa - ther in me. Ah! my
Fl.
Don Octavio.
A.
O.
pa-dre, il pa-dre mio dov' è? Lascia, o ca-ra,
fa-ther, my fa-ther I would see! Hush, oh dearest,
cresc.
f
sfp

O.
La ri-mem-bren-za a-ma-ra! hai spo-so e pa - dre, hai
Breathe not the world thou fearest, thou'st hus-band and fa - ther, thou'st
mf
p
(D. Anna, going to the other side, stands with lofty demeanor opposite Don Octavio)
spo-so e pa - dre in me.
husband and fa - ther in me.
Tutti.
fp
f
Donna Anna.
A.
Ah! vendi - car, se il puo - i, giu - ra quel sangue ognor!
Ah! if thou canst, a-venge him, swear it by heav'n a - bove!
Strgs.
Maestoso.
Don Octavio. (raising his hand as for taking an oath)
Lo giu - ro, lo giu - ro, lo giu - ro a - gli oc-chi tuo - i, Lo giu - ro al no - stro a - mor!
I swear it, I swear it, by heav'n I will a - venge him, I swear it by our love!
Adagio in tempo.
3
p
Tempo I.
Donna Anna.
Che giu - ra - mento, oh
Oh vow of wrath and
Don Octavio.
Che giu - ra - mento, oh
Oh vow of wrath and
Tutti.
cresc.

A.
De - i! che bar - ba-ro mo-men-to!
ter - ror! Oh night of dread la-ment-ing!
O.
De - i! che bar - ba-ro mo-men-to!
ter - ror! Oh night of dread la-ment-ing!
Fl. Ob. Fag.
sfp
cresc.
sfp
A.
tra cen-to af-fet - ti e cen-to vammi on-deg-gian-do il cor, tra
Oh when will heav'n re - lent-ing grant us of hope a ray, Oh
O.
tra cen-to af-fet - ti e cen-to vammi on-deg-gian-do il cor, tra
Oh when will heav'n re - lent-ing grant us of hope a ray, Oh
Vln.
Cor.
Ob.
Fag.
A.
cen-to af - fet - ti e cen- -to vam-mi on - deg - gian - do il cor.
when will heav'n re - lent - ing grant us of hope a ray.
O.
cen-to af - fet - ti e cen- -to vam-mi on - deg - gian - do al cor.
when will heav'n re - lent - ing grant us of hope a ray.
Winds.
Strgs.
sfp
sfp
sf
sf
p
f
A.
Ven-di - car quel san-gue, giu - ra!
If thou canst, a - venge him, swear it!
O.
Lo giu - ro a -
I swear it, I
p
f

O.
gli oc - - chi tuo - i, al no - - stro a-mor!
will a - venge him, I swear it by our love!
Vlns.
p
p
D. Anna.
A.
Che giu - ra - men - to, oh De - i!
Oh vow of wrath and ter - ror!
D. Octavio.
O.
Che giu - ra - men - to, oh De - i!
Oh vow of wrath and ter - ror!
cresc.
fp
A.
che bar - ba-ro mo - men-to! Tra cen - to af-fet - ti e
Oh night of wild la - menting! Oh when will heav'n re-
O.
che bar - ba-ro mo - men-to! Tra cen - to af-fet - ti e
Oh night of wild la - menting! Oh when will heav'n re-
cresc.
sfp
p
p
A.
cen - to vam-mi on-deg-gian - do il cor, tra cen-to af - fet - ti e
lent-ing grant us of hope a ray, Oh when will heav'n re -
O.
cen - to vam-mi on-deg-gian - do il cor, tra cen-to af - fet - ti e
lent-ing grant us of hope a ray, Oh when will heav'n re -

A.
cen- -to vam-mi on-deg - gian - do il cor, vam-mi on - deg-
lent- -ing grant us of hope a ray, oh when will
O.
cen- -to vam-mi on-deg - gian - do il cor,
lent- -ing grant us of hope a ray,
fp
fp
f
p
A.
gian- - - - - -do, on - deg - gian- -do il
heav'n grant of hope a
O.
vam - mi on - deg - gian- -do il cor, vam- -mi on - deggian - do il
Oh when will heav'n re - lent - ing grant of hope a
cresc.
f
p
Viola.
A.
cor, vam-mi on-deg - gian- - - - - -do, on-deg-
ray, oh when will heav'n grant of
O.
cor, vam- -mi on-deg - gian- -do il cor, vam -
ray, oh when will heav'n re - lent - ing
cresc.
f
p
A.
gian- -do il cor, vam - mi on - deg - gian- -do il cor,
hope a ray, when will heav'n grant to us,
O.
mi on - deg-gian - do il cor, vam - mi on - deg - gian- -do il cor,
grant of hope a ray, when will heav'n grant to us,
f

A.
Vam-mi on - deg - gian - do il cor, vam - mi on - deg - gian-
Grant us of hope a ray, When will heav'n grant
O.
Vam-mi on - deg - gian - do il cor, vam - mi on - deg - gian-
Grant us of hope a ray, When will heav'n grant
p
A.
-do il cor, vammi on-deg-gian-do il cor, vam -
to us, Grant us of hope a ray, Oh!
O.
-do il cor, vammi on-deg-gian-do il cor, vam -
to us, Grant us of hope a ray, Oh!
f
p
A.
mi on - deggian - do il cor, vam - mi on - deggian - do il cor, on - deg - gian - do il
when will heav - en Grant to us of hope a ray, Grant of hope a
O.
mi on - deggian - do il cor, vam - mi on - deggian - do il cor, on - deg - gian - do il
when will heav - en Grant to us of hope a ray, Grant of hope a
cresc.
A.
cor!
ray!
(Exeunt slowly into palace)
O.
cor!
ray!
(Curtain falls rapidly.)
f
f

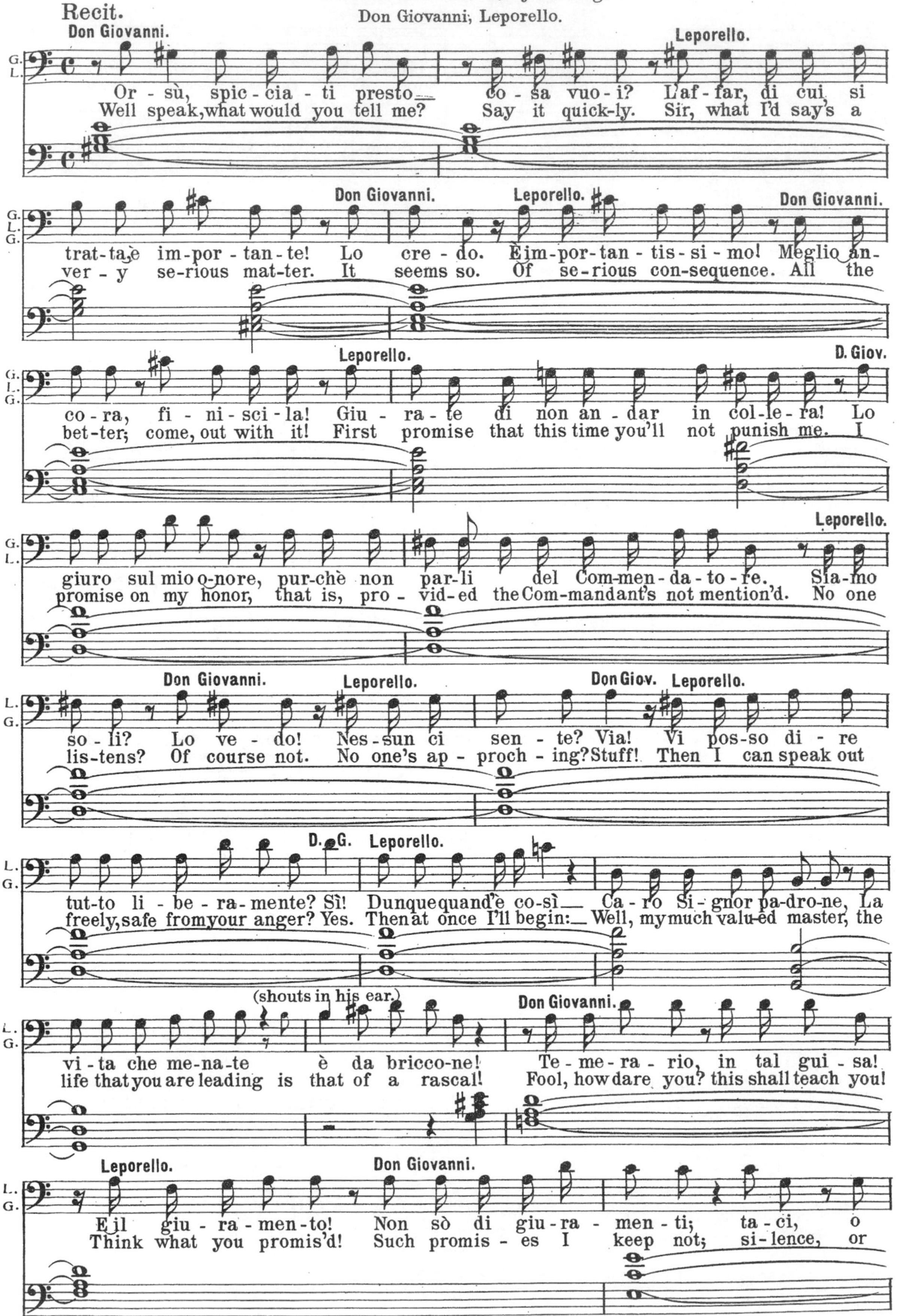
Scene.__A Street; Early morning.
Recit.
Don Giovanni; Leporello.
Don Giovanni.
Or - sù, spic - cia - ti presto__ co - sa vuo - i?
Well speak, what would you tell me? Say it quick-ly.
Leporello.
L'af - far, di cui si trat - ta, e im - por - tan - te!
Sir, what I'd say's a ver - y se-rious mat-ter.
Don Giovanni.
Lo cre - do.
It seems so.
Leporello.
È im - por - tan - tis - si - mo!
Of se - rious con-sequence.
Don Giovanni.
Meglio an - co - ra, fi - ni - sci - la!
All the bet-ter; come, out with it!
Leporello.
Giu - ra - te di non an - dar in col - le - ra!
First promise that this time you'll not punish me.
D. Giov.
Lo giuro sul mio o-nore, purchè non par-li del Com-men - da - to - re.
I promise on my honor, that is, pro - vid - ed the Com-mandant's not mention'd.
Leporello.
Sia-mo so - li?
No one lis-tens?
Don Giovanni.
Lo ve - do!
Of course not.
Leporello.
Nes-sun ci sen - te?
No one's ap - proch - ing?
Don Giov.
Via!
Stuff!
Leporello.
Vi pos-so di - re tut-to li - be - ra-mente?
Then I can speak out freely, safe from your anger?
D. G.
Sì!
Yes.
Leporello.
Dunque quand'e co-sì__ Ca - ro Si - gnor pa-dro-ne, La vi - ta che me-na-te è da bricco-ne!
Then at once I'll begin:__ Well, my much valu-ed master, the life that you are leading is that of a rascal!
(shouts in his ear.)
Don Giovanni.
Te - me - ra - rio, in tal gui - sa!
Fool, how dare you? this shall teach you!
Leporello.
E il giu - ra - men - to!
Think what you promis'd!
Don Giovanni.
Non sò di giu - ra - men - ti; ta - ci, o
Such promis - es I keep not; si - lence, or

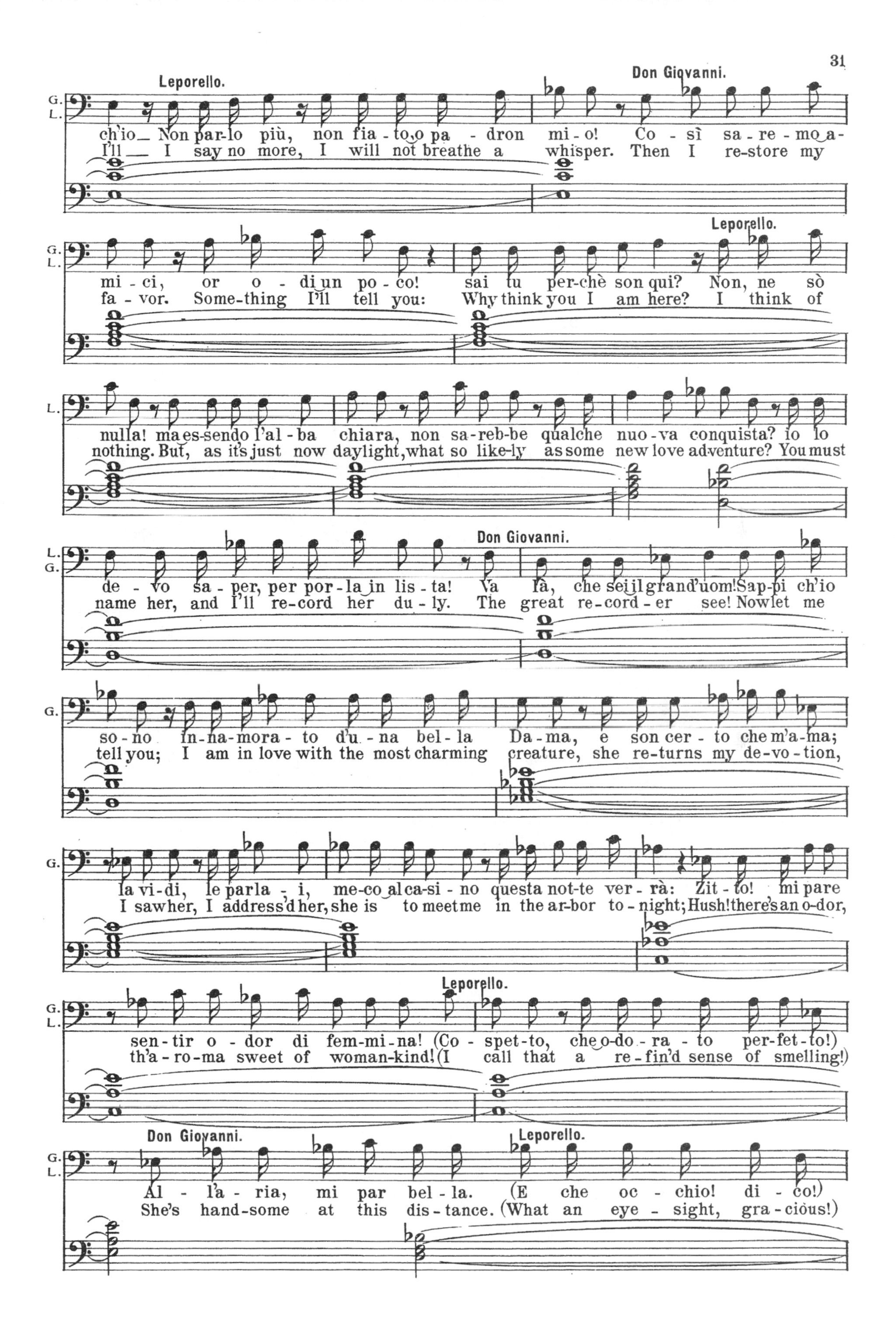
Leporello.
Don Giovanni.
ch'io_ Non par-lo più, non fia-to o pa - dron mi-o! Co - sì sa-re-mo a-
I'll _ I say no more, I will not breathe a whisper. Then I re-store my
mi-ci, or o - di un po-co! sai tu per-chè son qui?
Leporello.
Non, ne sò
fa-vor. Some-thing I'll tell you: Why think you I am here? I think of
nulla! ma es-sendo l'al-ba chiara, non sa-reb-be qualche nuo-va conquista? io lo
nothing. But, as it's just now daylight, what so like-ly as some new love adventure? You must
de - vo sa - per, per por-la in lis-ta!
Don Giovanni.
Va là, che sei il grand'uom! Sap-pi ch'io
name her, and I'll re-cord her du-ly. The great re-cord-er see! Now let me
so-no in-na-mora-to d'u-na bel-la Da-ma, e son cer-to che m'a-ma;
tell you; I am in love with the most charming creature, she re-turns my de-vo-tion,
la vi-di, le parla - i, me-co al ca-si-no questa not-te ver-rà: Zit-to! mi pare
I saw her, I address'd her, she is to meet me in the ar-bor to-night; Hush! there's an o-dor,
sen-tir o-dor di fem-mi-na!
Leporello.
(Co-spet-to, che o-do-ra-to per-fet-to!)
th'a-ro-ma sweet of woman-kind! (I call that a re-fin'd sense of smelling!)
Don Giovanni.
Al - l'a-ria, mi par bel-la.
Leporello.
(E che oc - chio! di - co!)
She's hand-some at this dis-tance. (What an eye - sight, gra-cious!)

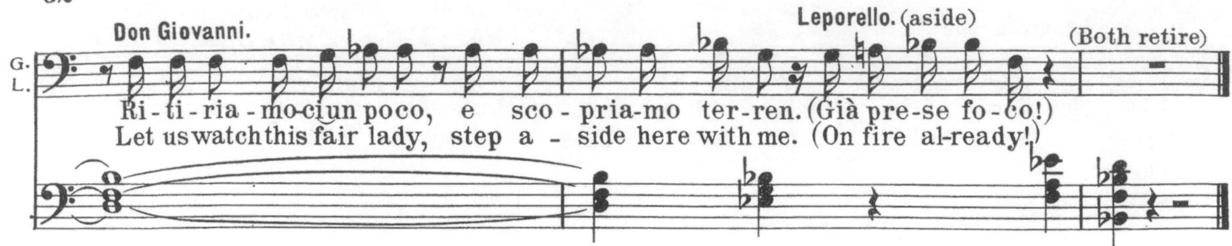
Don Giovanni.
Leporello. (aside)
(Both retire)
G.
L.
Ri-ti-ria-mo ci un poco, e sco-pria-mo ter-ren. (Già pre-se fo-co!)
Let us watch this fair lady, step a-side here with me. (On fire al-ready!)

Nº 3. "Ah! chi mi dice mai."

Trio.

Donna Elvira (in a travelling-dress); Don Giovanni, and Leporello.

Allegro.
Tutti.
Vlns.
Tutti.
Vlns.
Cl. Fag.
Donna Elvira. (facing the auditorium throughout the entire scene)
E.
Ah! chi mi di-ce ma-i, quel bar-ba-ro dov' è? che
Where shall I find a to-ken to guide my steps to thee? My
E.
per mio scor-no a-ma-i, che mi man-cò di
heart is near-ly bro-ken, the world is dark to

E.
fè? che mi man - cò di fè?
me, all, all is dark to me!
cresc.
sf
sfp
(D. Giovanni and Leporello reappear)
Ah! se ri - tro- -vo l'empio,
Ah! If he stood be - fore me,
(Leporello busies himself with Don Giovanni's attire, helps him draw on
e a me non tor- -na an - cor, vo'
Pierce - ly his vows I'd spurn, The
his gloves, etc.)
far- -ne or - ren- -do scem- -pio, gli
love that once he bore me, Can
fp
vo' ca - var il cor, gli vo' ca - var il
nev- -er - more re - turn, can nev - er - more re -
f

Don Giovanni. (to Leporello)
E.
G.
cor! U - di - sti? qualche bel - la, dal_ va - go ab-ban - do -
turn! Look yon-der, 'tis a dam-sel Who's by her swain for-
p
Donna Elvira.
G.
E.
na - ta? Vo' far - - ne or-ren - - do scem - pio, gli
sak-en! The love that once he bore me Can
fp
fp
fp
fp
Don Giovanni. (with contemptuous pity)
E.
G.
vo' ca-var il cor! Po - ve - ri - na! Po - ve - ri - na!
nev - er-more re - turn! Ah, poor girl, her grief be - comes her!
fp
fp
p
Donna Elvira.
E.
Gli vo' ca - var il__ cor, sì, gli vo' ca - var il__
Can nev-er - more re - turn, no, can nev-er - more re -
f
p
f
Don Giovanni. (to Leporello)
Leporello. (aside)
E.
G.
L.
cor! Cerchiam di con-so - la - re il suo tor - men-to. Co - sì ne con-so -
turn! I think I'll go and try just to con - sole her. No doubt, like man-y
p

L.
E.
Donna Elvira.
lò mil-le e ot-to cen-to. Ah! chi mi di-ce
oth-ers you'll ca-jole her. Where shall I find a
(Leporello steals about Donna Elvira to catch sight of her face; unsuccessful, he informs his
master pantomimically of his failure)
ma-i, quel bar-ba-ro dov' è? che per mio scor-no a-
token to guide my steps to thee? My heart is near-ly
ma-i, che mi man-cò di fè? che
bro-ken, the world is dark to me, all,
mi man-cò di fè?
all is dark to me!
Ah, se ri-tro-vo l'em-pio,
Ah, if he stood be-fore me,
f
p
cresc.
sfp

E.
e a me non for - na an - cor, vo'
Fierce - ly his vows I'd spurn, The
cresc.
fp
far - ne or-ren - do scem - pio, gli vo' ca-var il
love that once he bore me Can nev - er-more re -
fp
Don Giovanni.
Donna Elvira.
E.
G.
cor! Po - ve - ri - na! Po - ve - ri - na! Gli vo' ca - var il
turn. Ah, poor girl, her grief be - comes her! Can nev-er - more re -
p
f
Don Giovanni.
cor, sì, gli vo' ca - var il cor! Cerchiam di con - so -
turn, no, can nev-er - more re - turn. I think I'll go and
Leporello (aside)
G.
L.
la - re il suo tor - men - to. Co - sì ne con - so - lò mil - le e ot - to
try just to con - sole her. No doubt like many oth - ers you'll ca -

Donna Elvira.
E.
Gli vo' ca-va - - - - - re il cor, gli vo' ca-va-
His love can ne'er re - turn, his love can ne'er
L.
cen-to.
jole her.
f
p
(Don Giovanni clears his throat several times, to attract
- - - - - - re il cor, gli
re - turn, his
Donna Elvira's notice; she does not hear him, but grows more and more excited. Finally his patience
vo' cavar il cor, ca - - var il
love can ne'er re - turn, can ne'er re - -
cresc.
gives way, and he steps up to Donna Elvira boldly, but politely.)
Don Giovanni.
(raising his hat)
D. Elvira.
E.
G.
cor! Si - gno - ri - na! Si - gno - ri - na! Chi è
turn! Fair Se - ño - ra! fair Se - ño - ra! That
cresc.

Recit.
Don Giovanni. (starting back; mezza voce)
Leporello. (aside)
Donna Elvira. (indignantly)
là? Stel - le! che ve - do! O bel - la! Don-na El-vi-ra! Don Gio -
voice! She? oh! con - fu - sion! How charming! Don-na El-vi-ra! Don Gio -
van-ni! sei qui? mostro! fel-lon! ni-do d'in - ganni! Che ti-to-li cruscan-ti!
van-ni! You here? Falsest of men! Monster of baseness! (Now compliments are passing!
man-co ma - le che lo co - no - sce be - ne. Via, ca - ra Donna El -
Waste of words, she by this time ought to know him.) El - vi - ra dear, I
vi - ra, cal - ma - te que - sta col - le - ra! sen - ti - te, la -
pray you, re - strain that voice im - pet - u - ous! now lis - ten, and
sciа - te-mi par - lar! Co - sa puoi di - re, do-po a-zion si ne - ra? In ca-sa
I will tell you all. What can you say that will ex - cuse your falsehood? First you be -
mi - a en-tri fur-ti-va-men-te, a for - za d'ar - te, di giu-ramen-ti e
sought me se-cret-ly to re-ceive you, with vows of fond-ness, oaths of de-vo-tion,
di lu - sin-ghe ar - ri - vi a se - dur - re il cor mi - o; m'in - na -
love e - ter - nal pro - fess - ing, I be - lieved that you loved me, in your

E.
mo - ri, o cru-de - le! mi di - chia - ri tua spo - sa, e poi, man-
hon - or con-fid-ing when your wife you de-clared me; then on a
E.
can-do del-la ter-ra e del ciel al san - to drit-to, con e-nor - me de-lit - to
sud-den, cast-ing off ev-'ry tie of earth and heaven that our hearts had u-ni-ted,
E.
do - po tre dì da Bur-gos t'al - lon - ta - ni, m'ab-ban-do - ni, mi
af - ter three days from Bur-gos you de - part-ed; I, for-sa-ken, dis -
E.
fug - gi, e la-sci in pre-da al ri-mor - so ed al pian - to per pe-na for - se
tract-ed, was left a prey to re-morse and bit - ter weep-ing, for I, a-las, had
Leporello (aside)
Don Giovanni.
E.
L.
G.
che t'a-mai co - tan - to. (Pa-re un li - bro stam-pa-to!) Oh in quanto a que-sto
learnt to love you dear-ly. (She says it off like a les-son.) For my de-par-ture
(to Leporello)
Leporello. (ironically)
G.
L.
eb - bi le mie ra - gio - ni! è ve - ro? È ve - ro!
I had im-port - ant rea-sons. You know them? I know them.
Donna Elvira. (to Don Giovanni)
L.
E.
e che ra-gio - ni for - ti! E qua - li so - no, se non la tua per-
Oh, such im-port-ant rea-sons! What oth - er rea-sons than your in-con-stant

E.
fi - dia, la leg-ge - rez-za tu - a? Ma il giu - sto cie - lo vol - le ch'io ti tro -
heart, that will fol-low ev-'ry fan-cy? But heav'n has led me hither that I might
E.
G.
Don Giovanni.
vas - si, per far le sue, le mie ven - det - te. Eh vi - a, sia - te più ra - gio -
warn you to stay your wild career of fol - ly. Come, come, you'll not let me ex - cul -
G.
ne - vo - le: (mi po - ne a ci - men - to co - stei.) se non cre - de - te al lab - bro
pate my - self (This woman will soon drive me mad.) Since you, a - las, will not be -
G.
L.
Leporello.
D. Giov. (to Lep. aloud)
mi - o, cre - de - te a que - sto ga - lant - uo - mo. (Sal - vo il ve - ro.) Via, dil - le un
lieve me, Then let this hon - est fel - low tell you. (Honest tru - ly.) Go, tell her
G.
L.
E.
Leporello. (aside to Don Giovanni)
Don Giovanni. (aloud)
D. Elv. (to Lep.)
po - co. (E co - sa de - vo dir - le?) Sì, sì, dil - le pur tut - to. Eb -
plain - ly. (What - ev - er shall I tell her?) Yes, yes, keep nothing from her. Pro -
E.
L.
(Don Giovanni escapes.)
Leporello.
ben, fa pre - sto! Ma - da - ma, ve - ra - men - te, in que - sto
ceed, what is it? Well, Ma - dam, it is cer - tain this world we
L.
E.
Donna Elvira.
mon - do con - cios - sia - co - sa quan - do fos - se che Il quadro non è ton - do! Scia - gu -
live in I mean to say, perhaps, that is, I mean, You cannot square a circle! Heartless
E.
(Turning as if to Don Giovanni)
ra - to! Co - sì del mio do - lor gio - co ti pren - di? Ah
vil - lain! Dare you thus to in - sult my just re - sent - ment? And

Leporello.
E.
L.
voi! stel-le! l'i-ni-quo fug-gì! mi-se-ra me! do-ve? in qual par-te? Eh, la-
you, oh heav'n! he basely has fled! oh wretched me! whither? was it that way? Come, be
L.
E.
Donna Elvira.
scia-te che va-da; e-gli non mer-ta che di lui ci pen-sia-te. Il scel-le-
thankful he's left you; waste not your an-ger, he's not worth a re-gret. But by his
Leporello. (Donna Elvira turns to the bench before the
E.
L.
ra-to m'in-gan-no, mi tra-dì! Eh, con-so-la-te-vi! non sie-te
falsehood I'm deceiv'd, I'm be-tray'd! Pray, Ma'am, be com-fort-ed, for you are
house, and seats herself sadly.)
L.
voi, non fo-ste, e non sa-re-te nè la pri-ma, nè
not, nor have been, and nei-ther will be or the first, or
(Leporello takes out a book, or a long, narrow roll of paper, covered with silhouettes and names.)
L.
l'ul-ti-ma; guar-da-te, que-sto non pic-ciol li-bro è tut-to
last of them. Look here now, see this not too small vol-ume, 'tis al-most
L.
pie-no dei no-mi di sue bel-le; O-gni vil-la, o-gni bor-go, o-gni pa-
full of the names of his fair ones; town and vil-lage, distant countries, yes, foreign
L.
e-se, È te-sti-mon di sue don-ne-sche im-pre-se.
na-tions, Can wit-ness bear to his in-fat-u-a-tions.

Nº 4. "Madamina."

Aria.
Allegro.
Leporello.
L.
Strs
p
Ma-da-mi-na! Il ca-ta-lo-go è
Pretty la-dy! Here's a list I would
que-sto, del-le bel-le, che a-mo il padron mi-o; un ca-ta-lo-go e-
shew you, Of the fair ones my mas-ter has courted, Here you'll find them all
gli è, che ho fat-to i-o; os-ser-va-te, leg-ge-te con
du-ly as-sort-ed, In my writing, will't please you to
me! os-ser-va-te, leg-ge-te con me!
look, in my writ-ing, will't please you to look.
Fl.
Fag.
In I-ta-li-a sei cen-to e qua-ran-ta;
Here is It-a-ly six hun-dred and for-ty,
p Cor.
f

L.
in Al - ma-gna due cen-to e trent' u - na,
France is down for five hun-dred and twen - ty,
3
p
f
L.
cen - to in Francia, in Turchia no-vant' u - na; ma, in I -
On - ly two hun-dred the Rhine - land supplied him, But mark the
p
fp
L.
spa - gna, ma in I - spa-gna son già mille e tre! mil - le e tre!
cli - max, Spain has al-rea-dy one thousand and three, thousand and three,
Tutti
Vlns.
p
sfp
p
L.
mil - le e tre! V'han fra que-ste con-ta - di - ne,
thousand and three! Here are Countesses in plen - ty,
L.
ca - me-rie - re, cit - ta-di - ne, V'han contesse, ba-ro-nes-se,
Waiting-maids nineteen or twenty, Rustic beauties, Marchionesses,

L.
marchesa - ne, prin-ci-pesse, e v'han don-ne d'o-gni gra-do, d'o-gni for-ma, d'ogni e-
Ev'ry grade his pow'r confesses. Here are courtly dames and maidens, Young and handsome, old and
cresc.
tà, d'o - gni for-ma, d'o-gni e-tà, In I - ta-li-a
plain, Young and handsome, old and plain. Here is It - a - ly,
f
Vln.
p
Cello & Bass
sei cen-to e qua-ran - ta, in Al-ma-gna
Six hun-dred and for - ty, France is down for
due cen-to e trent' u-na, cen - - to in Fran - cia, in Tur-
five hun-dred and twenty On - - ly two hun - dred the
chia no - vant' u-na, ma, ma, ma in I - spa-gna! ma in I -
Rhine - land sup-plied him, But, but Spain is the cli-max! Here are al-

L.
spagna son già mil-le e tre, mil-le e tre, mil-le e
ready one thousand and three, thousand and three, thousand and
sfp
tre! V'han fra queste conta - di-ne, ca-me - rie - re, ci-ta-di-ne, v'han contesse, ba-ro -
three! Here are countesses in plenty, Waiting-maids nineteen or twenty, Rustic beauties, Marchio -
Vln.
Cl. Fag.
f sf p
nesse, marchesa - ne, prin-ci-pesse, e v'han donne d'o-gni gra-do, d'o-gni for-ma, d'ogni e-
nesses, Ev'ry grade his pow'r confesses, Here are courtly dames and maidens, young and handsome, old and
Tutti.
cresc.
f
tà! d'o - gni for - ma, d'o - gni e -
plain, Young and hand - some, old and
tà! d'o - gni for - ma, d'o - gni e - tà!
plain, young and hand - some, old and plain.
cresc.

Andante con moto.
L.
Nel - la bionda e - gli ha l'u - san-za di lo - dar-la
Is a maiden fair and slender, He will praise her
Str.
p
Fl.
fp
la gen-ti - lez - za, nel - la bru - na la co -
for modest sweetness, Then the dark ones are so
Tutti
Cor.
f
stanza, nel - la bian - ca la dol - cez - za.
tender! Lint - white tress - es shew dis - creetness;
Str.
p
Fl. Fag. Vln.
Vuol d'in - ver - no la grassot - ta, vuol d'e - sta - te la ma -
When 'tis cold he likes her port - ly, In the sum - mer, slim and
cresc.
grotta, e la gran - de ma - e -
courtly, Tall and haugh - ty, ne'er she a -
f
p
f
p

L.
sto - sa, e la gran - de ma - e -
larmshim, tall and haugh - ty, ne'er she a -
f
p
cresc.
sto - - - - - sa. La pic - ci - na, la pic -
larms him. If she's ti - ny, if she's
Fl.
Ob.
Bassi
Vln.
ci - na, la pic - ci - na, la pic - ci - na, la pic - ci - na, la pic -
ti - ny, if she's ti - ny, ver - y ti - ny, ver - y ti - ny, ti - ny,
Fag.
ci - na, la pic - ci - na, la picci - na, la pic - ci - na è ognor vez - zo - sa, è ognor vez -
ti - ny, If she's ti - ny, very ti - ny, ti - ny, ti - ny, no less she charms him, no less she
Tutti
zo - sa, è ognor vez - zo - sa; del - le vecchie fa con - qui - sta
charms him, no less she charms him. Ripe du - en - nas he en - gag - es,
fp

L.
pel pia - cer_ di por-le in li-sta, sua passion pre-do-mi-
That their names may grace these pag-es, But what most he's bent on
p
Fag.
nan - te_ è la gio-vin prin-ci-pian-te;
win - ning,_ is of youth the sweet be-ginning,
Fl.
Fag.
Vln.
non si pic - ca, se sia ric - ca, se sia brut - ta, se sia
Poor or wealth - y, wan or health - y, State-ly dame or mod-est
tr
cresc.
bel - la, se sia ric-ca, brut-ta, se sia bel-la, pur-chè_
beau - ty, State-ly dame, or youthful modest beau-ty, He to_
Ob.
Vln.
p
por-ti la_ gon-nel-la, voi sa-pe-te
win them makes his du-ty, And, you know it,

L.
quel che fa, voi sa - pe - te quel che
not in vain, and, you know it, not in
Fl.
Fag.
fa, pur che por - ti la gon - nel - la, voi sa - pe - te quel che
vain, He to win them makes his du - ty, And, you know it, not in
Vln.
fa, voi sa - pe - te, voi sa - pe - te quel che fa,
vain. Yes, you know it, yes, you know it, not in vain,
Ob.
Vln.
Fl.
Fag.
mf
p
quel che fa, quel che fa, voi sa-
not in vain, not in vain, Well you
f
f
pe - te quel che fa.
know it, not in vain.
(Exit hastily into villa.)

Recit.
Donna Elvira. (alone)
E.
In que-sta for-ma dun-que mi tra-dì il scel-le-ra-to! è questo il
This is the man I trusted, he betrays and de-rides me; and shall I
pre-mio che quel bar-ba-ro ren-de all' a-mor mi-o! Ah, ven-di-car vo-
bear it, that his in-so-lent ser-vant mocks my anguish? No, I will call on
gl'i-o l'in-gan-na-to mio cor! pria ch'ei mi fug-ga, si ri-cor-ra, si
justice! and my wrongs I'll a-venge, Ere he escape me, friends shall aid me to
(Exit into the house.)
va-da; io sento in pet-to sol ven-det-ta par-lar, rab-bia e dispet-to!
find him, and to chastise him. Love has fled from my heart! Miscreant! I despise him!
Nº 5. "Giovinette, che fate all' amore."
Duet and Chorus.
Scene. — The open Country.
Zerlina, Masetto, and Chorus of Villagers, dancing and singing.
Allegro.
Tutti.
f
p
f
p
f

(turning to the maidens, who press about her, while Masetto,
Zerlina. on the other side, is surrounded by the lads.)
Z.
Gio-vi-net-te, che fa-te all'a-mo-re, che fa-te all' a-mo-re, non la-
Let's en-joy, while the season in-vites us, the season in-vites us. 'Tis not
Str.
p
Fl. Ob.
Fag.
scia-te, che pas-si l'e-tà, che pas-si l'e-tà, che pas-si l'e-tà! Se nel
long that its pleasure will stay, its pleasure will stay, its pleasure will stay. While the
Opp. fair dream of youth yet de-lights us,
se-no vi bu-li-ca il co-re, vi bu-li-ca il co-re, il ri-
fair dream of youth yet de-lights us, while youth yet de-lights us, To her
me-dio ve-de-te-lo quà! che pia-
swain let no maid-en say nay, to her
cer, che piacer che sa-rà!
swain let no maiden say nay!
(the maidens form a ring, and dance around Zerlina.)
Chorus. SOPRANO & ALTO.
Ah! che pia-cer, che pia-cer che sa-
Ah! to her swain let no maiden say
Tutti.
f

Masetto. (to the lads.)
M.
Gio-vi - net - ti leg-gieri di
Oh ye swains and young lasses, take
rà, la-la - re-la - la, la-la - re-la - la!
nay, la la re la la, la la re la la!
sf p
sf p
f
Str.
p
te-sta, leg-gie-ri di te-sta, non an-da-te gi-ran-do di quà e là e
warning, ye lasses take warning, Lest your true love ye tri-fle a - way, a-way in
là, e quà e là; po-co du-ra de' mat-ti la fe-sta, de' mat-ti la
play, a way in play, And the season of joy turn to mourning, and joy turn to
fe - sta, ma per me co-min-cia - to non ha, co - min-cia - to non
mourning, When your youth's gid-dy vi-sions de - cay, when its vi-sions de -
ha! che pia-cer, che piacer che sa-rà!
cay, when your youth's giddy visions de - cay!
Chorus. TENOR & BASS.
(ring and dance)
Tutti
Ah
Ah
f

che pia-cer, che pia-cer che sa-rà; la-la-re-la-la, la-la-re-la-
Let us car-ol and dance and be gay, la la re la la, la la re la
sf p
sf p
(Zerlina and Masetto leave the groups and advance to centre, where the young chorus forms a great ring around them.)
Zerlina.
Z.
Vie-ni, vie-ni ca-ri-no, go-dia-mo, e can-tiamo, e bal-liamo, e suo-
Ev-er hap-py with thee, oh, my treasure, All our days are contentment and
Masetto.
M.
Vie-ni, vie-ni ca-ri-no, go-dia-mo, e can-tiamo, e bal-liamo, e suo-
Ev-er hap-py with thee, oh, my treasure, All our days are contentment and
la!
la!
Vln.
p
Z.
nia-mo, vie-ni, vie-ni ca-ri-no, go-dia-mo, che pia-cer, che pia-cer che sa-
pleasure, Ev-er hap-py with thee, oh, my treasure, Let us car-ol and dance and be
M.
nia-mo, vie-ni, vie-ni ca-ri-no, go-dia-mo, che pia-cer, che pia-cer che sa-
pleasure, Ev-er hap-py with thee, oh, my treasure, Let us car-ol and dance and be
Z.
rà! Ah! che pia-cer, che pia-cer che sa-
gay! Ah! Let us car-ol and dance and be
M.
rà! Ah! che pia-cer, che pia-cer che sa-
gay! Ah! Let us car-ol and dance and be

Z.
rà!
gay!
M.
rà!
gay!
(D. Giovanni and Leporello come out of the villa; both stop to look on.)
SOPR. & ALTO.
Chorus.
Ah, che pia - cer, che pia - cer che sa -
Ah, Let us car - ol and dance and be
TENOR & BASS.
Ah, che pia - cer, che pia - cer che sa -
Ah, Let us car - ol and dance and be
f
rà! La - la - re - la - la, re - la - la, re - la - la, la - la - re - la -
gay. La la re la la, re la la re la la, la la re la
rà! La - la - re - la - la, re - la - la, re - la - la, la - la - re - la -
gay. La la re la la, re la la re la la, la la re la
sf f
la, re-la-la, re-la - la!
la, re la la re la la.
la, re-la-la, re-la - la!
la, re la la re la la.

Recit.
Don Giovanni. (to Leporello.)
G.
(Man-co male,è par-ti-ta). Oh guarda, guarda che bel-la gio-ventù! che bel-le
(That's a mer-ci-ful riddance). But softly, see there, in hol-i-day attire, what pretty
G.
L.
Leporello.
don-ne! (Fra tan-te, per mia fè, vi sa-rà qual-che co-sa an-che per
fac-es! (A-mongst so man-y, I, 'pon my faith, may find some-thing for my-
Don Giovanni. (stepping between Zerlina and Masetto, while Leporello turns to the maidens.)
L.
G.
me). Ca-ri a-mi-ci, buon gior-no! se-gui-ta-te a sta-re al-le-gra-
self). Friends, I bid you good morn-ing, I am glad to see you so light-
G.
men-te, se-gui-ta-te a suo-nar, o buo-na gen-te! C'e qualche spo-sa-li-zio?
hearted, pray contin-ue your singing and your dancing. This surely is a wedding?
Z.
G.
Zerlina. (with a self-satisfied curtsey.)
Don Giovanni.
Sì, Si-gno-re, e la spo-sa son i-o. Me ne con-so-lo- Lo
'Tis in-deed, Sir, and 'tis I am the bride. Much joy I wish you! The
G.
M.
Masetto. (with scrape.)
Don Giovanni.
spo-so? Io, per ser-vir-la. Oh, bra-vo! per ser-vir-mi; questo è
bridegroom? I, at your ser-vice. Oh, charming, at my ser-vice; 'pon my
G.
L.
Z.
Leporello.
Zerlina.
ve-ro par-lar da ga-lant-uo-mo. (Ba-sta, che sia ma-ri-to)! Oh, il mio Ma-
life, that's the word of a true gal-lant. (Quite like a mod-el husband). Yes, my Ma-
Z.
G.
Don Giovanni.
set-to è un uom d'ot-ti-mo co-re. Oh anch'io, ve-de-te! vo-glio che sia-mo a-
set-to is al-ways so good-natur'd. Just like my-self, then; we are good friends al-

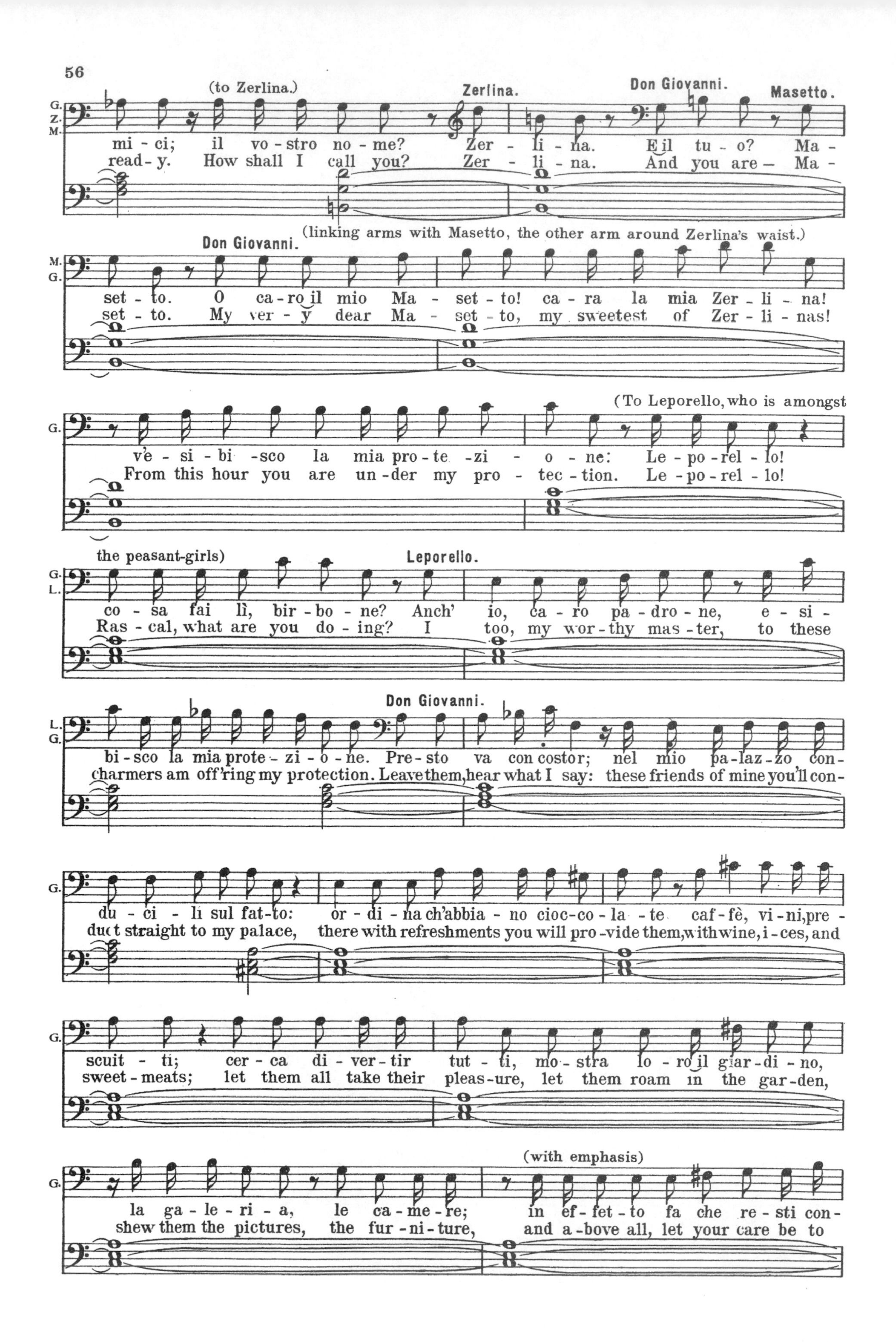
G.
Z.
M.
(to Zerlina.)
Zerlina.
Don Giovanni.
Masetto.
mi - ci; il vo - stro no - me? Zer - li - na. E il tu - o? Ma -
read - y. How shall I call you? Zer - li - na. And you are — Ma -
M.
G.
Don Giovanni.
(linking arms with Masetto, the other arm around Zerlina's waist.)
set - to. O ca - ro il mio Ma - set - to! ca - ra la mia Zer - li - na!
set - to. My ver - y dear Ma - set - to, my sweetest of Zer - li - nas!
G.
(To Leporello, who is amongst
v'e - si - bi - sco la mia pro - te - zi - o - ne: Le - po - rel - lo!
From this hour you are un - der my pro - tec - tion. Le - po - rel - lo!
the peasant-girls)
G.
L.
Leporello.
co - sa fai lì, bir - bo - ne? Anch' io, ca - ro pa - dro - ne, e - si -
Ras - cal, what are you do - ing? I too, my wor - thy mas - ter, to these
L.
G.
Don Giovanni.
bi - sco la mia prote - zi - o - ne. Pre - sto va con costor; nel mio pa - laz - zo con -
charmers am off'ring my protection. Leave them, hear what I say: these friends of mine you'll con -
G.
du - ci - li sul fat - to: or - di - na ch'abbia - no cioc - co - la - te caf - fè, vi - ni, pre -
duct straight to my palace, there with refreshments you will pro - vide them, with wine, i - ces, and
G.
scuit - ti; cer - ca di - ver - tir tut - ti, mo - stra lo - ro il giar - di - no,
sweet - meats; let them all take their pleas - ure, let them roam in the gar - den,
G.
(with emphasis)
la ga - le - ri - a, le ca - me - re; in ef - fet - to fa che re - sti con -
shew them the pictures, the fur - ni - ture, and a - bove all, let your care be to

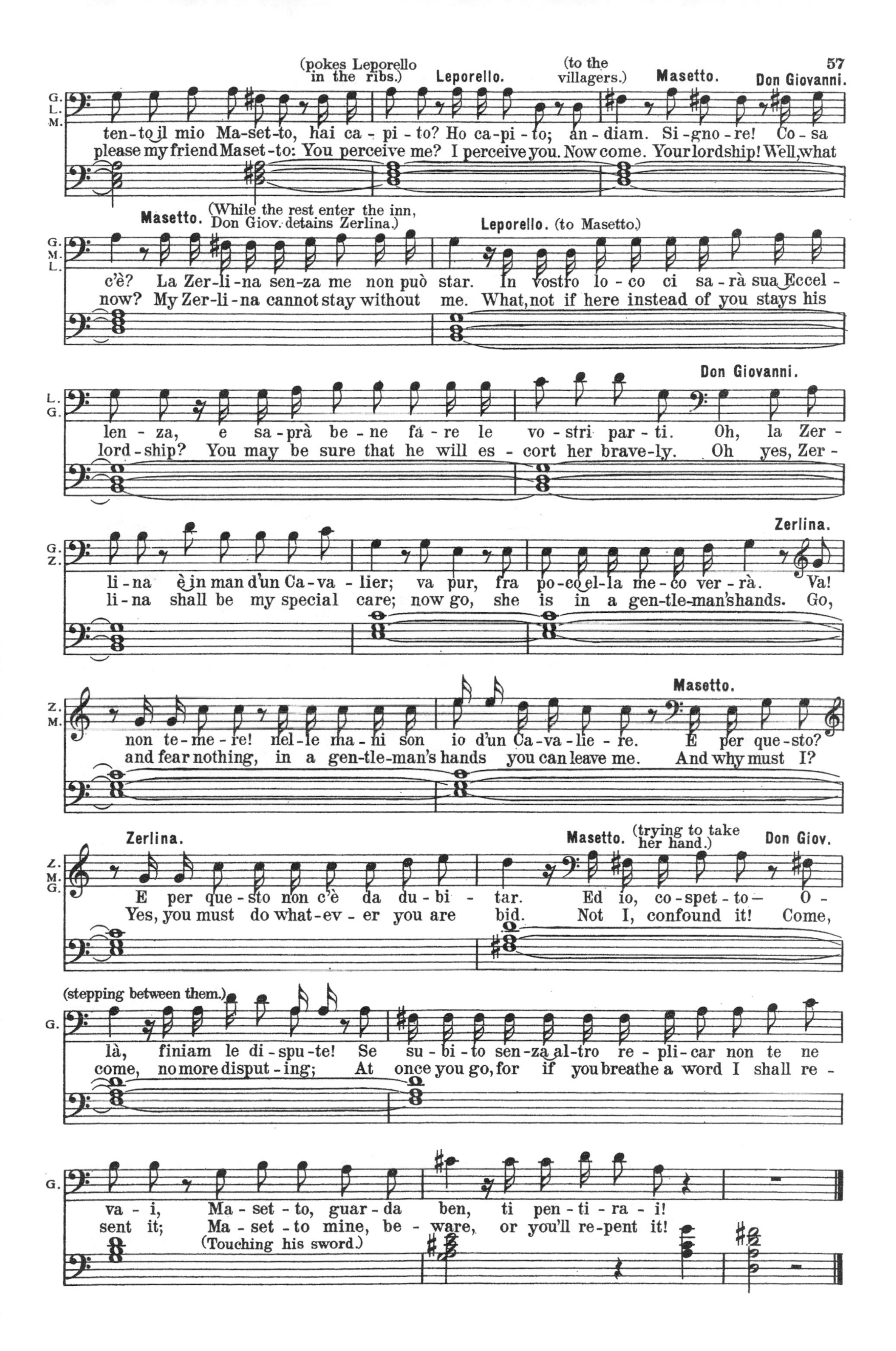
57
(pokes Leporello in the ribs.) Leporello. (to the villagers.) Masetto. Don Giovanni.
G. L. M.
ten-to il mio Ma-set-to, hai ca - pi - to? Ho ca-pi - to; an - diam. Si - gno - re! Co - sa
please my friend Maset - to: You perceive me? I perceive you. Now come. Your lordship! Well, what
Masetto. (While the rest enter the inn, Don Giov. detains Zerlina.) Leporello. (to Masetto.)
G. M. L.
c'è? La Zer - li - na sen - za me non può star. In vostro lo - co ci sa - rà sua Eccel -
now? My Zer - li - na cannot stay without me. What, not if here instead of you stays his
Don Giovanni.
L. G.
len - za, e sa - prà be - ne fa - re le vo - stri par - ti. Oh, la Zer -
lord - ship? You may be sure that he will es - cort her brave - ly. Oh yes, Zer -
Zerlina.
G. Z.
li - na è in man d'un Ca - va - lier; va pur, fra po - co el - la me - co ver - rà. Va!
li - na shall be my special care; now go, she is in a gen - tle - man's hands. Go,
Masetto.
Z. M.
non te - me - re! nel - le ma - ni son io d'un Ca - va - lie - re. E per que - sto?
and fear nothing, in a gen - tle - man's hands you can leave me. And why must I?
Zerlina. Masetto. (trying to take her hand.) Don Giov.
Z. M. G.
E per que - sto non c'è da du - bi - tar. Ed io, co - spet - to - O -
Yes, you must do what - ev - er you are bid. Not I, confound it! Come,
(stepping between them.)
G.
là, finiam le di - spu - te! Se su - bi - to sen - za al - tro re - pli - car non te ne
come, no more disput - ing; At once you go, for if you breathe a word I shall re -
G.
va - i, Ma - set - to, guar - da ben, ti pen - ti - ra - i!
sent it; Ma - set - to mine, be - ware, or you'll re - pent it!
(Touching his sword.)

Nº 6. "Ho capito."
Aria.

Allegro di molto.
Masetto.(dumbfounded, staring at Don Giovanni.)
M.
Piano.
Tutti.
Vlns.& Cor.
Wind.
f
p
Ho ca-pi - to, Si-gnor, sì!
Oh, of course, Sir, I perceive,
Si-gnor, sì! Chi - no il ca - po e me ne vo, giacche
I perceive! At your wish I'm deaf and dumb, I will
Cor.
pia-ce a voi co - sì, al-tre re-pli-che non fo, no, no, no, no, no, no, non
hum-bly take my leave, ne'er to common sense suc - cumb. No, no, no, no, no nev-er-
tr
Tutti.
cresc.
fo, Ca-va-lier voi sie-te già, du-bi-
more. You're a gen-tle-man, I know, That to
Vlns.
tar non pos-so af-fè, me lo di-ce la bon - tà che vo - le-te a-ver per
doubt were wrong in-deed, Vul-gar loves you can't al - low Gen-tle wish-es to im-

(aside to Zerlina.)
M.
me, a - ver per me, a - ver per me. Bricco-naccia, malan-dri-na, fostio-
pede, gen-tle wish-es to im - pede. By the Powers, I will shun thee, Oh thou
cresc.
f
p
(To Leporello who wants to lead him off.)
gnor la mia ru-i-na, fos-tio-gnor la mia ru-i-na! Ven-go, vengo!
flirt, thou hast un-done me, oh, thou flirt, thou hast un-done me! Yes, di-rectly!
fp
fp
cresc.
f
p
(to Zerlina.)
(aside, bitterly.)
Re-sta, re-sta! È u-na co-sa mol-to o-ne-sta!
Stay be-hind here! 'Tis not what I thought to find here!
cresc.
f
Strings.
p
(to Zerlina and Don G.)
(sarcastically to Zerlina.)
Faccia il nostro Ca-va-lie-re Ca-va-lie-ra anco-ra te, Ca-va-
Al-ways trust a no-ble's hon-or, this should be the vassal's creed, this should
Tutti.
f
p
(aside to Zerlina.)
liera an-co-ra te. Bric-co-nac-cia, ma-lan-dri-na! fo-sti-o-
be the vas-sal's creed. By the Powers, I will shun thee, Oh thou

M.
gnor la mia ru - i - na, fo - sti o - gnor la mia ru - i - na!
flirt, thou hast un - done me, oh thou flirt thou hast un - done me!
cresc.
f
p
(to Leporello.)
(to Zerlina.)
Ven - go, ven - go! Re - sta, re - sta! è u - na co - sa
Yes, di - rect - ly! Stay be - hind here, 'Tis not what I
cresc.
mol - to o - ne - sta! faccia il nostro Ca - va - lie - re Ca - va -
thought to find here! Al-ways trust a no-ble's hon-or. This should
(to Zerlina.)
liera an - co - ra te, Ca - va - liera an - co - ra te, faccia il no - stro Ca - va -
be the vassal's creed, This should be the vas-sal's creed, Al-ways trust a no-ble's
ten.
f
p
cresc.

M.
lie - re Ca - va - lie - ra an - co - ra te, faccia il no - stro Ca - va -
hon - or, This should be the vas - sal's creed, Al - ways trust a no - ble's
ten.
f
p
cresc.
M.
lie - re Ca - va - lie - ra anco - ra te, Ca - va - lie - ra an - co - ra
hon - or, This should be the vas - sal's creed, This should be - the vas - sal's
f
p
f
M.
te, Ca - va - lie - ra an - co - ra te! (Exit with Leporello, who hurries him into the Tavern.)
creed, this should be the vas - sal's creed.
p
f
Recit.
Don Giovanni.
G.
Al - fin siam li - be - ra - ti, Zerli - net - ta gen - til, da qual scioc - co - ne, che ne di - te, mio
At last we have dispatch'd him, Zerli - net - ta, to leave the boo - by liked not; did I manage it
(trying to embrace her.) Zerlina. (drawing back.) Don Giovanni.
G.
Z.
G.
ben? sò far pu - li - to? Si - gno - re, è mio ma - ri - to! Chi? co - lui? vi par che un o - nest'
well, my pret - ty dai - sy? My lord, he's my af - fi - anc'd! Who? that clown? think you a man of

G.
uo - mo, un no - bil Ca - va - lier, qual io mi van - to, pos - sa sof -
feel - ing, a well - born Ca - va - lier, such ev'n as I am, tame - ly can
G.
frir che qual vi - set - to d'o - ro, qual vi-so in-zuc-che - ra - to da un bi - fol-cac-cio
see such sweet and dain-ty freshness, such de-li-cate per-fec - tions all thrown a-way up-
G.
Z.
Zerlina.
vil sia stra - paz- za - to? Ma Si - gnor, io gli die - di pa -
on a sense - less rus - tic? But, my Lord, I have prom - is'd to
Z.
G.
Don Giovanni.
ro - la di spo-sar - lo. Tal pa - ro - la non va-le un ze - ro: voi non
mar - ry him to-mor-row. Who could help break-ing such a prom-ise? You were
G.
sie - te fat - ta per es-ser pa - e - sa - na, un al - tra sor - te vi pro -
not in - tend - ed by na-ture for a peasant; a brighter for - tune is in
G.
cu - ran que - gli oc-chi bric - con-cel - li, quei lab-bret - ti si bel - li, quel - le di - tuc - cia
store for those balm - y cheeks of ros - es, where sly Cu - pid re - poses, that snowy brow where
G.
Z.
Zerlina.
can-di-de e o-do - ro - se; par - mi toc-car giun - ca - ta, e fiu - tar ro - se. Ah, non vor -
not a shadow low-ers, that pret-ty mouth of cor - al, that breathes of flowers. Ah, but I -

Don Giovanni.
Zerlina.
Z.
G.
Z.
re - i— Che non vor - re - ste? Al - fi - ne in-gan - na - ta re -
would not— What is't you would not? I would not in my love be de -
Z.
star. Io sò che ra - ro col - le don - ne voi al - tri ca - va - lie - ri sie - te o -
ceiv'd. I know how sel - dom you great lords with us sim - ple country maid - ens court with
Don Giovanni.
Z.
G.
ne - sti e sin - ce - ri. Eh, un im - po - stu - ra del - la gen - te ple - be - a! la no - bil -
loy - al in - ten - tion. That's a vile slan - der, a ma - li - cious in - ven - tion; with no - ble
G.
tà ha di - pin - ta ne - gli oc - chi l'o - ne - stà. Or - sù, non per - diam
birth, no - ble man - ners go al - ways hand in hand, I'll shew you an ex -
Zerlina.
G.
Z.
tem - po; in que - sto i - stan - te io vi vo - glio spo - sar. Voi?
am - ple; this ver - y in - stant I will make you my wife. You?
Don Giovanni.
(pointing to his castle.)
G.
Cer - to, i - o. Quel ca - si - net - to è mi - o, so - li sa - re - mo. E
I, for cer - tain: Come to my qui - et dwell - ing, if you don't dread me, oh
G.
là, gio - jel - lo mi - o, ci spo - se - re - mo.
come, my fair - est an - gel, there I will wed thee.

Nº 7. "Là ci darem la mano.,,

Duettino.

Andante.
Don Giovanni.
G.
Là ci da-rem la ma-no, là mi di-rai di sì;
Give me thy hand, oh fair-est, Whisper a gen-tle "Yes,"
p Strings.
G.
Z.
ve-di, non è lon-ta-no, par-tiam, ben mio, da- qui.
Come, if for me thou car-est, With joy my life to- bless.
Zerlina.
Vor-rei, e non vor-
I would, and yet I
Strings.
p
Strings.
Z.
re-i, mi trema un po-co il cor, fe-li-ce, è ver, sa-re-i,
would not, I dare not give as-sent, A-las! I know I should not,
Z.
G.
ma può burlar-mi an-cor, ma può bur-lar-mi an-cor!
Too late I may re-pent, Ah! too late I may re-pent!
Don Giovanni.
Vie-ni, mio bel di-
Come, dearest, let me
Tutti.
mf
G.Z.
G.
let-to!
guide thee.
Zerlina.
Mi fa pie-tà Ma-set-to!
Ma-set-to sure will chide me!
Don Giovanni.
Io can-gie-rò tuo-
Dan-ger shall ne'er come
p
Tutti.

Zerlina.
G.
Z.
sor — te! Pre - sto non son — più for - te, non son più for - te, non son — più
nigh thee! Ah — that I could dè - ny thee, oh, that I — could, that I could de -
p
Cor.
Tutti.
p
(Donna Elvira appears on the verandah of the main building, and watches what is going on.)
Z.
for - te! Vor -
ny thee! I
Don Giovanni.
G.
Vie - ni! vie - ni! Là ci da - rem la ma - no,
Come then, Come then! Give me thy hand, oh fair - est!
3
sfp
Z.
rei, e non vor - re - i, Mi trema un po - co il
would, and yet I would not, I dare not give as -
G.
Là mi di - rai di sì,
Whisper a gen - tle "yes."
p
Z.
cor; ma — può bur - lar - mi an -
sent. Ah, — but I may — re -
G.
par - tiam, ben mio, da qui.
With joy my life thou'lt bless.

(disengaging
Z.
cor. Mi fa- pie - tà— Ma - set - to; pre -
pent! Ma - set - to— sure will chide me. Ah,—
(putting his arm around her.)
G.
Vie - ni, mio bel di - let - to! io can-gie - rò tuo
Come, dearest, let me guide thee, Dan - ger shall ne'er come
mf
p
mf
herself, and escaping to other side.)
- sto non son più for - te, non son più for - te, non son— più— for - te!
— that I could de - ny thee, oh that I— could, that I could de - ny thee.
sor - te.
nigh thee.
An -
Oh
p
(throwing herself into his arms.)
Allegro.
(insistently)
An - diam! An - diam, an - diam, mio be - ne,— a
I come! With thee, with thee, my treasure,— This
diam! An - diam!
come, Oh come!
An - diam, an - diam, mio be - ne,— a
With thee, with thee, my treasure,— This
Allegro.
ri - sto - rar le pe - ne— d'un' in - no - cen - te a - mor!
life is naught but pleasure,— My heart is— fond - ly thine!
ri - sto - rar le pe - ne— d'un' in - no - cen - te a - mor!
life is naught but pleasure,— My heart is— fond - ly thine!

Z.
An - diam, an - diam, mio be - ne, — a ri - sto - rar le pe - ne — d'un'
With thee, with thee, my treasure, — This life is naught but pleasure, — My
G.
An - diam, an - diam, mio be - ne, a ri - sto - rar le pe - ne — d'un'
With thee, with thee, my treasure, This life is naught but pleasure, — My
(Donna Elvira descends the steps, and
Z.
in - no - cen - te a - mor!
heart is — fond - ly thine!
G.
in - no - cen - te a - mor! An - diam!
heart is — fond - ly thine! Oh come!
Fl.
p
tr
3
pizz.
posts herself at centre, back.)
Z.
An - diam! An - diam!
I come! I'm thine!
G.
An -
Thou'rt
tr
3
arco
Z.
An - diam, mio bene, an - diam, le pe - ne a ri - sto - rar d'un
My heart is fond - ly thine, my heart is fond - ly thine, my
G.
diam! An - diam, mio bene, an - diam, le pe - ne a ri - sto - rar, d'un
mine! My heart is fond - ly thine, my heart is fond - ly thine, my
3
tr

in - no - cen-te a - mor!
heart is fond-ly thine!
(Exeunt, arm in arm.)
in - no - cen-te a - mor!
heart is fond-ly thine!
Recit.
Donna Elvira (desperately, intercepting Don Giovanni.)
Fer - ma - ti, scel - le - ra - to! il ciel mi fe - ce u - dir le tue per -
Leave her, thou vile se - du - cer! By heav'n I'm sent, thy per - fi - dy to
fi - die; io so - no a tem - po di sal - var que - ste mi - se - ra in - no -
wit - ness, and to pre - vent thee from de - lud - ing this poor girl's in - ex -
cen - te dal tuo bar - ba - ro ar - ti - glio!
pe - rience with thy treach - er - ous lan - guage!
Zerlina.
Me - schi - na! co - sa
I won - der, says she
sen - to!
tru - ly!
Don Giovanni. (aside.)
(Amor, con - si - glio!)
(Cupid inspire me!)
(softly to Elvira.)
I - dol mio, non ve - de - te, ch'io vo - glio di - ver -
Can you chide, dear El - vi - ra, a lit - tle harmless
tir - mi?
pas - time?
Donna Elvira (aloud.)
Di - ver - tir - ti? è ve - ro! di - ver - tir - ti! io sò, cru -
Harmless pas - time? In - deed, Sir! harmless pas - time! De - ceit - ful

Zerlina. (anxiously, to Don G.)
E.
Z.
de - le, co - me tu ti di - ver - ti. Ma, Si - gnor Ca - va - lie - re, è ver quel ch'el - la
man, I know too much of your pas-time. But, my lord, please to tell me, has she the right to
Don Giovanni (softly to Zerlina.)
Z.
G.
di - ce? La po-ve - ra in-fe - li - ce è di me in - na - mo - ra - ta, E per pie-
say this? She's so in - fat - u - at - ed! But I must treat her kindly, she cannot
G.
tà deg-gio fin - ge - re amo - re; ch'io son per mia dis - gra - zia uom di buon co - re. Attacca
bear from my side to be parted, un - fort - u - nate - ly I am too tenderhearted. l'Aria

Nº 8. "Ah! fuggi il traditor!"
Aria.

Allegro.
Donna Elvira.
E.
Ah! fug - - gi il tra - di -
The trai - - tor means de -
Strings throughout.
f
p
E.
tor! Non lo las - ciar più dir; il lab - bro è men - ti -
ceit! His flatt'ry heed thou not, While yet there's time, re -

E.
tor, fal-la - - - ce il ci - - glio!
treat, Or woe be-fall thee!
f
Da miei tor-men-ti im-pa-ra a
From wrong un-just and cru-el, From
p
cre - der a quel cor; e na - - sca il tuo ti - mor dal mio
long remorse and tears, From wast - - ed, lone - ly years I would
— pe-ri - - glio, ah fug-gi, fug - - gi! ah
— re-call thee. Ah, fly him, fly him! The
fug - gi il tra - di - tor! non lo la-sciar più dir; il
trai - tor means de-ceit! His flatt'ry heed thou not, While
tr

E.
labbro è men - ti - tor, fal-la - - ce il ci - glio, il
yet there's time, re - treat, Or woe be - fall thee. While
E.
lab - bro è men - ti - tor, fal - la - - - -
yet there's time, re-treat, Or woe
E.
ce il ci - glio, sì, fal - la - - -
be-fall thee, Yes, or woe
(Exit, leading off Zerlina.)
E.
- ce il ci - glio!
be-fall thee!
Recit. Don Giovanni.
(Enter Donna Anna and D. Octavio, dressed in mourning.)
G.
Mi par ch'oggi il de-mo-nio si di-ver-ta d'op-por-si a' miei pia-ce-vo-li pro-
It seems as if the ver-y imp of mischief, this day were bent on thwarting all my

Don Octavio.
G.
O.
gres - si; van - no mal tut - ti quan - ti. Ah ch'o - ra, i - do - lo mio, son va - ni i
pleasures; nothing goes as I wish it. Now dear - est, weep no more, look to the
(perceiving Don G.)
O.
pian - ti, di ven - det - ta si par - li! Oh Don Gio - van - ni!
fu - ture, let us speak but of vengeance! Ah, Don Gio - van - ni!
Don Giovanni. (aside.)
Donna Anna. (to D. Giovanni.)
G.
A.
(Man - ca - va questo in ver!) Si - gno - re, a tem - po vi ri - tro -
(Here comes the fi - nal blow!) Good Sir, this meet - ing is op - por -
Don Giovanni.
A.
G.
viam: a - ve - te co - re? a - ve - te a - ni - ma ge - ne - ro - sa? (Sta a ve -
tune: I know your courage, have you a heart that can feel com - passion? (Now I
(aside.)
(aloud, to D. Anna.)
G.
de - re che il dia - vo - lo le ha det - to qual - che co - sa.) Che do - man - da! per - chè?
wonder if that same fiend has set her on to track me.) What a question! And why?
Donna Anna.
Don Giovanni. (aside.)
A.
G.
Bi - so - gno abbia - mo del - la vo - stra ami - ci - zia. (Mi torna il fia - to in
We are in trouble, and have need of your friendship. (This time I'm out of
(aloud)
G.
cor - po.) Co - man - da - te; i con - giun - ti, i pa - ren - ti, que - sta
dan - ger.) Pray command me, all I can do, friends and vassals, My right
(With much warmth.)
G.
man, que - sto fer - ro, i be - ni, il san - gue spen - de - rò per ser -
hand, my pos - sessions, my sword, nay, life it - self I give to your

vi - vi: ma voi, bel - la Donn' An - na, per - chè co - sì pian -
ser - vice: but why, fair - est Donn' An - na, why thus for ev - er
ge - te? il cru - de - le chi fù che o - sò la cal - ma tur - bar del vi - ver
mourning? Who has dar'd to in - vade the tranquil peace of that heart, with grief in -
Donna Elvira (entering).
vo - stro? Ah, ti ri - tro - vo an - cor, per - fi - do mo - stro?
si - dious? Ah, do we meet a - gain? Mon - ster per - fi - dious!
Nº 9. "Non ti fidar, o misera."
Andante.
Quartet.
Donna Elvira. (to D. Anna.)
Voice.
Piano.
Strings.
Non ti fi - dar, o mi - se - ra, di quel ri - bal - do cor!
Oh, ere thou trust in him, beware, His heart is cold as stone,
me già tra - dì quel bar - ba - ro, te vuol tra - dir an - cor.
Know that his vows are writ in air, I their de - ceit have known.
p cresc.
mf
p
Vln.
Donna Anna. (aside, withdrawing a little.)
Cie - li! che aspetto no - bi - le! che dol - ce ma - es - tà! Il
Heaven! a no - ble la - dy this! She sore - ly seems dis - traught! Her
Don Octavio.
Cie - li! che aspetto no - bi - le! che dol - ce ma - es - tà! Il
Heaven! a no - ble la - dy this! She sore - ly seems dis - traught! Her
Cl.
Fl.

(Don G. tries to persuade Donna Elvira to step aside, but she refuses; finally he grasps her right hand, and draws her away toward his right.)
A.
suo do-lor, le la-gri-me m'empiono di pie-tà, m'em-piono di pie-
warn-ing voice, her mien of woe, By bitter grief were taught! by bitter grief were
O.
suo do-lor, le la-gri-me m'empiono di pie-tà, m'em-piono di pie-
warn-ing voice, her mien of woe, By bitter grief were taught! by bitter grief were
Cl.
Fl.
cresc.
mf
p
A.
tà!
taught!
Don Giovanni (whispers, D. Elvira listens.)
O.
G.
tà! La po-ve-ra ra-gaz-za è pazza, a-mi-ci mie-i! lascia-te-mi con
taught! Poor girl, she's quite de-mented, believe me, quite de-mented, I sore-ly do la-
cresc.
G.
le-i, è paz-za, a-mi-ci mie-i, for-se si cal-me-rà, for-
ment it! The fit may be pre-vent-ed If she's by me be-sought, if
f
p cresc.
mf
p
Donna Elvira.
E.
Ah! non cre-de-te al per-fi-do!
The trai-tor, oh be-lieve him not!
G.
-se si cal-me-rà!
she's by me be-sought.
È paz-za, non ba-
Poor thing, she's quite de-
Fl.
Cl.

Donna Anna. (aside.)
A.
A chi si cre-de-rà? a chi si cre-de-
Can I believe in aught? can I be-lieve in
E.
Re-sta - te, oh Dei — re - sta - te!
I pray you, friends, stay near — me!
Don Octavio. (aside.)
O.
A chi si cre-de-rà? a chi si cre-de-
Can I believe in aught? can I be-lieve in
G.
da - te!
ment-ed!
è pazza!
demented!
A.
rà? a chi si cre-de-rà? si cre - de - rà?
aught? can I be-lieve, can I believe in aught?
E.
Re-sta-te!
Stay near me!
Ah non cre-de-te al per-fi-do! re -
The traitor, oh be-lieve him not, stay
O.
rà? a chi si cre-de-rà? si cre - de - rà?
aught? can I be-lieve, can I believe in aught?
G.
tr
tr

A.
Cer - to mo - to d'i - gno - to tor - men - to
Sure some cause there must be for this rav - ing!
E.
sta - te!
near me!
Sde - gno, rabbia, di-spet-to, pa-
Scorn, distrac-tion and in-fam-y
O.
Cer - to mo - to d'i - gno - to tor - men - to
Sure some cause there must be for this rav - ing!
(aside)
G.
Cer - to mo - to d'i - gno - to tor - men - to
Would to heav'n I could stop all this rav - ing!
Fl. Vlns.
cresc.
f
p
A.
Den-tro l'al-ma gi - ra - re mi sen - to,
Al-most like one de-ment-ed be - hav - ing!
E.
ven - to
braving!
den-tro l'al-ma gi - ra - re mi
I'll pur-sue thee, for vengeance
C.
Den-tro l'al-ma gi - ra - re mi sen - to,
Al-most like one de-ment-ed be - hav - ing!
G.
Den-tro l'al-ma gi - ra - re mi sen - to,
Quite like one who is mad she's be - hav - ing!
cresc.
f
p

A.
che mi di - ce per quel - la in - fe - li - ce
None can tell, none can tell what be - fell thee,
E.
sen - to, Che mi di - ce di quel tra - di -
crav-ing! Who will tell thee, who'll tell what be -
O.
Che mi di - ce per
None can tell, none can
G.
Che mi di - ce per quel - la in - fe -
None can tell, none can tell what be -
Vln.
Cor.
Viol
A.
cen - to co - se, che in - ten - der, che inten - der non sa, no,
None can tell what this grief, what this grief on thee brought, No,
E.
to - re cen - to co - se, che inten - der non sa, no, Che mi
fell me! Who this grief, who this grief on me brought, No, none can
O.
quel-la in - fe - li - ce cen - to co - se, che in - ten - der non sa, no,
tell what be-fell thee, what this grief, what this grief on thee brought, No,
G.
li - ce cen - to co - se, che inten - der non sa, no,
fell her, But be cer - tain, her sor-rows are naught, No,

A.
no!
che in - ten - der non
no!
ah no, none can
E.
di - ce di quel tra - di - to - re, di quel tra - di - to - re cen - to co - se, che intender non
tell thee, ah no, none can tell thee, ah no, none can tell thee who this grief hath up - on me —
O.
p
no!
che in - ten - der non
no!
ah no, none can
G.
p
no!
cen - to co - se, che inten - der non
no!
oh be cer - tain, her sor - rows are
p
A.
sa,
che in - ten - der non sa!
tell!
Ah no, none can tell!
E.
sa, che mi di - ce, mi di - ce di quel tra - di - to - re, cen - to co - se che intender non sa!
brought, none can tell, none can tell thee, ah no, none can tell thee who this grief hath up - on me brought!
O.
sa,
che in - ten - der non sa!
tell.
Ah no, none can tell!
G.
sa,
cen - to co - se che inten - der non sa!
naught,
Oh be cer - tain; her sor - rows are naught.
Vln.
Cl.
Fag.

Don Octavio (aside.)
O.
Io di quà non va - do vi - a, se non so com' è l'af - far!
Is she in-jur'd or de - ceiv-ing, ere we part from here I'd know!
Donna Anna (aside.)
A.
Non ha l'a-ria di paz - zi - a il suo tratto, il suo par - lar.
Great her sorrow, past re - lieving, But no madness doth she shew.
Don Giovanni.
G.
Se men
While they
Donna Elvira. (to
E.
Da quel
Friends, his
G.
va - do, si po - tri - a qual-che co - sa so-spet - tar.
scan me, un-be - lieving, From their presence I'll not go.
Don G., in exasperation.)
E.
O.
cef - fo si do - vri - a la ner' al-ma giu - di - car.
wiles are past con-ceiving, Falsehood he will ne'er for - go.
Don Octavio (to D. Giov.)
Dunque quella?
Is this madness?
G.
È paz - za -
To my great

Donna Anna (to Donna Elvira.)
A.
Dun-que que-gli?
I'd befriend thee!
Donna Elvira.
E.
(to Don G.)
È un tra - di - to - re, men - ti -
Don Giovanni.
Oh heed my prayer! Vile be-
G.
(tries to seperate D. Anna and Elvira.)
rel-la! In - fe - li - ce!
sor-row! quite de-ment-ed!
sf
A.
In - co-
Soon, me-
E.
O.
Don Octavio.
to - re, men - ti - to - re, men - ti - to - re! In - co-
tray-er, vile be-tray-er, vile be - tray - er! Soon me-
G.
Vlns.
f
p
A.
min - cio a du - bi - tar.
thinks, the truth we'll know.
O.
min - cio a du - bi - tar.
thinks, the truth we'll know.
G.
(softly to Donna Elvira.)
Zit - ta, zit - ta, che la gen - te si ra - duna a noi d'in-
Hush, be still, thy sil - ly rav-ing will a rab-ble gath-er
Fl. & Strings.
pp

G.
tor - no. Sia-te un po - co più pru - den - te, vi fa - re - te cri - ti -
round us, thy un - wom - an - ly be - hav - ing makes me quite of thee a -
Donna Elvira (to Don Giovanni.)
E.
Non sperarlo, o sce - le - ra - to, ho per - du - ta la pruden - za,
Vil - lain, darest thou to blame me? Through the world I will pur - sue thee,
G.
car.
shamed.
E.
le tue colpe ed il mio sta - to voglio a tut - ti pa - le - sar, vo - glio a
As a traitor I'll proclaim thee, For by thee I am de - fam'd, for by
Donna Anna (aside, observing Don Giovanni.)
A.
Que - gli ac - cen - ti sì som -
Is he threat - 'ning? is he
E.
tut - ti pa - le - sar! Non sperarlo, o sce - le - ra - to!
thee I am defam'd! Villain! darest thou to blame me?
Don Octavio.
(aside)
O.
Que - gli ac - cen - ti sì som -
Is he threat - 'ning? is he
Don Giovanni.
G.
Zit - ta, zit - ta, che la gen - te si ra - du - na a noi d'in -
Silence, hush, thy sil - ly raving. Will a rabble gather
Vlns.

A.
E.
O.
G.
mes - - si, quel can -
plead - - ing? Why those
ho per - du - ta la pru - den - za!
Thro' the world I will pur - sue thee!
mes - - si, quel can -
plead - - ing? Why those
tor - no, siate un po - co più pru -
round us, Thy un - wom - an - ly be -
cresc.
f
p
giar - - - - - si di co - lo - re, son in -
loud and an - gry whispers? These are
le tue col-pe ed il mio sta - to vo - glio a tut - ti pa - le -
as a trai - tor I'll pro-claim thee, For by thee I am de -
giar - - - - - si di co - lo - re, son in -
loud and an - gry whispers? These are
den - te, vi fa - re - te cri - ti - car,
hav-ing makes me quite of thee a-shamed,
Clar.

A.
di - zi trop - po e - spres - si, che mi
signs not hard in read - ing, That her
E.
sar, ho per-du - ta la pru-den-za!
fam'd. Thro' the world I will pur sue thee.
O.
di - zi trop - po e - spres - si, che mi
signs not hard in read - ing, That her
G.
sia-te un po - co più pru-den - te!
Hush and stay thy sil - ly rav - ing!
A.
fan de - ter - mi - nar, che mi
griefs by him were fram'd, That her
E.
Non spe-rar-lo! ho per-du - ta la pru-
As a trai-tor! As a trai-tor I'll pro-
O.
fan de - ter - mi - nar, che mi
griefs by him were fram'd, That her
G.
zit - to, zit - to! si ra-du-na a noi d'in-tor - no!
Hush, be si-lent! Thou'lt a rab-ble gath-er round us!
Vln.

A.
fan de - ter - mi - nar, che mi
griefs by him were fram'd, That her
E.
den-za, non sperarlo, o scele - ra - to! le tue colpe, ed il mio
claim thee! Villain, darest thou to blame me! As a trai-tor I'll pro-
O.
fan de - ter - mi - nar, che mi
griefs by him were fram'd, That her
G.
zit-to, zit - to! che la gen-te siate un poco più pruden - te!
Hush and stay thy sil-ly raving, Thou'lt a rabble gather round us!
A.
fan de - ter - mi - nar!
griefs by him were fram'd!
E.
sta - to vo - glio a tut - ti pa - le - sar!
claim thee, For by thee I am de-fam'd!
O.
fan de - ter - mi - nar!
griefs by him were fram'd!
(Don G. mastering Donna Elvira by his gaze, leads her away, and then returns.)
G.
vi fa - re - te, vi fa - re - te cri - ti - car!
Thy be-hav-ing makes me quite of thee a-sham'd!
Fl.
Cl.
pp

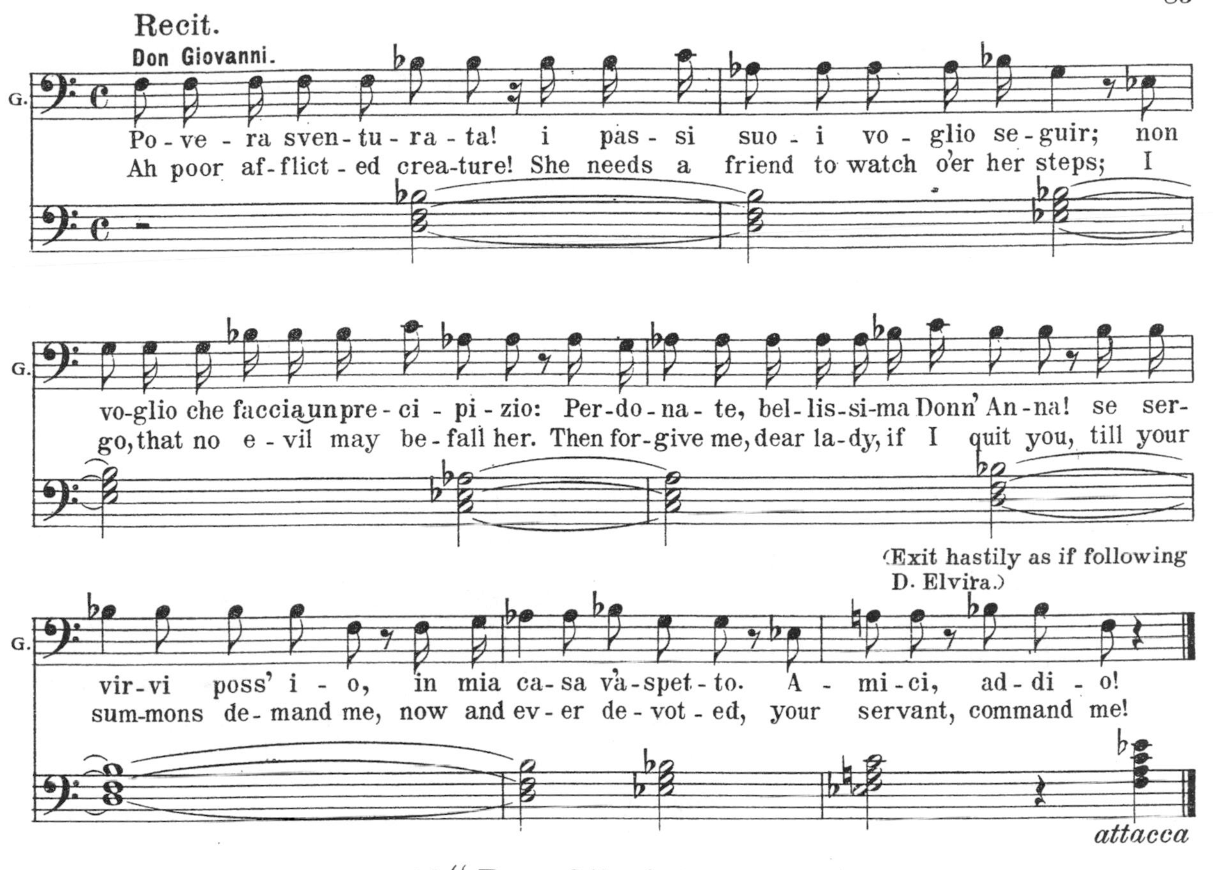
Recit.
Don Giovanni.
G.
Po-ve-ra sven-tu-ra-ta! i pas-si suo-i vo-glio se-guir; non
Ah poor af-flict-ed crea-ture! She needs a friend to watch o'er her steps; I
vo-glio che faccia un pre-ci-pi-zio: Per-do-na-te, bel-lis-si-ma Donn' An-na! se ser-
go, that no e-vil may be-fall her. Then for-give me, dear la-dy, if I quit you, till your
(Exit hastily as if following D. Elvira.)
vir-vi poss' i-o, in mia ca-sa v'a-spet-to. A-mi-ci, ad-di-o!
sum-mons de-mand me, now and ev-er de-vot-ed, your servant, command me!
attacca

Nº 10a "Don Ottavio! son morta!"

Recitative.

Allegro assai.
Donna Anna. (in extreme agitation.)
A.
Don Ot-ta-vio! son
Don Oc-ta-vio, oh
Tutti
p
f
Basso
(throwing herself into his arms)
Don Octavio.
Donna Anna.
A.
O.
A.
mor-ta! Co-sa è sta-to?
help me! What dis-turbs thee?
Per pie-tà, soc-cor-
I can not com-pre-

Don Octavio.
Donna Anna.
re-te-mi! Mio be-ne, fa-te co-rag-gio! O De-i!
hend it yet! My dear-est, say, what hath hap-pend? Oh Heav-en!
(Pointing after Don G., with uplifted arm.)
O De-i! Quegli è il car-
Oh Heav-en! That was the
Don Octavio.
Donna Anna.
ne-fi-ce del pa-dre mi-o! Che di-te? Non du-bi-ta-te
mur-der-er of my dear Fa-ther! What say'st thou? No long-er can I
più; gli ul-ti-mi ac-cen-ti che l'em-pio pro-fe-rì, tut-ta la
doubt: his words at part-ing his soft and hon-ey'd voice, all bring be-
Basso only
D. Oc-
vo-ce, ri-chia-mar nel cor mio di quell' in-deg-no, che nel mio apparta-mento Oh
fore me, past the chance of a doubt, the vile in-tru-der, who dar'd in-to my chamber Oh
tavio.
ciel! pos-si-bi-le, che sot-to il sa-cre man-to d'a-mi-ci-zia ma co-me
Heav'n, is't pos-si-ble that 'neath the sa-cred man-tle of long friend-ship but pro-

Donna Anna. (quieter, repressing her emotions).
fù, nar-ra-te-mi lo strano av-ve-ni-men-to. E-ra già al-quanta a-van-
ceed! the whole, oh tell me, of this dark ad-venture. Shadows of mid-night all a-
Str
f
Andante.
p
za-ta la not-te, quando nel-le mie stan-ze, o-ve so-let-ta mi trovai per sven-
round me were gathered; in my own qui-et cham-ber (sit-ting a-lone by mis-adven-ture, and
tu-ra, en-trar io vi-di in un man-tello av-vol-to un uom che al primo i-
dreaming,) when all at once there came in, wrapp'd in a mantle, a man, whom for the
stan-te a-vea pre-so per voi; ma ri-co-nob-bi poi, che un' in-
mo-ment I had ta-ken for thee. But soon I had dis-covered how
Don Octavio. (agitated)
Donna Anna.
gan-no e-ra il mi-o! Stel-le! se-gui-te! Ta-ci-to a me s'ap-
great was my er-ror! Hor-ror! con-ti-nue! Si-lent-ly he drew
p Andante.
pres-sa, e mi vuo-le ab-brac-ciar; scio-glier-mi cer-co, ei più mi
near me, and my hand would ca-ress; quick I with-drew it, an then he
stringendo il tempo
cresc.

88
stringe- io grido! non viene al-
seized me- I struggled: No one was
Tempo I.
Tutti
cun; con una mano cerca d'impedire la voce,
near- one hand upon my mouth he placed, my screaming to stifle,
Str.
p Andante.
e coll' altra m'afferra stretta così, che già mi credo
with the other he press'd me close in his grasp; I scarcely could re-
Don Octavio (in extreme agitation) Donna Anna.
vinta. Perfido! e alfin? Alfine il duol, l'orrore dell' infame atten-
sist him. Miscreant! and then? At last my dread, my horror of the dastardly
tato accrebbe sì la lena mia, che a forza di svinco-
ruffian, lent strength unwonted for the moment; I struggled with tortuous
larmi, torcermi e piegarmi da lui mi sciolsi! Ohimè! re-
writhings fearfully, with an effort I flung him from me. Oh joy! that
Don Octavio.

Donna Anna.
O.
A.
spi - ro. Al - lo - ra rin-for-zo i stri - di mie - i, chia - mo soc-
sav'd thee! A-loud then I clam-or'd for as-sistance, call'd on the
f Tempo I.
cor - so, fug - ge il fel - lon, ar-
household, he sought to fly, but
di - ta-men-te il se-guo fin nel-la stra - da per fer - mar - lo, e
bold - ly I pur-sued him in - to the street, that we might trace him, be-
so-no as-sa - li-tri - ce d'as-sa - li - ta; Il pa - dre vac-
com-ing of my as-sail - ant the as-sail-er, 'Twas there that my
cor-re, vuol co - no - scer - lo, e l'in - de - gno, che del po - ve - ro
fa - ther straight-way chal-leng'd him, and the vil - lain, by whose strength he was
vec - chio e - ra più for - te, com-pie il mi - sfat - to su - o,
ea - si - ly o - ver-pow-er'd, stay'd not his guil-ty mad-ness,

(in an agony of grief, almost collapsing.)
A.
com - pie il mi - sfat - to su - o, col dar - gli mor - te.
stay'd not his guil - ty mad - ness, gave him the death - blow.
"Or sai, chi l'onore.,,
Aria.
Andante.
Donna Anna. (collecting herself, with lofty energy.)
Voice.
Piano.
Strings.
p
Or sai, chi l'o - no - re ra - pi - re a me vol - se, che fù il tra - di - to - re, che il padre, che il pa - dre mi tol - se. Vendet - ta ti chieg - gio, la
The wretch now thou know - est Who sought my be - tray - ing, And ven - geance thou owest my father's, my fa - ther's foul slay - ing. For jus - tice I sue thee, I
Ob.
Fag.
Strings.
Corni sustain.

A.
chie - de il tuo cor, la
ask of thy troth, I
chie - de il tuo cor. Ram - men - ta la
ask of thy troth. Re - mem - ber when
pia - ga del mi - se - ro se - no, ri -
wound - ed, His life - blood was flow - ing, Un -
mi - ra di san - gue co - per - to, coper - to il ter -
sol - aced, un - shriv - en, He heard not, he heard not my
re - no, se l'i - rain te lan - gue d'un giu - sto fu - ror,
cry ing, My heart will be riv - en, If thou break thy oath!
Ob.
Vlns.
Fag.
Bassi.
Tutti.
f

largamente
d'un giu - sto fu - ror! Or sai chi lo - nore ra - pi - re a me vol - se, chi fù il tra - di - to - re, che il padre, che il pa - dre mi tol - se, vendet - ta ti chieg - gio, la chie - de il tuo cor, la chie - de il tuo cor! Ram - men - ta la pia - ga, ri -
Re - mem - ber thy oath! The wretch now thou know - est who sought my be tray - ing, and ven - geance thou ow - est my fa - ther's, my fa - ther's foul slay - ing. For jus - tice I sue thee, I ask of thy troth, I ask of thy troth! Re - member, when wounded, his
Ob. Fag.
Bassi
p
f

A.
mi-ra di san-gue! Ven-det - ta ti chieg-gio, la
life-blood was flowing. For jus - tice I sue thee, I
chie-de il tuo cor, la
ask of thy troth, I
chie-de il tuo cor, ven-det - ta ti chieg-gio, la chie - de il tuo
ask of thy troth, For jus - tice I sue thee, I ask of thy
Winds sustain
cor, ven-det - ta ti chieg-gio, la chie - de il tuo cor, la chie - de il
troth, For jus - tice I sue thee, I ask of thy troth, for jus - tice
tuo cor, la chie - de il tuo cor, la chie - de il tuo
I sue, I ask of thy troth, for jus - tice I

A.
cor, la chie - de il tuo cor; ven - det - ta ti chieggio, la
sue, for jus - tice I sue, for jus-tice I sue thee, I
cresc.
chie - de il tuo cor!
ask of thy troth!
(Exit.)
f
p
Recit.
Don Octavio. (alone.)
O.
Co - me mai cre - der deg - gio, di sì ne - ro de - lit - to ca -
I can scarce - ly be - lieve it, that of crimes so de - grad - ing a
pa - ce un ca - va - lie - re! Ah, di - sco - pri - re il ve - ro o - gni
no - ble can be guil - ty! Close - ly I will pur - sue him, till the
mez - zo si cer - chi; io sen - to in pet - to e di spo - so e da -
truth is dis cov - er'd, ev - 'ry e - mo - tion, my al - le - giance to the
mi - co il do - ver che mi par - la; Dis - in - gan - nar la vo - glio, o ven - di - car - la!
dear one whom my faith I have plighted, bids me a - venge her wrongs and see her righted.

Nº 10b "Dalla sua pace."

Aria.

Don Octavio.
Dal-la sua pa-ce la mia di-pen - de, quel che a lei
On her, my trea-sure, All joy de-pend - eth, Life hath no
Str
p
pia-ce vi-ta mi ren-de, quel che le in-cre-sce, mor-te mi dà,
plea-sure, But that she sendeth, Sor-rows that grieve her Tor-ture my heart,
cresc.
mf
f
Cor.
mor - te, mor-te mi dà.
tor - ture, tor-ture my heart.
Fl.
Fag.
S'el-la so-
E'en when she
Str
p
cresc.
stacc.
spi-ra, so-spi-ro an-ch'i-o, è mia quell' i-ra, quel
sigh-eth, My sighs a waken, And joy it di-eth, By
Ob.
fp
pian - to è mi-o; e non ho be-ne, s'el-la non l'ha, e non ho
her for-saken, Oh, worst of tor-ments, from her to part, Oh worst of
Vlp.
Fag.
sfp
sfp
p

O.
be-ne, s'el-la non l'ha, e non ho be-ne, s'el-la non l'ha!
torments, From her to part, Oh worst of tor-ments, From her to part!
Wind
cresc.
f
Dal-la sua pa-ce la mia di-pen-de, quel ch'a lei pia-ce,
On her, my trea-sure, all joy de-pend-eth, life hath no plea-sure,
Str
p
vi-ta mi ren-de, quel che le in-cre-sce, mor-te mi dà, mor-te,
but that she sendeth, sorrows that grieve her, tor-ture my heart, tor-ture,
cresc.
mf
f
Cor.
p
cresc.
Str
mor-te mi dà; dal-la sua pa-ce la mia di-pen-de, quel che a lei
tor-ture my heart. On her, my trea-sure, all joy de-pend-eth, life hath no
p
Ob.
Fag.
pia-ce, vi-ta mi ren-de, quel che le in-cre-sce, mor-te mi dà,
pleasure, but that she sendeth, sor-rows that grieve her, tor-ture my heart,
Fl.
Wind
mf
f

O.
mor - - te, mor - te mi dà, mor - te mi dà, quel che le in-
tor - - ture, tor - ture my heart, tor - ture my heart; sorrows that
p
Cor.
O.
cre - sce, morte mi dà!
grieve her, torture my heart.
(Exit.)
Tutti.
cresc.
f
tr
Recit.
Leporello (enters from the tavern; after him Don Giovanni, from his villa.)
L.
Io deggio ad o - gni pat - to per sempre abbandonar questo bel mat - to! ec - co - lo quì;
I'll stay with him no longer, I will not have this mad-man for a master! See, there he comes,
L. G.
guarda - te, con qual in - dif - fe - ren - za se ne vie - ne!
look at him, so cool, just as if nothing e'er had happen'd.
Don Giovanni. (gaily)
Oh, Le - po - rel - lo mi - o! va tutto
Well, how are matters going, my Lepo -
L. G.
bene?
rello?
Leporello. (crossly)
Don Gio - va - ni - no mi - o, va tut - to male!
Much worse they scarcely could be, my gay young master.
Don Giovanni.
Co - me va tut - to ma - le?
Worse, say'st thou, how can that be?
Leporello.
Vado a
To your
L. G.
ca - sa, co - me m'or - di - na - ste, con tut - ta quel - la gen - te.
pal - ace I took all those peasants, ac - cording to your or - ders.
Don Giovanni.
Bra - vo!
Bra - vo!

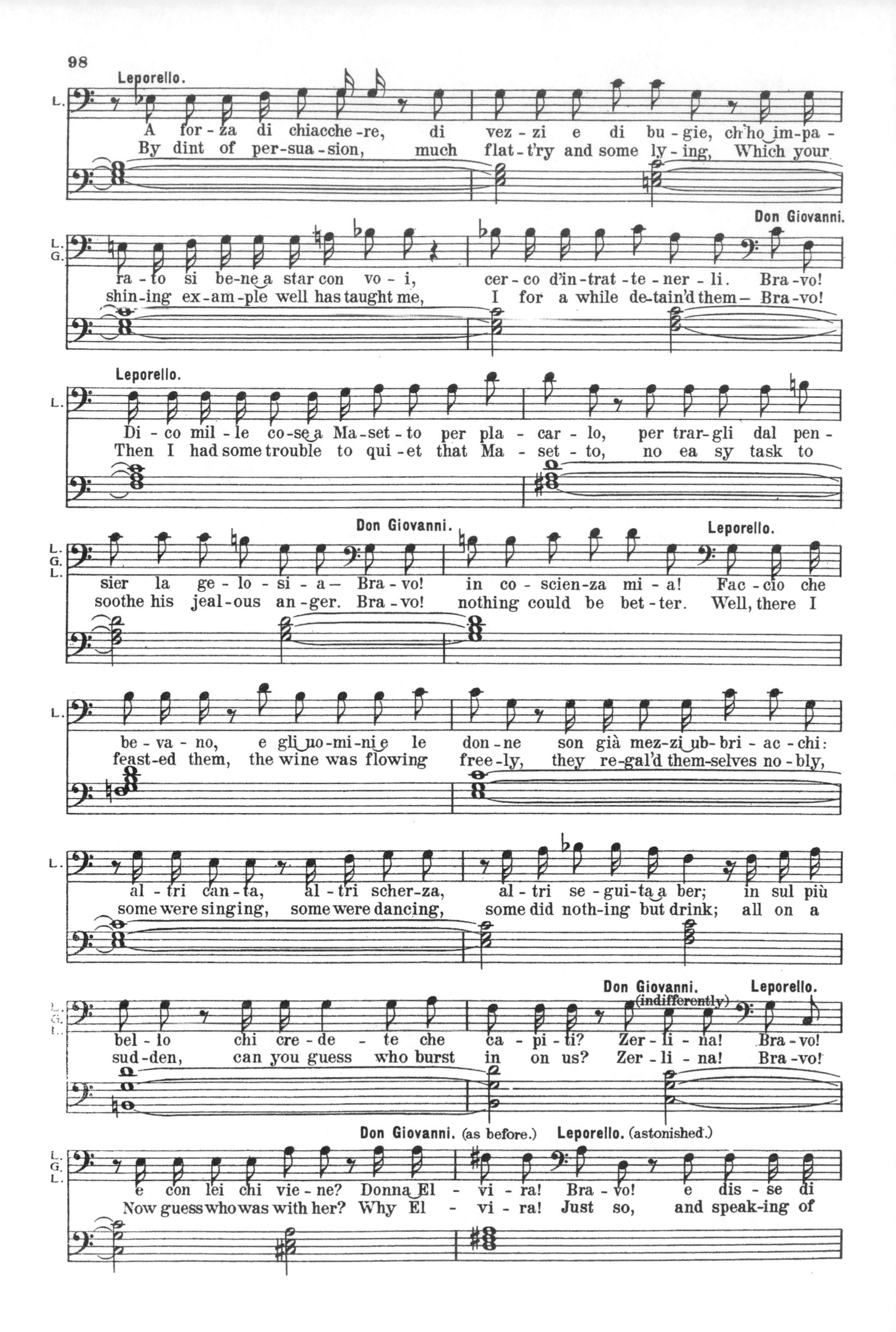
Leporello.
L.
A for - za di chiacche - re, di vez - zi e di bu - gie, ch'ho im - pa -
By dint of per - sua - sion, much flat - t'ry and some ly - ing, Which your
Don Giovanni.
L.
G.
ra - to si be - ne a star con vo - i, cer - co d'in - trat - te - ner - li. Bra - vo!
shin - ing ex - am - ple well has taught me, I for a while de - tain'd them - Bra - vo!
Leporello.
L.
Di - co mil - le co - se a Ma - set - to per pla - car - lo, per trar - gli dal pen -
Then I had some trouble to qui - et that Ma - set - to, no ea sy task to
Don Giovanni.
Leporello.
L.
G.
L.
sier la ge - lo - si - a - Bra - vo! in co - scien - za mi - a! Fac - cio che
soothe his jeal - ous an - ger. Bra - vo! nothing could be bet - ter. Well, there I
L.
be - va - no, e gli uo - mi - ni e le don - ne son già mez - zi ub - bri - ac - chi:
feast - ed them, the wine was flowing free - ly, they re - gal'd them - selves no - bly,
L.
al - tri can - ta, al - tri scher - za, al - tri se - gui - ta a ber; in sul più
some were singing, some were dancing, some did noth - ing but drink; all on a
Don Giovanni.
Leporello.
(indifferently)
bel - lo chi cre - de - te che ca - pi - ti? Zer - li - na! Bra - vo!
sud - den, can you guess who burst in on us? Zer - li - na! Bra - vo!
Don Giovanni. (as before.)
Leporello. (astonished.)
L.
G.
L.
e con lei chi vie - ne? Donna El - vi - ra! Bra - vo! e dis - se di
Now guess who was with her? Why El - vi - ra! Just so, and speak - ing of

Don Giovanni. (humorously)
Leporello.
voi– Tutto 'quel mal che in boc-ca le ve-ni-a! Bra-vo, in co-sci-en-za
you– As of a wretch whom hanging were too good for! Shrewdly guess'd, nothing could be
Don Giovanni.
Leporello. Don Giovanni. Leporello. D. Giov.
mi-a! E tu, co-sa fa-ce-sti? Tacqui. Ed el-la? Seguì a gri-dar. E
better! What said you to her raving? Nothing. She scolded? Yes, that she did; And
Leporello.
tu? Quan-do mi par-ve che già fos-se sfo-ga-ta, dol-ce-men-te fuor del-
you? When it appear'd as if the storm were sub-sid-ing, from the house I gen-tly
l'or-to la tras-si, e con bell' ar-te, chiu-sa la por-ta a chia-ve a mi sot-
led her convers-ing, and there I left her, lock'd fast the door, put the key in-to my
Don Giovanni.
tra-i, e sul-la via so-let-ta la la-scia-i. Bra-vo!
pock-et; out-side she may pur-sue her lam-en-ta-tions, Le-po-
bra-vo! ar-ci-bra-vo! l'af-far non può andar me-glio; in-co-min-
rel-lo, thou'rt a gen-ius! 'twas managed to per-fect-ion. Soon I will
cia-sti, io sa-prò ter-mi-nar. Trop-po mi pre-mo-no
fin-ish what so well you've be-gun. But now these coun-try-girls
que-ste con-ta-di-not-te; le vo-glio di-ver-tir finchè vien not-te.
with their gay sports invite me, we will return to them, I'll now de-light me.

Nº 11. "Finch' han dal vino."

Aria.

Presto.
G.
Flauti., Ob., Cl., Fag., Corni & Strings.
Don Giovanni.
Finch'han dal vi - no cal - da la te - sta, u - na gran
For a ca - rousal Where all is madness, Where all is
(to Leporello)
fe - sta fa pre - pa - rar! Se tro - vi in piaz - za qual - che ra - gaz - za,
gladness, Do thou pre - pare. Maids that are pret - ty, Dames that are wit - ty,
te - co an - cor quel - la cer - ca me - nar, te - co an - cor quel - la
All to my cas - tle Bid them re - pair, All to my cas - tle
cer - ca me - nar, cer - ca me - nar, cer - ca me - nar. Senza alcun
Bid them re - pair, bid them re - pair, bid them re - pair. I'll have no
Cl.

G.
or-di-ne la danza si-a, chi'l menu-et-to, chi la fo-li-a,
dis-cipline, Fol-ly shall rule it, Some minu-etting, Each one shall fool it,
f p
Ob. Fag. Fl.
chi l'a-le-ma-na fa-rai bal-lar, chi'l me-nu-et-to fa-rai bal-
Some a fan-dango, So they are fair, Some minu-et-ting, so they are
Ob. Cl. Fag. Vln.
lar, chi la fol-li-a fa-rai bal-lar, chi l'a-le-ma-na
fair, Each one shall fool it, so they are fair, Some a fan-dan-go,
fa-rai bal-lar! Ed io frat-tan-to dall' altro can-to con questa e quella
so they are fair! Then in the gloaming, Pen-sively roaming, Some pretty damsel
Ob. Cl. & Cor. sustain.
tr
vo'a-moreggiar, vo'a-mo-reg-giar, vo'a-mo-reg-giar; Ah, la mia
With me will stray, with me will stray, with me will stray, Beauties in

G.
li - sta do-man mat - ti - na d'u - na de - ci - na de - vi aumentar,
plenty My list a - dorning, Will, ere the morning, Not say me nay,
G.
Ah, la mia li - sta d'u - na de - ci - na de - vi aumen-
Beauties in plenty Will, ere the morning, Not say me
f
p
tr
G.
tar. Se trovi in piazza qual - che ra - gaz - za, te - co ancor quel - la cer - ca me -
nay. Maids that are pret - ty, Dames that are wit - ty, All to my cas - tle bid them re -
Tutti.
fp
G.
nar. Ah la mia li - sta do - man mat - ti - na
pair. For a ca - rousal where all is madness,
Fl.
Vln.
Fl. & Str.
fp
p
tr
G.
d'u - na de - ci - na de - vi aumen - tar! Sen - za al - cun or - di - ne,
Where all is gladness, do thou pre - pare! I'll have no dis - cipline,
Tutti
fp

G.
la danza si - a, chi'l menu - et - to, chi la fol - li - a, chi l'a - le - ma - na
Fol - ly shall rule it, Some minu - et - ting, Each one shall fool it, Some a fan - dan - go,
fp
fa - rai bal - lar.
So they are fair.
Fl. Vln.
Ob. Cl. Fag.
Ah, la mia li - sta do - man mat - ti - na
Beauties in plenty My list a - dorning,
d'u - na de - ci - na de - vi aumen - tar, d'u - na de - ci - na de - vi aumen -
Will, ere the morning, Not say me nay, Will, ere the morn - ing, Not say me
tr
f
p
tar, d'u - na de - ci - na de - vi aum - tar, de - vi aumen - tar,
nay, Will, ere the morn - ing, Not say me nay, none say me nay
de - vi aumen - tar, de - vi, de - vi au - men - tar!
none say me nay, none, none say me nay!
(signs to Leporello to
cresc.

104 fetch the peasants from the tavern; he then hastens into his villa, Leporello going to the tavern.)
tr
Scene.—A Garden. Two closed doors in the wall. Two alcoves.
Zerlina, Masetto. Chorus of Peasants, scattered here and there, sitting or lying on banks of turf.
Recit.
Zerlina. (coming with Masetto from tavern; tries to take his hand.)
Masetto.
Z.
M.
Ma-set-to, sen-ti un po'! Ma-set-to, di-co! Non mi toc-
Ma-set-to, hear me speak, I say, Ma-set-to– Let me a-
Zerlina.
Masetto.
M.
Z.
M.
car! Per-chè? Per-chè mi chie-di? per-fi-da! il
lone! And why? And why, you ask me? Faith-less girl! No
M.
Z.
tat-to sop-por-tar do-vre-i d'u-na man in-fe-de-le? Ah
long-er I'll bear your ca-pric-es since no long-er you love me. No,
Zerlina.
Z.
M.
no, ta-ci, cru-de-le, io non mer-to da te tal trat-ta-men-to. Co-me?
no, you are mis-tak-en, Oh, how can you be-have with such un-kindness? How so?
Masetto.
M.
ed hai l'ar-di-men-to di scu-sar-ti? star so-la con un
And have you the face to make ex-cus-es? A stranger leads you

M.
uom: ab-bando-nar-mi il dì del-le mie noz-ze! porre in fron-te a un vil-la-no d'o-
on, for him you leave me on the eve of our marriage, both your faith and my honor for-
M.
no-re que-sta mar-ca d'in-famia! Ah, se non fos-se, se non fos-se lo scanda-lo,
getting, you rush on to your ru-in! Oh it is too much, if I did not contain my-self
(goes exitedly to other side.)
Zerlina. (interrupting him)
M.
Z.
vor-re-i— Ma se col-pa io non ho, ma se da lui in-gan-na-ta ri-
I'd strike you. But it was not my fault; if for the mo-ment his flatter-y
Z.
ma-si, e poi che te-mi? tran-quil-la-ti, mia vi-ta: non mi toc-
pleased me, how could I help it? Now think of him no long-er, there was no
Z.
cò la pun-ta del-le di-ta: non me lo cre-di? In-gra-to! vien
harm, his words I scarcely answered. Say you be-lieve me! un-grateful! come
(agitatedly)
Z.
qui: sfo-ga-ti, a-maz-za-mi, Fa tut-to di me quelche ti
here, strike me then, I'll bear it all, kill me if you think my fault so
(tenderly)
Z.
pia-ce; Ma poi, Ma-set-to mi-o, ma poi fa pa-ce.
heinous, and then, my own Ma-set-to, peace be be-tween us.
attacca l'aria

No. 12. "Batti, batti, o bel Masetto."

Aria.

Andante grazioso.
Zerlina.
Z.
Bat - ti, bat - ti, o bel Ma - set - to, la tua po - ve - ra Zer -
Canst thou see me, un - for - giv - en, Here in sor - row stand and
p sempre legato
li - na: sta - rò qui come a - gnel - li - na le tue bot - te ad a - spet -
languish? Oh Ma - set - to, end my an - guish, Come, and let's be friends a -
tar. Bat - ti, bat - ti la tua Zer - li - na; sta - rò
gain. Canst thou see me here stand and languish, Oh Ma -
Fl.
Ob.
Fag.
p
Cor.
(Masetto crosses over.)
qui, sta - rò qui le tue botte ad a - spet - tar.
set - to, end my anguish, Come, and let's be friends a - gain.
Vln.
tr
Wood
Lascie - rò straziar mi il cri - ne,
Oh believe, I sore re - pent it,

Z.
tr
Lascie-rò cavar-mi gli occhi, e le ca - re tue ma -
But I did not under - stand. Come, no long - er then re -
ni - ne lie - ta poi sa-prò ba - ciar, sa - prò ba -
sent it, give me kind - ly thy dear hand, oh give thy
f p
ciar, ba - ciar, sa - prò, sa - prò ba -
hand, thy hand, Oh give me thy dear
fp
(Masetto goes away again, but not so crossly; he even steals a few glances at Zerlina.)
ciar. Bat - ti, batti o bel Ma -
hand. Canst thou see me, un - for -
Wood Cor: sustain.
Str.
set - to, la tua po - ve - ra Zer - li - na! sta - rò qui come a - gnel -
giv - en, Here in sor - row stand and languish? Oh Ma - set - to, end my

(still trying to get one of Masetto's hands; he always draws back.)
li - na le tue botte ad a - spet - tar. O bel Ma - set - to!
anguish, Come and let's be friends a - gain. O canst thou see me
Wood
Bat - ti, bat - ti! sta - rò qui, sta - rò qui le tue botte ad a - spet -
Stand and languish, Oh Ma - set - to, end my anguish, Come, and let's be friends a -
tar. Ah, lo ve - do,
gain. Ah, con - fess it,
Vln.
non hai co - re, ah non hai
ah, con - fess it, Ah thou no
(here Zerlina seizes one of his hands.)
Allegro.
co - re, ah, lo ve - do, non hai co - re. Pa - ce, pa - ce, o vi - ta
long - er, thou no long - er canst withstand me. Peace and joy once more shall
cresc.
Cello

Z.
mi - a! pa-ce, pa - ce,o vi - ta mi - a! in — con - ten - to,ed al - le -
bless us, Not a frown shall e'er dis-tress us, While u - nit - ed and de -
Z.
gri - a not - te,e dì — vo - gliam pas - sar,
light - ed All — our days shall sweet - ly glide,
Ob.
Fag.
Z.
not - te,e dì — vo - gliam pas - sar,
All — our days shall sweet - ly glide,
not - te,e
All our
Wood.
Z.
dì — vo - gliam pas - sar,
days shall sweet - ly glide,
not - te,e dì — vo - gliam pas -
All our days shall sweet - ly
Z.
sar. Pa - ce, pa - ce,o vi - ta mi - a! Pa - ce, pa - ce,o vi - ta
glide. Peace and joy — a - gain shall bless us, Peace and joy — a - gain shall
Str.

Z.
mi - a! in con - ten - to ed al - le - gri - a not - te e
bless us, Not a frown shall e'er dis - tress - us, All our
Fl.
Fag.
Cor. sost.
(Masetto, quite persuaded, gazes joyfully on his bride.)
dì vo - gliam pas - sar, sì, sì, sì, sì, sì, sì, not - te e
days shall sweet - ly glide, yes, yes, yes, yes, yes, yes, All our
dì vo - gliam pas - sar, sì, sì, sì, sì, sì, sì, not - te e dì vo - gliam pas -
days shall sweet - ly glide, yes, yes, yes, yes, yes, yes, All our days shall sweet - ly
sar, vo - gliam, vo - gliam pas - sar, vo - gliam, vo - gliam pas -
glide, shall sweet - ly sweet - ly glide, shall sweet - ly, sweet - ly
sar.
glide.
pp

Recit.
Masetto. (gaily.)
M.
Guarda un po', co-me sep-pe que-sta stre-ga se-dur-mi! sia-mo
'Tis no use my re-sist-ing, lit-tle witch, you've ca-jol'd me! When a
M.
G.
Don Giovanni (within.)
pu-re i de-bo-li di te-sta! Sia pre-pa-ra-to tut-to a u-na gran
woman's de-termin'd, who can stay her? Soon will the guests as-sem-ble, let all be
G.
Z.
Zerlina. (frightened.)
fe-sta. Ah, Ma-set-to, Ma-set-to, o-di la vo-ce del Mon-
read-y. Ah, Ma-set-to, Ma-set-to, hark, 'tis his lord-ship, how his
Z.
M.
Masetto. (suspiciously.)
Zerlina.
Masetto.
sù Ca-va-lie-ro! Eb-ben, che c'è? Ver-rà! La-scia che
voice makes me tremble! Why should it, pray? He comes. I do not
M.
Z.
Zerlina.
Masetto.
ven-ga. Ah, se vi fos-se un bu-co da fug-gir! Di co-sa te-mi, per-
mind him. Oh, for a corner to hide my-self from him! Why do you tremble? Why
M.
chè di-ven-ti pal-li-da? Ah, ca-pi-sco! ca-pi-sco, bric-concel-la: hai ti-
do you thus change countenance? Ah, I see it, there is something between you, and you
(it gradually grows dark.)
M.
mor ch'io com-pren-da com' è tra voi pas-sa-ta la fac-cen-da.
dread I should know it, flirt that you are, your terrors plainly shew it.

Nº 13. "Presto, presto, pria ch'ei venga."

Finale.

Allegro assai.
Masetto.
M.
Pre-sto, pre-sto, pria ch'ei venga, por-mi vo' da qual - che
Quickly, quickly I'll out-wit him, In some nook I'll creep and
Strs. Fl. & Fag.
p
(pointing at the arbor)
la - to; c'è u-na nic-chia qui ce - la - to, che - to, che - to
watch him; None will see me, I will watch him, Here in safe - ty
Fag. Cor.
Fl. Ob. Cl.
Vln.
(going)
Zerlina. (retains him)
M. Z.
mi vo' star. Sen-ti, sen-ti! do-ve va - i? ah non t'a - sconder, o Ma -
I can wait. Softly, softly, Why this hiding? Oh dear Ma - set-to, do not
mfp
Z.
set - to! se ti tro-va, po - ve - ret - to! tu non sai quel che può
grieve me, Think that if my lord perceive thee, Sure his an-ger will be
Masetto. (angrily)
Z. M.
far, po - ve - ret-to! tu non sai quel che può far. Faccia, di - ca quel che
great, sure his anger, oh his an - ger will be great. Let him say what-e'er he
cresc.
f

Zerlina.
Z.
M.
(Ah, non gio - van le pa - ro - le!)
(All he wish - es straight he seiz - es.)
vuo - le. Par - la for - te, e qui t'ar -
pleas - es. Why, speak out, what art thou
p
cresc.
f
Che ca - pric - cio ha nel - la te - sta, che ca - pric - cio ha nel - la
Do not bawl so in my hear - ing, Do not bawl so in my
re - sta! Par - la for - te, e qui t'ar -
fear - ing? Why, speak out, what art thou
p
cresc.
cresc.
(sotto voce)
te - sta? quell' in - gra - to, quel cru - de - le, og - gi
hearing! He doth use me most un - kind - ly, He's to -
(sotto voce)
re - sta! Ca - pi - rò se m'è fe - de - le, e in qual modo
fear - ing? I must know if she would blind me, and my anger
p
vuol pre - ci - pi - tar; quell' in - gra - to, quel cru - de - le, og - gi vuol pre - ci - pi -
day in sur - ly mood, He doth use me most un - kindly, He's to - day in sur - ly
an - dò l'affar! Ca - pi - rò se m'è fe - de - le,
shall be subdued, I must know if she would blind me,

Z.
tar, quell' in-gra-to, quel cru-de-le,
mood. He doth use me most un-kind-ly,
M.
se m'è fe-de-le, e in qual mo-do an-dò l'af-far, in qual
Yes I must know it, And my an-ger shall be sub-dued, yes, my
Z.
og-gi vuol pre-ci-pi-tar. (Enter Don Giovanni with four gaily dressed servants)
He's to-day in surly mood.
M.
G.
Don Giovanni. (to the peasants)
mo-do an-dò l'af-far. (Hides in the arbor) Sù! sve-
an-ger shall be sub-dued. Come, let
Tutti
f
G.
glia-te-vi da bra-vi! Sù! co-rag-gio, o buo-na
all be mirth and gladness! Deep-ly quaff the draught of
f
p
G.
gen-te! vogliam sta-re al-le-gra-men-te, vogliam ri-de-re, e scher-
pleas-ure! Let your rev-els have no meas-ure, We will turn the night to
f
f
p
(to the servants)
G.
zar. Al-la stan-za del-la dan-za con-du-ce-te tut-ti
day. Those who are for pi-rou-et-ing, give them mu-sic in the
tr

G.
quan-ti, ed a tut-ti a ab-bon-dan-za, gran ri-fre-schi fa-te
ball-room, Those whose turn is for co-quett-ing, in the gar-den let them
dar! gran ri-fre-schi fa-te dar!
stray, gai-ly pass the time a-way.
(Don Giovanni, looking everywhere for Zerlina, at last discovers her, and then gives Leporello a sign to take the peasants and servants into the villa)
cresc.
f
Chorus of Servants.
TENOR & BASS.
Sù, sve-glia-te-vi da bra-vi!
Come let all be mirth and glad-ness!
Sù! co-rag-gio, o buo-na gen-te! vo-gliam sta-re al-le-gra-
Deep-ly quaff the draught of pleasure! Our de-lights shall have no
men-te, vo-gliam ri-de-re, e scher-zar, Vo-gliam sta-re al-le-gra-
measure, We will turn the night to day, Our de-lights shall have no

(going off.)
men-te, vo-gliam ri-de-re e scher-zar, vo-gliam ri-de-re e scher-
measure, We will turn the night to day, we will turn the night to
(exit.)
zar, vo-gliam ri-de-re e scher-zar, vo-gliam
day, we will turn the night to day, we will
poco a poco piano
Andante.
Zerlina (trying to hide herself.)
Z.
Tra quest'
In this
(exeunt peasants.)
ri-de-re e scher-zar!
turn the night to day!
Andante.
Vln.
p
Z.
ar-bo-ri-ce-la-ta, si può dar che non mi
ar-bor I will hide me, None my pres-ence here per-
Don Giovanni.
(detains her.)
Z.
G.
ve-da. Zer-li-net-ta, mia gar-ba-ta,
ceiving. Sweet Zer-li-na, I'm be-side thee.
Cor.
f

G.
Z.
Zerlina. (trying to escape).
t'ho già vi-sto, t'ho già vi - sto, non scop-par. Ah, la-scia - te-mi andar
To escape a lov-er's glance will ne'er suc-ceed! Ah my Lord, I'm greatly
tr
p
Don Giovanni.
Zerlina.
vi - a! No, no, re - sta, gio - ja mi - a! Se pie - ta - dea-ve-te in
frighten'd! Oh how fair! with co-lor heighten'd! If thou'rt kind, I pray thee,
Don Giovanni.
(indicating the arbor, which
co - re Sì, ben mio, son tut-to a - mo - re; vie - - - ni un
leave me All my heart's thine own, be - lieve me, To yon
he approaches backwards, drawing Zerlina after him)
po - co in que - sto lo - co! for - tu - na - ta io ti vo'
ar - bor let me guide thee, There a ten - der tale I'll
Zerlina.
Ah! sei ve - de il spo - so mi - o, so ben
Ah, how would Ma - set - to chide me, If thy
far! vie - ni un po - co in que - sto lo - co, for - tu -
plead, To yon ar - bor let me guide thee, There a

Z.
io quel che può far, sò ben io, sò ben io, sò quel che può
flatt-'ries I should heed, he would chide, he would chide, if thee I could
G.
na - ta io ti vo' far! for - tu - na - ta io ti vo'
ten - der tale I'll plead, There a ten - der tale I'll
Z.
far, sò ben io, sò ben io, sò quel che può far!
heed, he would chide, he would chide, if thee I could heed.
G.
far! for - tu - na - ta io ti vo' far!
plead, There a ten - der tale I'll plead.
Str. & Corni
M.
Masetto.
(Don Giovanni goes towards the arbor, sees Masetto, and stands petrified.)
Sì, Ma - set - to!
Yes, Ma - set - to!
Don Giovanni (a little confused)
G.
Ma - set - to?
Ma - set - to?
E chiu - so là, per - chè?
So sur - ly? Wherefore pray?
(recovering himself)
La bel - la tua Zer -
Zer - li - na here, is

G.
li - na non può, la po - ve - ri - na, più
sigh - ing, Be - cause the hours are fly - ing. And
star sen - za di te, non può più star sen - za di
thou from her a - way, and thou, and thou from her a -
Masetto. (ironically)
Don Giovanni.
te. Ca - pi - sco, sì, Si - gno - re. A - des - so fa - te
way. Your kind - ness would I might re - pay! Come, think of no un -
Cl.
cresc.
Allegretto.
(steps between Masetto and Zerlina, giving each an arm).
co - re, fa - te co - re. I suo - na - to - ri u - di - te, ve -
kindness, no un - kindness. Where mu - sic gay in - vites us, We'll
Quartet, Ob. and horns
(on stage, at a distance)
Zerlina.
Sì, sì, fac - cia - mo co - re, sì, sì, fac - ciamo
He means us no un - kindness, he means us no un -
Masetto.
ni - te o - mai con me! Sì, sì, fac - ciamo
fro - lic, dance and play. He means us no un -
Orchestra

Z.
co-re, ed a bal-lar co-gli al-tri an-dia-mo tut-ti tre, an-
kind-ness, Where mu-sic gay in-vites us, Come let us haste a-way, Where
Don Giovanni.
G.
Ve-ni-te o-mai, ve-ni-te o-mai con me, ve-
To mu-sic gay, Come let us haste a-way, Where
M.
co-re, ed a bal-lar co-gli al-tri an-dia-mo tut-ti tre, an-
kind-ness, Where mu-sic gay in-vites us, Come let us haste a-way Where
cresc.
f
dia-mo, an-dia-mo tut-ti tre, an-dia-mo, an-dia-mo
mu-sic in-vites us, haste a-way, Where mu-sic in-vites us,
ni-te, ve-ni-te o-mai con me, ve-ni-te, ve-ni-te o-
mu-sic in-vites us, haste a-way, Where mu-sic in-vites us,
dia-mo, an-dia-mo tut-ti tre, an-dia-mo, an-dia-mo
mu-sic in-vites us, haste a-way, Where mu-sic in-vites us,
tut-ti tre, an-dia-mo tut-ti tre, an-dia-mo tut-ti tre!
haste a-way, Come let us haste a-way, Come let us haste a-way!
mai con me, ve-ni-te o-mai con me, ve-ni-te o-mai con me!
haste a-way, Come let us haste a-way, Come let us haste a-way!
tut-ti tre, an-dia-mo tut-ti tre, an-dia-mo tut-ti tre!
haste a-way, Come let us haste a-way, Come let us haste a-way! (Exeunt.)
(Enter Don Octavio, Donna Anna, and Donna Elvira, masked.)
Str.
Wind
p

Donna Elvira.
E.
Bi - sog - na a - ver co - rag - gio, o ca - ri a - mi - ci mie - i! e i
We come in night and darkness, By just re - sent - ment guid - ed, To
Vlns in 8ve
E.
O.
Don Octavio.
suoi mi - sfat - ti re - i sco - prir, sco - prir po - tre - mo al - lor. La -
heav'n we have con - fid - ed Our trust, our trust this woe to end. His
O.
mi - ca di - ce be - ne! co - raggio a - ver con - vie - ne; di - scac - cia o vi - ta
dar - ing crimes re - sent - ing, Her grevious wrongs la - ment - ing, Al - lay thy fears, oh
O.
mi - a, l'af - fan - no ed il ti - mor!
dear - est, Thy cause I will de - fend.
Corni sustain.
Donna Anna.
A.
Il pas - so è pe - ri - glio - so,
My heart with hope thou cheer - est,
A.
può na - scer qual - che im - bro - glio.
Our path is full of dan - ger,
Str.

A.
Io te - mo pel ca - ro spo - so, pel
I trem - ble for thee, oh dear - est, for
A.
ca - ro spo-so, e per noi te - mo an - cor!
thee, oh dearest, And thee, oh gen - tle friend!
A.
te - - mo pel ca - ro spo - so, pel ca - ro
I fear for thee, oh dear - est, for thee, oh
Wood.
Fag.
A.
spo - so, e per noi te - mo an - cor!
dear - est, And thee, oh gen - tle friend!
(Leporello opens the window from within.) Leporello.
L.
Menuetto. (in the distance, on the stage)
Si-gnor guar-da-te un po - co, che mas-che-re ga-
Sir, see those charming maskers, here standing just be-
p
Don Giovanni. (at the window.)
L.
G.
lan - ti! Fal - le pas-sar a - van - ti, dì, che ci fan - no o-
low us, Hop-ing they may not know us, Ask, will they please as-

Donna Anna. p (all three have seen Don Giovanni; aside).
A.
Al vol - to ed al - la vo - ce si sco - pre il tra - di - to - re!
Donna Elvira. That voice, and manner, sure-ly 'Tis he whom we are seek - ing!
E.
p
Al vol - to ed al - la vo - ce si sco - pre il tra - di - to - re!
Don Octavio. That voice, and manner, sure-ly 'Tis he whom we are seek - ing!
O.
p
Al vol - to ed al - la vo - ce si sco - pre il tra - di - to - re!
That voice, and manner, sure-ly 'Tis he whom we are seek - ing!
G.
L.
Leporello.
nor!
cend!
Zi!
'St
A.
Via ri - spon - de - te.
What would he ask us?
(to Don Octavio _ softly.)
E.
Via ri - spon - de - te.
What would he ask us?
L.
zi! Si - gno - re ma - schere! Zi! zi!
'st! ye gen - tle maskers, stay, 'st! 'st!
Zi!
'St!
Don Octavio.
O.
Co - sa chie - de - te?
What is your pleasure?
L.
zi! Si - gno - re ma - schere!
'st! ye gentle maskers, stay.
Al bal - lo, se vi
My mas - ter sends t'in -

Don Octavio. (to Leporello).
(to Donna
L.
O.
pia - ce, v'in - vi - ta il mio Si - gnor. Gra - zie di tan - to o - no - re! an -
vite you An hour with him to spend. Thanks, we ac - cept with plea - sure His
Anna and D. Elvira)
Leporello. (aside)
O.
L.
diam, compagne bel - le. L'a - mi - co anche su quel - le
cour - teous in - vi - ta - tion. With - out pre - me - di - ta - tion,
Adagio.
Donna Anna. (all three unmask, and
A.
Pro - teg - ga il giu - sto
Thou pow'r a - bove, be
Don Octavio.
L.
O.
pro - va fa - rà d'a - mor! Pro - teg - ga il giu - sto
Straightway they condes - cend! (Goes in and shuts the window) Thou pow'r a - bove, be
Adagio.
Str.
Orchestra p
advance to front.)
A.
cie - lo il ze - lo del mio cor! pro -
near us, Our hopes on thee de - pend! Thou
Donna Elvira.
E.
Ven - di - chi il giu - sto cie - lo il mio tra - di - to a -
Thou wilt a - venge and hear us! To me thou'lt jus - tice
O.
cie - lo il ze - lo del mio cor!
near us, Our hopes on thee de - pend!
Wind.

A.
teg - ga il giu - - sto cie - - - lo il
pow'r a - bove, be near us, Our
E.
mor, ven-di-chi il giu-sto cie-lo il mio tra-di-to a-
send! Thou wilt a - venge and hear us: To me thou'lt jus-tice
O.
pro-teg-ga il giu-sto cie-lo il ze-lo del mio
Thou pow'r a - bove, be near us: Our hopes on thee de-
Cl.
Fag.
A.
ze - - - - - - - lo del mio cor, pro-
hopes on thee de - pend, Oh
E.
mor, il mio tra - di-to, tra-di-to a-mor!
send, to me for - lorn thou'lt jus-tice send!
O.
cor, il ze-lo il ze-lo del mio cor!
pend, our hopes, our hopes on thee de - pend!
A.
teg - ga il giu - - sto cie - - - lo il
pow'r a - bove, be near us, Our
E.
Ven-di-chi il giu-sto cie-lo il mio tra - di - to a-
Thou wilt a - venge and hear us, To me thou'lt jus-tice
O.
pro-teg-ga il giu-sto cie-lo il ze-lo del mio
Oh pow'r a - bove, be near us, Our hopes on thee de-
Cl.

A.
ze - - - - lo del mio cor, pro -
hopes on thee de - pend! Thou
E.
mor, il mio, il mio tra-di - to a-mor, ven-di-chi, ven-di-chi il giusto
send, to me for - lorn thou'lt jus - tice send! Thou wilt avenge, wilt avenge and
O.
cor, il zelo, il ze - lo del mio cor, pro -
pend, our hopes, our hopes on thee de - pend! Thou
A.
teg-ga il giu - sto cie-lo il ze - lo del mio
pow'r a - bove, be - near us, Our hopes on thee de -
E.
cie - lo il mio tra-di - to, tra - di - to a - mor, tra-di - to a -
hear us, To me forlorn, thou wilt jus-tice send, thou'lt jus - tice
O.
teg - ga il giu - sto cie-lo il ze - lo del mio
pow'r a - bove be - near us, Our hopes on thee de -
A.
cor!
pend! (All resume their masks.)
E.
mor!
send! (Exeunt.) (Scene changes to a brilliantly lighted ballroom.)
O.
cor!
pend!
Ob
Fl.
Cl.
sfp
Fag.

(Don Giovanni is handing some young girls to seats. Leporello is amongst the men; a dance is just over.)
Allegro.
Don Giovanni.
Ri-po-sa-te, vez-zo-se ra-gaz-ze!
Pret-ty maidens, now rest from your dancing,
Leporello.
Rin-fre-sca-te-vi, bei gio-vi-
Cooling drinks ye all want to re-
Tor-ne-re-te a far presto le paz-ze, tor-ne-re-te a scher-zar e bal-
If I lose now your presence en-tranc-ing, you must promise me soon to re-
net-ti! Tor-ne-re-te a far presto le paz-ze, tor-ne-re-te a scher-zar e bal-
fresh ye, If he los-es your presence en-tranc-ing, you must promise him soon to re-
(to the servants)
lar, a scher-zar e bal-lar! Ehi, Caf-fè! (Refreshments are handed.)
turn, pro-mise soon to re-turn. Here, some ice!
lar, a scher-zar e bal-lar!
turn, pro-mise soon to re-turn.
cresc.
Vln.

Leporello.
Masetto.(holding Zerlina anxiously by her gown) Don Giovanni.
L.
M.
G.
Cioc-co-la-te! Ah, Zer-li-na! giu-di-zio! Sor-
Give champagnehere! Oh Zer-li-na, be pru-dent! More
Wind.
Vln.
Leporello.
Masetto.
G.
L.
M.
bet-ti! Con-fet-ti! Ah, Zer-li-na! giu-di-zio!
wine here! I come,sir! Oh Zer-li-na, be pru-dent!
Zerlina. (aside in great confusion).
Z.
Trop-po dol-ce co-min-cia la sce-na, in a-
There's too much of this gid-dy ca-reer-ing, You will
Masetto. (aside.)
M.
Trop-po dol-ce co-min-cia la sce-na, in a-
There's too much of this gid-dy ca-reer-ing, You will
tr
Z.
ma-ro po-tria ter-mi-nar, sì, in a-ma-ro po-
see that to grief it will turn, yes, you will see that to
M.
ma-ro po-tria ter-mi-nar, sì, in a-ma-ro po-
see that to grief it will turn, yes, you will see that to

Zerlina. (smiling shyly)
tria ter-mi-nar! Sua bon-tà!
grief it will turn. You're so kind!
Don Giovanni. (caressingly.)
tria ter-mi-nar! Sei pur va-ga, brillan-te Zer-li-na!
grief it will turn. E-ver charming, my pretty Zer-li-na!
Wind.
Vlns
Cl.
Fag.
Leporello. (Amongst the girls, imitating his master.)
Sei pur ca-ra, Gia-not-ta, San-dri-na!
Al-ways love-ly, my fine Al-phon-si-na!
Masetto. (aside, enraged)
La bric-co-na fa fe-sta! Toc-ca pur, che ti ca-da la te-sta.
How the flirt is co-quet-ting! That my cane to thy back I were set-ting!
Zerlina (aside; looking at Masetto).
Quel Ma-set-to mi par stra-lu-na-to, brut-to, brut-to si fa quest' af-far!
That Ma-set-to will get in-to trou-ble, All my plans he is sure to o'er-turn!
cresc.
Quel Ma-set-to mi par stra-lu-
That Ma-set-to will get in-to
Don Giovanni. (aside)
Quel Ma-set-to mi par stra-lu-na-to,
That Ma-set-to will get in-to trou-ble,
Leporello. (aside)
Quel Ma-set-to mi par stra-lu-na-to,
That Ma-set-to will get in-to trou-ble,
f
p

Z.
na-to! Brut-to, brut-to si fa quest'af-
trou-ble, All my plans he is sure to o'er-
G.
Qui bi-so-gna cer-vel-lo-a-do-prar.
How to pun-ish this rus-tic I burn!
L.
Qui bi-so-gna cer-vel-lo-a-do-prar.
How to pun-ish this rus-tic I burn!
Masetto. (growing angrier.)
M.
La bric-co-na fa fe-sta!
How the flirt is co-quet-ting!
Wind.
Vln.
Z.
far! Quel Ma-set-to mi par stra-lu-
turn! That Ma-set-to will get in-to
G.
Quel Ma-set-to mi par stra-lu-
That Ma-set-to will get in-to
Masetto.
Lep.
M.
L.
Toc-ca pur, che ti ca-da la te-sta! Quel Ma-set-to mi par stra-lu-
That my cane to thy back I were set-ting! That Ma-set-to will get in-to
f
p
Z.
na-to, brut-to, brut-to si fa quest'af-far, si fa quest' af-far! quel Ma-
trou-ble, All my plans he is sure to o'er-turn, sure to o-ver-turn! That Ma-
G.
na-to, qui bi-so-gna cer-vel-lo-a-do-prar, cer-vel-lo-a-do-prar! quel Ma-
trou-ble, How to pun-ish this rus-tic I burn, to pun-ish I burn! That Ma-
L.
na-to, qui bi-so-gna cer-vel-lo-a-do-prar, cer-vel-lo-a-do-prar! quel Ma-
trou-ble, How to pun-ish this rus-tic I burn, to pun-ish I burn! That Ma-
Masetto.
M.
Toc-ca, toc-ca!
Oh, I see thee!
f
p
cresc.
f
p

Z.
set-to mi par stralu - na - to, brutto, brut-to si fa quest' af - far, si
set-to will get in-to trou - ble, All my plans he is sure to o'er - turn, is
G.
set-to mi par stralu - na - to, qui bi - sogna cervello a-do - prar, cer-
set-to will get in-to trou - ble, How to punish this rustic I burn, to
L.
set-to mi par stralu - na - to, qui bi - sogna cervello a-do - prar, cer-
set-to will get in-to trou - ble, How to punish this rustic I burn, to
M.
Ah bricco - na! ah bric-co - na! mi
flirt, I see thee! Faith-less flirt, thy af -
f
p
cresc.
fa quest'af-far, brut-to, brut - to si fa quest'af-far!
sure to o'er-turn, All my plans he is sure to o'er-turn.
vel - lo a-do - prar, qui bi - so - gna cer-vel - lo a-do-prar!
pun - ish I burn, How to pun - ish this rus- tic I burn!
vel - lo a-do - prar, qui bi - so - gna cer-vel - lo a-do-prar!
pun - ish I burn, How to pun - ish this rus - tic I burn!
(Enter Don Octavio, Donna Anna, and Donna Elvira, masked.)
vuoi di-spe-rar; ah bric-co - na! mi vuoi di-spe-rar!
fec - tion I spurn, yes I spurn, yes I spurn, yes I spurn!
p
Maestoso.
Leporello. (to the three.)
Ve - ni - te pur a - van-ti, vez - zo - se ma-sche-
Ye mask-ers fair, to greet you My mas-ter is ad -
Tutti.
tr
Str.
p
Wind.

L.
G.
Don Giovanni. (saluting them.)
ret-te!
vanc-ing,
È a-per-to a tut-ti quan-ti,
Come near-er, I en-treat you,
tr
f Tromb.
tr
p
fp
Donna Anna. (curtseying.)
A.
Siam gra-ti a tan-ti se-gni di ge-ne-ro-si-
We thank your kind-ly greet-ing, We join your fes-tive
Donna Elvira.
E.
Siam gra-ti a tan-ti se-gni di ge-ne-ro-si-
We thank your kind-ly greet-ing, We join your fes-tive
Don Octavio. (bowing.)
G.
O.
vi-va la li-ber-tà. Siam gra-ti a tan-ti se-gni di ge-ne-ro-si-
Wel-come. I say to all! We thank your kind-ly greet-ing, We join your fes-tive
tr
A.
tà, di ge-ne-ro-si-tà; siam gra-ti
ball, We join your fes-tive ball, We thank you,
E.
tà, di ge-ne-ro-si-tà; siam gra-ti
ball, We join your fes-tive ball, We thank you,
O.
tà, di ge-ne-ro-si-tà; siam gra-ti
ball, We join your fes-tive ball, We thank you,
Don Giovanni.
G.
È a-per-to a tut-ti, a tut-ti
I pray you en-ter, I pray come
f

A.
a tan-ti se-gni di ge-ne-ro-si-tà!
your kind-ly greet-ing, We join your fes-tive ball.
E.
a tan-ti se-gni di ge-ne-ro-si-tà!
your kind-ly greet-ing, We join your fes-tive ball.
O.
a tan-ti se-gni di ge-ne-ro-si-tà!
your kind-ly greet-ing, We join your fes-tive ball.
G.
quanti, vi-va, vi-va la li-ber-tà!
nearer, Wel-come, wel-come I say to all.
Strings Corni Fag. & Tympani.
p
mf
f
(servants place three chairs at left, front.)
Donna Anna.
A.
E.
Donna Elvira.
Vi-va la li-ber-tà! la li-ber-tà,
Wel-come is said to all, is said to all,
Don Octavio.
O.
Vi-va la li-ber-tà! la li-ber-tà,
Wel-come is said to all, is said to all,
Don Giovanni.
G.
Vi-va la li-ber-tà! la li-ber-tà,
Wel-come I say to all, I say to all,
Leporello.
L.
Vi-va la li-ber-tà! la li-ber-tà,
Wel-come is here for all, is here for all,

A.
E.
Vi-va la li-ber-tà, la li-ber-tà, vi-va,
Wel-come is said to all, is said to all, Wel-come,
O.
Vi-va la li-ber-tà, la li-ber-tà, vi-va,
Wel-come is said to all, is said to all, Wel-come,
G.
Vi-va la li-ber-tà, la li-ber-tà, vi-va,
Wel-come I say to all, I say to all, Wel-come,
L.
Vi-va la li-ber-ta, la li-ber-tà, vi-va,
Wel-come is here for. all, is here for all, Wel-come,
A.
E.
vi-va la li-ber-tà, vi-va, vi-va la li-ber-tà, la li-ber-tà, la li-ber-
Welcome is said to all, Welcome, Welcome is said to all, is said to all, is said to
O.
vi-va la li-ber-tà, vi-va, vi-va la li-ber-tà, la li-ber-tà, la li-ber-
Welcome is said to all, Welcome, Welcome is said to all, is said to all, is said to
G.
vi-va la li-ber-tà, vi-va, vi-va la li-ber-tà, la li-ber-tà, la li-ber-
Welcome I say to all, Welcome, Welcome I say to all, I say to all, I say to
L.
vi-va la li-ber-tà, vi-va, vi-va la li-ber-tà, la li-ber-tà, la li-ber-
Welcome is here for all, Welcome, Welcome is here for all, is here for all, is here for

Minuetto.
A.
E.
tà!
all!
O.
tà!
all!
(to the musicians.)
(To Leporello.)
G.
tà!
all!
Ri-co-min-cia-te il suo-no!
Now play an-oth-er measure!
tu accoppia i bal-le - ri-ni!
Go thou and place the dancers!
L.
tà!
all!
Minuetto.
p
★ Don Giovanni. (to Zerlina.)
(Me-co tu dei bal-la-re;
(I've chos-en thee for part-ner.
Zer-
Zer-
Cor.
Donna Elvira. (to Donna Anna.)
Quel-la è la con-ta-
That is the peas-ant
(Here Don Giovanni begins to dance with Zerlina.)
li-na, vien pur quà!)
li-na, dance with me!)
Leporello. (to the peasants.)
Da bra-vi via bal-la-te!
Quite joy-ous they ap-pear not.

*) These two phrases in small notes are not included in the score, but are found in the earliest copied voice-parts, and were probably inserted at the first rehearsals.

Donna Anna. (agitatedly, to Don Octavio.)
A.
Io mo - ro!
I trem-ble!
E.
di - na.
maiden.
Don Octavio. (to Donna Anna.)
O.
Si - mu - la - te.
Cour - age, fear not.
Don Giovanni.
G.
Va be - ne in ve - ri - tà!
She's mine, be-yond re - call!
Leporello.
Masetto. (ironically.)
L.
M.
Va be - ne in ve - ri - tà!
She's his be-yond re - call!
Va be - ne, va
What says he? What
(To Leporello.)
G.
A ba - da tien Ma - set - to.
Just keep a-way Ma - set - to.
M.
be - ne, va bene in ve - ri - tà!
says he? She's his be-yond re - call?
(to Zerlina.)
G.
Leporello. (compassionately, to Masetto.)
Il tuo compagno io so - no, Zer-
Ne'er such a charming part - ner, Zer-
L.
Non bal - li, po - ve - ret - to, po - ve - ret - to!
Why don't you dance, Ma - set - to? Poor Ma - set - to!
Vien quà, Ma - set - to
Come, let us dance a

(embraces her, and tries to kiss her; Zerlina opposes him, escapes, and hides behind the dancers.)
G.
li - na, Zer - li - na, vien pur quà!
li - na, Zer - li - na did I see!
(crossly, opposing him.)
Masetto.
L.
M.
ca - ro, ca - ro! fac-ciam quel ch'altri fa. No, no, ballar non
bit to-geth - er, Come, man, I say you shall. No, no, I will not
Leporello.
Masetto.
Leporello. (turn -
M.
L.
vo-glio! Eh, bal - la, ami - co mi - o! No! Sì!
bear it! Come dance, all eyes are on thee! No! Yes!
ing him.)
Donna Anna.
A.
Re-si - ster non poss' i - o!
My ter - ror hath un - done me!
Donna Elvira.
E.
Fin-ge - te per pie -
Be firm, thy wrongs re -
Don Octavio.
O.
Fin-ge - te per pie -
Be firm, thy wrongs re -
Leporello.
Masetto.
Leporello.
Masetto.
L.
M.
ca - ro Ma - set - to! Bal - la! No, no, non vo - glio! Bal - la! No, no, non
Come come, Ma - set - to! Dance then! I will not bear it! Dance then! I will not

E.
tà! (Zerlina, passing between the dancers, has gradually approached the door at right; here Don
call! Giovanni reaches her, puts his arm about her waist, and draws her towards the door.)
O.
tà!
call!
Leporello.
M.
L.
vo - glio. Eh, bal - la, ami - co mi - o! fac - ciam quel ch'al - tri
bear it! Come, dance, all eyes are on — thee, come, show thou'rt full of
tr
Don Giovanni.
G.
Vie - ni con me, — mia vi - ta! vie - ni,
Dear - est, a grace — con-cede me, let me
Masetto. (struggling.)
L.
M.
fa. La-scia-mi! Ah no! Zer-
glee. (Forces Masetto to dance with him.) Let me go! let go! Zer-
A.
Donna Anna.
.L'i-
His
Zerlina.
Z.
E.
O nu-mi! son tra - di - ta.
Ah whither dost thou lead me?
Donna Elvira.
L'i-
His
G.
O.
Don Octavio.
vie-ni!
lead thee. (Leads her off against her will.)
L'i-
His
Leporello.
M.
L.
li-na! Qui nasce u-na ru-i-na.
li-na! This fel-low will undo us! (Exit hastily after them.)

A.
ni - quo da se stes - so nel lac - cio se ne va!
guilt - y course ful - fill - ing, He rush - es on his fall!
E.
ni - quo da se stes - so nel lac - cio se ne va!
guil - y course ful - fill - ing, He rush - es on his fall!
O.
ni - quo da se stes - so nel lac - cio se ne va!
guilt - y course ful - fill - ing, He rush - es on his fall!
tr
Allegro assai.
Donna Anna & Donna Elvira.
A.
E.
Soc-cor-
Not an-
Zerlina. (from within.)
Z.
Gen - te, a - ju - to, a - ju - to! gen-te!
Help, oh help me, friends, oh haste ye!
Don Octavio.
O.
Soc-cor-
Not an-
(Tumult. The stage-orchestras cease, the main orchestra recommences.)
Allegro assai.
sfp
fp
(all turn towards door.)
ria-mo l'in-no - cen-te, Soc-cor - ria-mo l'in-no - cen - te!
oth-er mo-ment waste we, Not an - oth-er moment waste we!
ria-mo l'in-no - cen-te, Soc-cor - ria-mo l'in-no - cen - te!
oth-er mo-ment waste we, Not an - oth-er moment waste we!
Masetto.(terri-
M.
Ah, Zer-
Oh, Zer-
fp
fp
fp
p
cresc.

(her voice is heard at the other side.)
Zerlina.
Donna Anna & Donna Elvira.
Z. A. E.
Sce - le - ra - to! O - ra
Oh thou trai - tor! She is
Don Octavio.
O.
O - ra
She is
bly excited.)
M.
li - na, ah Zer - li - na!
li - na, Oh Zer - li - na!
p
cresc.
(all hasten to the door.)
A. E.
gri - da da quel la - to, da quel la - to!
there, oh let us haste to ex - tri - cate her!
Zerlina.
Z.
Sce - le - ra -
Oh thou trai -
O.
gri - da da quel la - to, da quel la - to!
there, oh let us haste to ex - tri - cate her!
cresc.
Donna Anna & Donna Elvira.
Zerlina.
Z. A. E.
to! Ah git - tia - mo giù la - por - ta, giù la - por - ta! Soc - cor -
tor! Force the lock, or let the door at once be - shat - ter'd! Ah a -
Don Octavio.
O.
Ah git - tia - mo giù la - por - ta, giù la - por - ta!
Force the lock, or let the door at once be - shat - ter'd!
f
p

Z.
re - te-mi! Ah soc - co - re - temi! son
way from me! Ah me, my sens - es all are
cresc.
(They try to force the door.)
Donna Anna.
A.
Siam qui noi per tua di -
We are near, thou art pro -
Donna Elvira.
E.
Siam qui noi per tua di -
We are near, thou art pro -
Don Octavio.
Z.
O.
mor - - - - ta! Siam qui noi per tua di -
scat - - - - ter'd! We are near, thou art pro -
Masetto.
M.
Siam qui noi per tua di -
We are near, thou art pro -
f
A.
fe - sa, siam qui noi per tua di - fe - sa, per tua di -
tect - ed, we are near, thou art pro - tect - ed, thou art pro -
E.
fe - sa, siam qui noi per tua di - fe - sa, per tua di -
tect - ed, we are near, thou art pro - tect - ed, thou art pro -
O.
fe - sa, siam qui noi per tua di - fe - sa, per tua di -
tect - ed, we are near, thou art pro - tect - ed, thou art pro -
M.
fe - sa, siam qui noi per tua di - fe - sa, per tua di -
tect - ed, we are near, thou art pro - tect - ed, thou art pro -

(they break open the door)
A.
fe - sa, per tua di - fe - sa!
tect - ed thou, art pro - tect - ed!
E.
fe - sa, per tua di - fe - sa!
tect - ed thou, art pro - tect - ed!
O.
fe - sa, per tua di - fe - sa!
tect - ed thou, art pro - tect - ed!
M.
fe - sa, per tua di - fe - sa!
tect - ed thou, art pro - tect - ed!

(Don Giovanni comes out holding Leporello by the arm, he pretends as though he would stab him, but does not take his sword out of the scabbard.)

Andante maestoso.
Don Giovanni.
G.
Ec - co il bir - bo chi t'ha of - fe - sa! ma da
Here's the scoundrel! just de - tect-ed! Now re-
f
p
me la pe - na a - vrà, la pe - na a - vrà! mo - ri, i - ni - quo!
ceive thy just re - ward, thy just re - ward! Wretch, thou di - est!
Leporello. (kneel-ing)
L.
Ah, co - sa
Oh pray, have
Wind
tr
f
p

G.
mo - ri, di - co!
Churl, thou li - est!
mo - ri, di - co!
churl, thou li - est!
L.
fa - te!
done, sir!
ah co - sa
oh pray, have
fa - te!
done, sir!
ah co - sa
oh pray, have
f
p
Don Octavio (taking out a pistol; to Don Giovanni.)
O.
No! spe-ra - te! no! spe - ra - te!
Get you gone, sir, get you gone, sir!
L.
fa - te!
done, sir!
cresc.
f
Donna Elvira.
(unmasking)
E.
L'em - pio cre - de con tal
False - hood here will not a -
Don Octavio. (unmasking)
O.
L'em - pio cre - de con tal fro - de, con tal
False - hood here will not a - vail thee! not a -
fp
fp
Donna Anna. (unmasking)
A.
L'em - pio cre - de con tal fro - de di nascon - der l'em - pie -
False - hood here will not a - vail thee! Thou thy-self art now en -
E.
fro - de, con tal fro - de di nascon - der l'em - pie -
vail thee, not a - vail thee! Thou thy-self art now en -
O.
fro - de, con tal fro - de di nascon - der l'em - pie -
vail thee, not a - vail thee! Thou thy-self art now en -
fp

A.
tà, l'em - - pie - tà!
snared, yes, en - snared!
E.
tà, l'em - - pie - tà! Sì, mal-vaggio!
snared, yes, en - snared! Yes, be-hold me!
O.
tà, l'em - - pie - tà! Sì, si -
snared, yes, en - snared! Sir, we
(disconcerted, lets Leporello go)
G.
Donna El-vi-ra? Don Ottavio?
Donna El-vi-ra? Don Octavio?
Wind. Strs.
f p p f p f
Donna Anna.
A.
Tra - di - to - re, tra - di - to - re, tra - di - to - re!
Shame up on thee, shame up-on thee, shame up-on thee!
Donna Elvira.
E.
Tra - di-to - re, tra - di - to - re!
Shame up-on thee, shame up-on thee!
Zerlina.
Z.
Tra - di-to - re, tra - di - to - re! Tut - to,
Shame up-on thee, shame up-on thee! Naught can
Don Octavio.
O.
gno-re. Tra - di-to - re, tra - di - to - re!
know you. Shame up-on thee, shame up-on thee!
Don Giovanni.
G.
(to Donna Anna) Ah credete!
On my honor _
Masetto.
M.
Tra - di-to - re, tra - di - to - re!
Shame up-on thee, shame up-on thee!
Strs. Wind sustain
f p

A.
Tut - to,tut - to già si sa,
Naught can now thy fate re - tard,
E.
Tut - to,tut - to già si sa,
Naught can now thy fate re-tard,
Z.
tut - to già si sà, tut - to, tut - to già si
now thy fate re - tard, Naught can now thy fate re -
O.
Tut - to,tut - to già si sa,
Naught can now thy fate re-tard,
M.
Tut - to, tut - to già si sa, tut - to
Naught can now thy fate re - tard Naught can
A.
tut - to,tut - to già si sa, tut - to, tut - to già si
Naught can now thy fate re - tard, Naught can now thy fate re -
E.
tut - to, tut - to già si sa, tut - to, tut - to già si
Naught can now thy fate re - tard, Naught can now thy fate re -
Z.
sà, tut - to, tut - to già si sa, già si
tard, Naught can now thy fate re - tard, Naught can
O.
tut - to, tut - to già si sa, tut - to,
Naught can now thy fate re - tard, Naught can
M.
tut - to già si sa,
now thy fate re - tard,

A.
sa, tut - to, tut - to, tut - to, tut - to già si
tard! No, thou trai - tor, Naught thy fate can now re -
E.
sa, tut - to, tut - to, tut - to, tut - to già si
tard! No, thou trai - tor, Naught thy fate can now re -
Z.
sa, tut - to, tut - to, tut - to, tut - to già si
fate! No, thou trai - tor, Naught thy fate can now re -
O.
tut - to già si sa, tut - to, tut - to già si
now thy fate re - tard, Naught thy fate can now re -
M.
tut - to, tut - to già si sa, tut - to, tut - to già si
Naught can now thy fate re - tard, Naught can now thy fate re -
f
cresc.
(All the men threateningly approach Don Giovanni, who calmly awaits them, leaning on his sword)
A.
sa, tut-to! tut-to! tut - to!
tard! traitor! traitor! trai - tor!
E.
sa, tut-to! tut-to! tut - to!
tard! traitor! traitor! trai - tor!
Z.
sa, tut-to! tut-to! tut - to!
tard! traitor! traitor! trai - tor!
O.
sa, tut-to! tut-to! tut - to!
tard! traitor! traitor! trai - tor!
M.
sa, tut-to! tut-to! tut - to!
tard! traitor! traitor! trai - tor!
3

Allegro.
Donna Anna and Zerlina.
A. Z.
Tre - ma, tre - ma,
Trem - ble, trem - ble,
Donna Elvira.
E.
Tre - ma, tre - ma,
Trem - ble, trem - ble,
Don Octavio.
O.
Tre - ma, tre - ma,
Trem - ble, trem - ble,
Masetto.
M.
Tre - ma, tre - ma,
Trem - ble, trem - ble,
Allegro.
sce - le - ra-to! tre - ma,
vile be - tray-er! trem - ble,
Don Giovanni. sotto voce
G.
È con-fu - sa la mia te-sta.
Not my cus - tom'tis to tremble.
Leporello. sotto voce
L.
È con-fu - sa la sua te-sta.
Not his cus - tom'tis to tremble.
Masetto.
sce - le - ra-to! tre - ma,
vile be - tray-er! trem - ble,

A. E. Z.
tre - ma, sce - le - ra - to, sa - prà
trem - ble, vile be - tray - er! To the
E.
tre - ma, sce - le - ra - to, sa - prà
trem - ble, vile be - tray - er! To the
O.
tre - ma, sce - le - ra - to, sa - prà
trem - ble, vile be - tray - er! To the
G.
Non sò più quel ch'io mi
What a storm on him has
L.
Non sa più quel ch'ei si
What a storm on him has
M.
tre - ma, sce - le ra - to, sa - prà
trem ble, vile be - tray - er! To the
tr
f
p
D. Anna, D. Elvira and Zerlina.
to - sto il mon - do in - te - ro il mi - sfat - to or - ren - do e - ne - ro, la tua
world we will pro - claim thee, As a vil - lian men will name thee, Be thou
Don Octavio.
to - sto il mon - do in - te - ro il mi - sfat - to or - ren - do e - ne - ro, la tua
world we will pro - claim thee, As a vil - lian men will name thee, Be thou
fac - cia, e un or - ri - bi - le tem - pe - sta mi - nac - ciando, o Dio, mi
brok - en I no long - er can dis - sem - ble, 'Tis a scrape, up - on my
fac - cia, e un or - ri - bi - le tem - pe - sta mi - nac - ciando, o Dio, lo
brok - en He no long - er can dis - sem - ble, 'Tis a scrape, up - on my
to - sto il mon - do in - te - ro il mi - sfat - to or - ren - do e - ne - ro, la tua
world we will pro - claim thee, As a vil - lian men will name thee, Be thou

A.
E.
Z.
fie-ra_cru-del-tà, la tua fie - ra cru - del-tà!
ev-er-more ab-horr'd, be thou ev - er-more ab-horr'd!
O.
fie-ra cru-del-tà, la tua fie - ra cru - del-tà!
ev-er-more ab-horr'd, be thou ev - er-more ab-horr'd!
G.
va! È con-fu-sa
word! Not my cus-tom
L.
va! È con-
word! Not his
M.
fie-ra_cru-del-tà, la tua fie - ra cru - del-tà!
ev-er-more ab-horr'd, be thou ev - er-more ab-horr'd!
cresc.
p
A.
E.
Z.
Tre - ma! tre - ma!
Trai - tor! trai - tor!
O.
Tre - ma! tre - ma!
Trai - tor! trai - tor!
G.
la mia te - sta, non sò più quel ch'io mi fac-cia, e un or -
'tis to tremble, I no longer can dis-sem-ble, Tem - pest
L.
fu - sa la sua te - sta, non sa più quel ch'ei si fac - cia, e un or-
cus - tom 'tis to trem-ble, He no longer can dis-sem-ble, Tem - pest
M.
Tre - ma! tre - ma!
Trai - tor! trai - tor!
Vlns
cresc.

Donna Anna and Zerlina.
A.
Z.
tre - ma, tre - - - ma sce - le - ra - to!
Trem - ble, trem - - - ble vile be - tray - er!
Donna Elvira.
E.
tre - ma, tre - ma, tre - ma, tre - ma, o sce - le - ra - to!
Trem - ble, trem - ble, trem - ble, trem - ble, oh vile be - tray - er!
Don Octavio.
O.
tre - ma, tre - ma, tre - ma, tre - ma, o sce - le - ra - to!
Trem - ble, trem - ble, trem - ble, trem - ble, oh vile be - tray - er!
G.
ri - bi - le tem - pe - sta mi - nac - cian - do, o Dio, mi va.
wild around me gathers, All my sense it doth ap - pal.
È con - fu - sa la mia te - sta, non sò più quel ch'io mi
But my courage ne'er for - sook me, And I'll face the matter
L.
ri - bi - le tem - pe - sta mi - nac - cian - do, o Dio, lo va.
wild around him gathers, All his sense it doth ap - pal.
È con - fu - sa la sua te - sta, non sa più quel ch'ei si
But his courage ne'er for - sook him, He will face the matter
M.
tre - ma, tre - ma, tre - ma, tre - ma, o sce - le - ra - to!
Trem - ble, trem - ble, trem - ble, trem - ble, oh vile be - tray - er!
f

D. Anna, D. Elvira and Zerlina.
A. E. Z.
O - di il tuon del-la ven - detta!
Fear the wrath of heav'n of - fended!
Don Octavio.
O.
O - di il tuon del-la ven - detta!
Fear the wrath of heav'n of - fended!
G.
faccia, e un or-ri - bi - le tempe-sta minacciando, o Dio, mi
boldly, All their threats shall not withhold me, Tho' a sign from heav'n should
L.
faccia, e un or-ri - bi - le tempe-sta minacciando, o Dio, lo -
boldly, All their threats shall not withhold him, Tho' a sign from heav'n should
M.
O - di il tuon del-la ven - detta!
Fear the wrath of heav'n of - fended!
tr
3
A. E. Z.
O - di il tuon del - la ven - det-ta, che ti fi-schia in-tor - no in
Fear the wrath of heav'n of - fend-ed, Fear its thun-ders o'er thee
O.
O - di il tuon del - la ven - det-ta, che ti fi-schia in-tor - no in
Fear the wrath of heav'n of - fend-ed, Fear its thun-ders o'er thee
G.
va! (Don Giovanni, behind whom Leporello shelters himself, attempts to clear a path for himself with
fall! his sword, but is hindered by Don Octavio.)
L.
va!
fall!
M.
O - di il tuon del - la ven - det-ta, che ti fi-schia in-tor - no in
Fear the wrath of heav'n of - fend-ed, Fear its thun-ders o'er thee
tr

A. E. Z.
tor - no, sul tuo ca - po in que - sto gior - no il suo ful - mi - ne ca -
breaking, That thy reck-less course o'er - tak - ing, On thy guilt - y head will
O.
tor - no, sul tuo ca - po in que - sto gior - no il suo ful - mi - ne ca -
breaking, That thy reck-less course o'er - tak - ing, On thy guilt - y head will
M.
tor - no, sul tuo ca - po in que - sto gior - no il suo ful - mi - ne ca -
breaking, That thy reck-less course o'er - tak - ing, On thy guilt - y head will
A. E. Z.
drà, il suo ful - mi - ne ca - drà!
fall, On thy guilt - y head will fall!
O.
drà, il suo ful - mi - ne ca - drà!
fall, On thy guilt - y head will fall!
Don Giovanni.
G.
È con-fu - sa la mia te - sta,
Not my cus - tom 'tis to trem-ble,
Leporello.
L.
È con-fu - sa la sua
Not his cus - tom 'tis to
Masetto.
M.
drà, il suo ful - mi - ne ca - drà!
fall, On thy guilt - y head will fall!
p

A.
E.
Z.
tre - ma! tre - ma!
Trai - tor! trai - tor!
O.
tre - ma! tre - ma!
Trai - tor! trai - tor!
G.
non sò più quel ch'io mi fac - cia, e un or - - ri - bi - le tem -
I no lon - ger can dissem - ble, Tem - pest wild a - round me
L.
te - sta, non sa più quel ch'ei si fac - cia, e un or - ri - bi - le tem -
tremble, He no lon - ger can dis - sem - ble, Tem - pest wild a - round him
M.
Tre - ma! tre - ma!
Trai - tor! trem - ble!
cresc.
Donna Anna.
A.
tre - ma, tre - - - - - ma,
Trem - ble, trem - - - - - ble,
Zerlina.
Z.
tre - ma, tre - - - - - ma, o
Trem - ble, trem - - - - ble,
Donna Elvira.
E.
tre - ma, tre - ma, tre - ma, tre - ma, o
Trem - ble, trem - ble, trem - ble, trem - ble, O
Don Octavio.
O.
tre - ma, tre - ma, tre - ma, tre - ma, o
Trem - ble, trem - ble, trem - ble, trem - ble, O
G.
pe - sta mi - nac - cian - do, o Dio, mi va!
gathers, All my sense it doth ap - pal!
L.
pe - sta mi - nac - cian - do, o Dio, lo va!
gathers, All his sense it doth ap - pal!
M.
tre - ma, tre - ma, tre - ma, tre - ma, o
Trem - ble, tremble, trem - ble, tremble, O

Donna Anna, Donna Elvira & Zerlina.
A. E. Z.
sce - le - ra - to!
vile be - trayer!
O - di il
Fear the
Z.
sce - le - ra - to!
vile be - trayer!
E.
sce - le - ra - to!
vile be - trayer!
O.
sce - le - ra - to!
vile be - trayer!
O - di il
Fear the
G.
È confu - sa la mia te - sta, non sò più quel ch'io mi faccia,
But my courage ne'er for - sook me, And I'll face the matter boldly,
L.
È confu - sa la sua te - sta, non sa più quel ch'ei si faccia,
But his courage ne'er for - sook him, And he'll face the matter boldly,
M.
sce - le - ra - to!
vile be - trayer!
O - di il
Fear the
tr
A. E. Z.
tuon del - la ven - det - ta!
wrath of heav'n of - fended!
O.
tuon del - la ven - det - ta!
wrath of heav'n of - fended!
G.
e un or - ri - bi - le tem - pe - sta mi - nacciando, o Dio, mi
all their threats shall not withhold me, Tho' a sign from heav'n should
L.
e un or - ri - bi - le tem - pe - sta mi - nacciando, o Dio, lo
all their threats shall not withhold him, Tho' a sign from heav'n should
M.
tuon del - la ven - det - ta!
wrath of heav'n of - fended!

A.
E.
Z.
O - di il tuon del - la ven - det - ta, che ti fi - schia in - tor - no in -
Fear the wrath of heav'n of - fend - ed, Fear its thunders o'er thee
O.
O - di il tuon del - la ven - det - ta, che ti fi - schia in - tor - no in -
Fear the wrath of heav'n of - fend - ed, Fear its thunders o'er thee
G.
va!
fall!
L.
va!
fall!
M.
O - di il tuon del - la ven - det - ta, che ti fi - schia in - tor - no in -
Fear the wrath of heavn of - fend - ed, Fear its thunders o'er thee
tr
tor - no, sul tuo ca - po in que - sto gior - no il suo ful - mi - ne ca -
breaking, That thy reckless course o'er - tak - ing, on thy guilt - y head will
Masetto.
drà, sì, ca - drà, il suo ful - mi - ne ca - drà!
fall, on thy head, on thy guilt - y head will fall!
Don Giovanni.
M.
G.
Ma non
No, my
Vln
p

A.
E.
Z.
O - di il tuon!
On thy head
O.
O - di il tuon!
On thy head
G.
man - ca in me co -rag - gio, non mi
cour - age ne'er for-sook me, And I'll
Leporello.
L.
Ma non manca in lui co-rag-gio,
No, his courage ne'er forsook him,
Masetto.
M.
O - di il tuon!
On thy head
f
p
più stretto
O - di il tuon!
They will fall!
O - di il tuon!
They will fall!
per - do, o mi con - fon - do. Se ca -
face the mat - ter bold - ly, All their
non si per-do, o si con-fon - do. Se ca -
And he'll face the matter bold - ly. All their
O - di il tuon!
They will fall!
f
ff più stretto
Bassi

A. E. Z.
Sul tuo ca-po in que-sto gior-no il suo ful-mi-ne cadrà, il suo ful-mi -
Fear the wrath of heav'n of-fend-ed, That thy reckless course o'ertaking, Up-on thy
O.
Sul tuo ca - po in que-sto gior - no il suo ful-mi -
Fear the thun - ders of heav'n of - fend - ed, That up-on thy
G.
des-se an-co-ra il mon-do, ca-desse an-co-ra il mon-do, nul-la mai te-mer, te -
threats shall not withhold me, their threats shall not with-hold me, Tho' a sign, a sign from
L.
des-se an-co-ra il mon-do, ca-desse an-co-ra il mon-do, nul-la mai te-mer, te -
threats will not withhold him, their threats will not with-hold him, Tho' a sign, a sign from
M.
Sul tuo ca - po in que-sto gior - no il suo ful-mi -
Fear the thun - ders of heav'n of - fend - ed, That up-on thy
A. E. Z.
ne ca - drà, sul tuo ca-po in que-sto gior-no, il suo ful-mi-ne ca -
head will fall, Fear the wrath of heav'n of - fend - ed, That thy reckless course o'er-
O.
ne ca - drà, sul tuo ca - po, in que-sto gior - no,
head will fall, Fear the thun - ders of heav'n of - fend - ed,
G.
mer mi fa, se ca-desse an-cora il mon-do, se ca-desse an-co-ra il mon-do,
heav'n should fall, All their threats shall not withhold me, all their threats shall not withhold me,
L.
mer lo fa, se ca-desse an-cora il mon-do, se ca-desse an-co-ra il mon-do,
heav'n should fall, All their threats will not withhold him, all their threats will not withhold him,
M.
ne ca - drà, sul tuo ca - po, in que-sto gior - no,
head will fall, Fear the thun - ders of heav'n of - fend - ed,

A.
E.
Z.
drà, il suo ful - mi - ne ca - drà, il suo ful-mi-ne ca-drà, il suo
taking Up - on thy head will fall, On thy guilt-y head will fall, on thy
O.
il suo ful - mi - ne ca - drà, il suo ful-mi-ne ca-drà, il suo
That up - on thy head will fall, On thy guilt-y head will fall, on thy
G.
nul - la mai te - mer, te - mer mi fa, nul - la mai te-mer mi fa, nul - la
Tho' a sign, a sign from heav'n should fall, tho' a sign from heav'n should fall, tho' a
L.
nul - la mai te - mer, te - mer lo fa, nul - la mai te-mer lo fa, nul - la
Tho' a sign, a sign from heav'n should fall, tho' a sign from heav'n should fall, tho' a
M.
il suo ful - mi - ne ca - drà, il suo ful-mi-ne ca-drà, il suo
That up - on thy head will fall, On thy guilt-y head will fall, on thy
A.
E.
Z.
ful-mi-ne ca-drà, il suo ful-mi-ne ca-drà!
guilt-y head will fall, on thy guilt - y head will fall!
O.
ful-mi-ne ca-drà, il suo ful-mi-ne ca-drà!
guilt-y head will fall, on thy guilt - y head will fall!
(Don Giovanni, seizing Leporello by the collar, and pushing him on before, makes his way through the peasants pressing upon him, and exit.)
G.
mai te-mer mi fa, nul-la mai te-mer mi fa!
sign from heav'n should fall, tho' a sign from heav'n should fall!
L.
mai te-mer lo fa, nul-la mai te-mer lo fa!
sign from heav'n should fall, tho' a sign from heav'n should fall!
M.
ful-mi-ne ca-drà, il suo ful-mi-ne ca-drà!
guilt-y head will fall, on thy guilt - y head will fall!
3
End of Act I.

Act II.

Nº 14. "Eh via, buffone, eh via.„

Duet.

Scene.— A Street.

Allegro assai.
Don Giovanni.
Leporello.
Voice.
G.
L.
Eh via, buf-fo - ne, eh via, buffo-ne, non mi sec-car! No, no, pa -
I'll not be-lieve thee, I'll not believe thee! Whate'er thou say! I would not
Ob. Corni & str.
Str.
Piano.
dro - ne, no, no, pa-dro - ne! non vo' re - star! Sen-ti-mi ami - co Vo' andar, vi
grieve ye, I would not grieve ye, but I'll not stay! Do I ill - use thee? Pray, sir, ex -
di - co! Va chi ti ho fatto, che vuoi la-sciar-mi? O niente affat-to, qua-si ammaz-
cuse me. My wrath I'll stifle, say what has chill'd thee? Oh, a mere trifle, You've near-ly
Va che sei mat-to, va che sei matto, matto, matto, fu per bur-lar.
Thou fool-ish fel - low, thou fool-ish, foolish, foolish fel-low, 'Twas all in fun.
zar-mi.
kill'd me.
Ed io non
Such fun I
Vln.
cresc.

G.
Eh via, buf -
I'll not be -
L.
bur - lo, ed io non bur-lo, bur-lo, bur - lo, ma vo-glio an - dar!
like not, such fun I like not, no, I thank you, With me you've done!
tr
cresc.
f
p
fp
G.
fo - ne, sen - ti-mi, a - mi - co; va che sei mat-to, va che sei
lieve thee, Do I ill - use thee! Thou fool-ish fel-low, thou foolish
L.
No, no, pa - dro - ne! vo' an - dar, vi di - co, No,
I would not grieve ye, pray, sir, ex - cuse me, No,
f.
p
fp
G.
mat-to, va che sei mat-to, va che sei mat-to, mat-to, mat-to, matto!
fel - low, thou fool-ish fel - low, thou fool-ish, fool - ish, fool-ish, fool-ish fel-low!
L.
no, no, no, no, no, no, no, no,
no, no, no, no, no, no, no, no,
cresc.
f
p
G.
Va che sei mat-to, va che sei
Thou fool-ish fel - low, 'twas all in
L.
no, no, no, no, no, no, non vo' re-star, no, non vo' re - star, sì,
no, no, no, no, no, no, Such fun I like not, With me you've done, yes,
cresc.
f
tr
p

G.
mat-to, va che sei mat-to, va che sei mat-to, mat-to, mat-to, mat-to!
fun, it was all in fun, it was all in fun, thou fool-ish, fool-ish fel-low!
L.
sì, sì, sì, sì, sì, sì, sì, sì,
yes, yes, yes, no, no, in-deed, in-
cresc.
f
p
G.
Eh via, buf-
Do I ill-
L.
sì, sì, sì, sì, sì, sì, sì, voglio an-dar, sì, sì, voglio an-dar! no, no, pa-
deed you must excuse me, such fun I like not, With me you've done. Pray, sir, ex-
cresc.
f
tr
p
G.
fo-ne, buf-fo-ne, non mi sec-car. Va che sei mat-to, va che sei
use thee, ill-use thee? 'Twas all in fun, thou fool-ish fel-low, thou fool-ish
L.
dro-ne, no, no, pa-dro-ne, non vo' re-star! ed io non burlo, ed io non
cuse me, pray, sir, ex-cuse me, With me you've done, such fun I like not, such fun I
cresc.
p
cresc.
G.
matto, fu per bur-lar, fu per bur-lar, fu per bur-lar, fu per bur-lar!
fel-low, 'Twas all in fun, 'twas all in fun, 'twas all in fun, 'twas all in fun!
L.
burlo, ma voglio andar, ma voglio an-dar, ma voglio an-dar, ma voglio an-dar!
like not, With me you've done, with me you've done, with me you've done, with me you've done!
p
f
f
f
(Lep. tries to go, Don Giovanni detains him.)

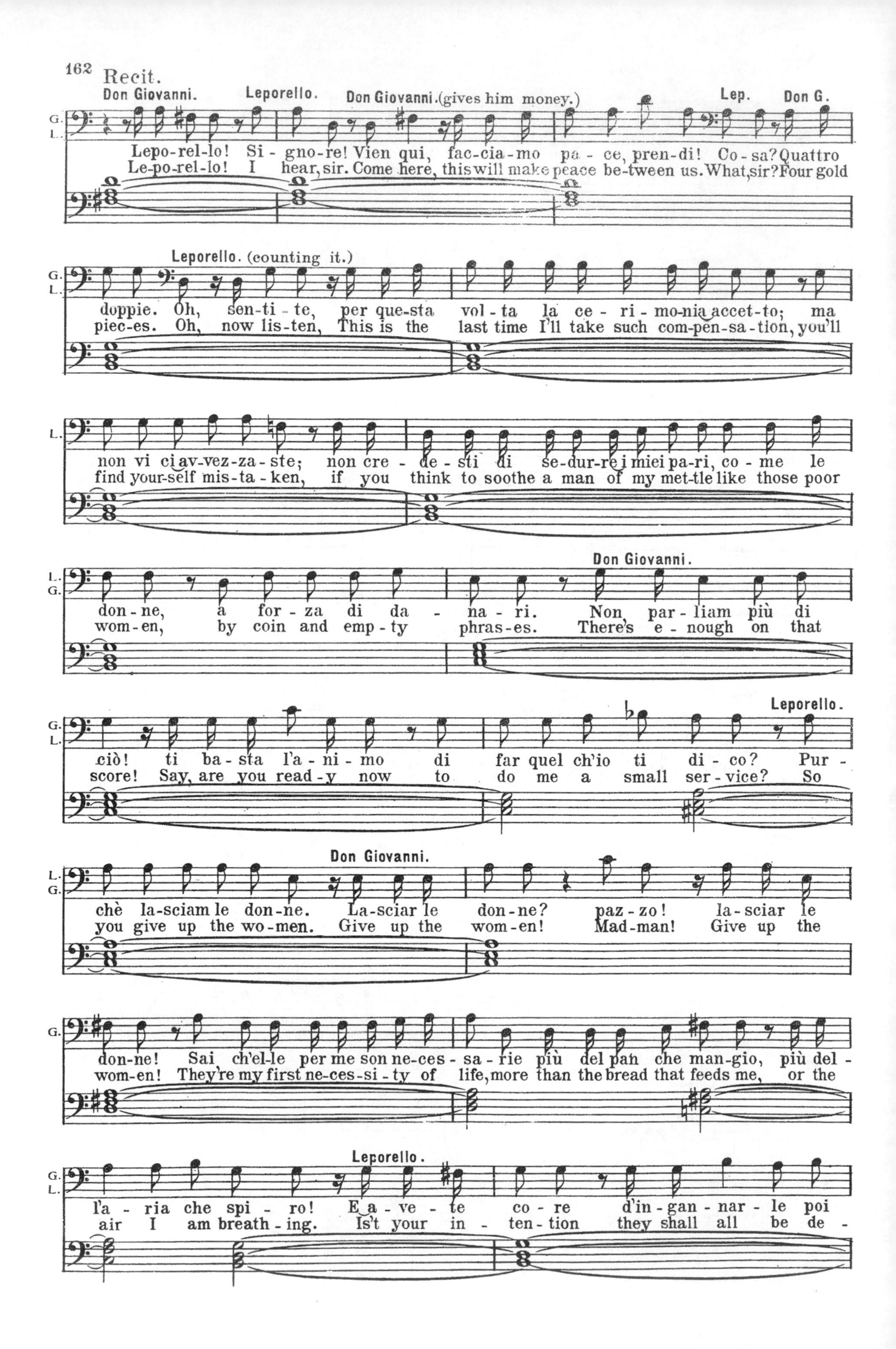
Recit.
Don Giovanni. Leporello. Don Giovanni. (gives him money.) Lep. Don G.
G.
L.
Lepo-rel-lo! Si - gno-re! Vien qui, fac-cia-mo pa - ce, pren-di! Co - sa? Quattro
Le-po-rel-lo! I hear, sir. Come here, this will make peace be-tween us. What, sir? Four gold
Leporello. (counting it.)
doppie. Oh, sen-ti - te, per que-sta vol-ta la ce - ri - mo-nia accet-to; ma
piec-es. Oh, now lis-ten, This is the last time I'll take such com-pen-sa-tion, you'll
non vi ci av-vez-za-ste; non cre - de - sti di se-dur-re i miei pa-ri, co - me le
find your-self mis-ta - ken, if you think to soothe a man of my met-tle like those poor
Don Giovanni.
don - ne, a for - za di da - na - ri. Non par - liam più di
wom - en, by coin and emp - ty phras - es. There's e - nough on that
Leporello.
ciò! ti ba - sta l'a - ni - mo di far quel ch'io ti di - co? Pur -
score! Say, are you read - y now to do me a small ser - vice? So
Don Giovanni.
chè la-sciam le don-ne. La-sciar le don - ne? paz - zo! la - sciar le
you give up the wo-men. Give up the wom - en! Mad-man! Give up the
don-ne! Sai ch'el-le per me son ne-ces - sa - rie più del pan che man-gio, più del -
wom-en! They're my first ne-ces-si - ty of life, more than the bread that feeds me, or the
Leporello.
l'a - ria che spi - ro! E a - ve - te co - re d'in - gan - nar - le poi
air I am breath - ing. Is't your in - ten - tion they shall all be de -

Don Giovanni.
L.
G.
tut - te? È tut - to a-mo-re; chi a u-na so-la è fe-de-le, ver-so l'al-tre è cru -
ceiv'd thus? For love I do it. Who to one is de-vot-ed, to the rest must be
G.
de - le; io che in me sen - to sì e-ste-so sen - ti-men-to, vo' be-ne a tut - te
faith-less; mine is a heart of such in - fi - nite af - fec-tion, there is not one I
G.
quan-te: le don-ne poi-chè cal - co - lar non san - no, il mio buon na - tu -
love not; and yet the wom-en, dear un-reas'n-ing crea - tures, my hap - py dis - po -
Leporello.
G.
L.
ral chia-ma-no in-gan-no. Non ho ve - du - to ma - i na - tu - ra - le più
si - tion call de - ceiv - ing. In - deed I can not fol - low such a huge dis - po -
Don Giovanni. (confidentially.)
L.
G.
va-sto, e più be-ni - gno! Or-sù, co-sa vor - re-ste? O-di! ve-de-sti
si-tion for deeds of kind-ness; but what is your small service? Listen! say, have you
Leporello. Don Giovanni. (ar-
G.
L.
tu la ca - me - rie - ra di Donn' El - vi - ra? Io, no. Non hai ve -
seen the pret - ty dam-sel of Donna El - vi - ra? Not I. It is your
dently.)
G.
du - to qual-che co - sa di bel - lo, ca-ro il mio Le - po - rel - lo; o - ra io con
loss then not to see what is charm-ing, my so - ber Le - po - rel - lo; with her this
G.
le - i vo' ten-tar la mia sor-te, ed ho pen-sa - to, giacchè siam verso sera, per a - guz -
instant I would fain try my fortune, and it has struck me, as ev'ning is upon us, 'twould make the

G.
zar-le me-glio l'ap-pe-ti-to di pre-sen-tar mi a lei col tuo ve-
jest both new and more di-vert-ing, if I put on thy cloak in this ad-
Leporello.
Don Giovanni.
G.
L.
sti-to. E per-chè non po-tre-ste pre-sen-tar-vi col vo-stro? Han po-co
ven-ture. I can see no oc-ca-sion for this strange mas-que-rad-ing! A-las, a
(takes off his cloak.)
Lep.
cre-di-to con gen-te di tal ran-go gli a-bi-ti si-gno-ri-li. Sbri-ga-ti, vi-a! Si-
gen-tle-man is apt to be sus-pected by people of her sta-tion. Give it me, make haste! Oh
Don Giovanni. (angrily.)
(they exchange cloaks and hats.)
L.
G.
gnor, per più ra-gio-ni- Fi-ni-sci-la! Non soffro op-po-si-zio-ni!
sir, for sev'ral rea-sons- De-lay me not! De-lays in love are treasons!

Nº 15. "Ah, taci, ingiusto core."

Trio.

Donna Elvira. (at the window.) **Don Giovanni. Leporello.** (It gradually becomes dark.)

Andantino.
Donna Elvira.
E.
Ah, ta-ci, in-giu-sto co-re!
Oh hush, sad heart, from griev-ing!
Str.
p
Cor.
Non pal-pi-tar-mi in se-no! è un
Thy days of joy are o-ver, The
tr
sf

E.
empio, è un tra-di-to-re, è col-pa a-ver pie-
traitor with wiles de-ceiving, Hath broke my heart in
Wind & Bass Vl.
mf
p
mf
p
E.
L.
Leporello. (aside to Don G.)
tà, è col-pa a-ver pie-tà. Zit-to! di Donna El-
twain, hath broke my heart in twain. Soft-ly, 'tis Donna El-
cresc.
p
Fag.
Bassi & Viola.
Don Giov. (aside to Leporello)
L.
G.
vi-ra, Si-gnor, la vo-ce io sen-to! Co-glie-re io vo' il mo-
vi-ra, Per-chance you might re-gain her. Thou here a while de-
Fl.
Cl.
Fag.
Bassi & Viola.
G.
men-to, tu fer-ma-ti un po' là! tu fer-ma-ti un po'
tain her, I'll soon come back a-gain, I'll soon come back a-
(stands behind Leporello.)
(making appropriate
G.
là! El-vi-ra, i-do-lo mi-o,
gain, El-vi-ra, hear my sighing!
tr
Wind.
gestures with Leporello's arms)
G.
El-vi-ra, i-do-lo mi-o!
El-vi-ra, hear my sigh-ing!
Strs
tr
sf

Donna Elvira.
E.
Non è co-stui l'in-gra-to?
Ah is it thou, un-grateful?
Don Giovanni.
G.
Sì, vi - ta mi - a, son'
'Tis I, and fond - ly re-
mf
p
mf
p
Strings & Cor sustain.
Donna Elvira.
E.
Nu-mi, che strano effet-to
Strangely his words af-fect me.
Don Giovanni.
G.
i - - o, e chie - do ca - ri - tà.
ly - - ing, My love thou'lt not dis - dain.
Leporello.
L.
(aside)
Sta-te a ve-der la
She must be of the
Cl.
Fag.
E.
mi si ri-sveglia in pet-to, mi si ri-sve- -glia in pet-to!
Love, oh do thou di-rect me! Love, oh do thou di-rect me!
G.
(poking
Di-
Oh
L.
(crossly, to Don Giovanni)
paz - za, che ancor gli cre-de-rà, gli cre-de-rà, gli cre-de-rà.
mad-dest, in him to trust a - gain, in him to trust, to trust a - gain.

Leporello in the ribs, and making more animated gestures)
167
G.
scen - di, o gio - ja bel - la, o gio - - ja
come in beau - ty beam - ing, In beau - - ty
p
legato
bel - la! ve - drai che tu sei quel - la, che a -
beam - ing, Oh come thro' star - light gleam - ing, My
do - ra l'al - ma mi - - - a, pen - ti - - to io
ten - der love re - quit - - ing, Oh, come o'er this
Donna Elvira.
E.
No, non ti cre - do, o bar - ba - ro!
Oh, ne'er can I believe a - gain!
so - - - no già! Ah,
heart to reign! Ah,
Tutti.
fp
no, non ti credo, o bar - ba - ro!
Oh, ne'er can I be - lieve again!
no, non ti credo, o bar - ba - ro!
Oh, ne'er can I be - lieve again!
cre - de - mi! ah, cre - de - mi! ah,
do believe! Ah, do believe! Ah,

E.
L.
G.
Leporello. (piano to Don Giovanni.)
non ti cre - do! Se se-gui-ta - te, io ri - do!
ne'er be - lieve thee! I cannot keep from laughing!
cre - de - mi! o m'uc - ci - do! (excitedly, almost in tears.) o m'uc -
do be - lieve! I con - jure thee! I con -
cresc.
p
mf
ci - do! ah m'uc - ci - do!
jure thee! I con - jure thee!
Leporello.
se se-gui-ta - te, io ri - do! se se-gui-ta - te, io ri - do, ri - do, ri - do,
I cannot keep from laughing! I cannot keep from laughing, oh, I cannot
un poco cresc.
i - do-lo mio, vien quà!
Ah, do not think I feign!
ri-do, ri-do, ri-do, ri-do, ri-do, ri-do, ri-do!
no, I cannot, cannot, cannot, cannot keep from laughing!
Wind
tr
Donna Elvira.
Dei, che ci-men-to è questo! non sò s'io va - do, o
For this my heart has panted! Shall I refuse or
Spe - ro che ca - da presto! che bel col-pet - to è
She thinks I have re-canted! Poor girl, she's quite en-
Già quel men-da - ce labbro tor-na a se-dur co -
Great is the pow'r of lying! Tru-ly the trick is

E.
re - sto? ah pro - - teg - ge - te
grant it? By some en - chantment
G.
que - sto? più fer - ti - le ta - len-to del mio no non si
chanted! To trick a thousand others, I feel quite in the
L.
ste - i, deh pro - - teg - ge - te, oh
clev - er, No great en - deavor now
sf
mf
p
mf
p
E.
vo - i la mia cre - du - li - tà, cre - du - li -
spell-bound, Quite fled is my dis - dain, is my dis-
G.
dà, più fer - ti - le ta - len-to, no, del mio no non si
vein, to trick a thousand others, yes, I feel quite in the
L.
De - i! la sua cre - du - li - tà, cre - du - li -
needs it Her sil - ly heart to gain, her heart to
mf
p
E.
tà! Dei, che cimen-to è questo, Dei, che cimen-to è questo, non sò s'io
dain! For this my heart has panted, for this my heart has panted, Shall I re -
G.
dà! Spe - ro che ca - da pre - sto! che bel col - pet - to è
vein! She thinks I have re - canted! Poor girl, she's quite en-
L.
tà! Già quel menda - ce
gain! Great is the pow'r of
Vl.
Cl.
Fag.

E.
va-do, non sò s'io re-sto! Dei! che ci-men-to è que-sto, non sò s'io va-do, o
fuse now, or shall I grant it? For this my heart has panted, Shall I re-fuse or
G.
que-sto, che bel col-pet-to, spe-ro che ca-da pre-sto, che bel col-pet-to è
chanted, she's quite en-chanted. She thinks I have re-cant-ed, Poor girl, she's quite en-
L.
labbro torna a se-dur co-ste-i; già quel men-da-ce labbro tor-na a se-dur co-
ly-ing, Truly the trick is clever, great is the pow'r of ly-ing, tru-ly the trick is
cresc.
f
p
E.
re-sto! Ah pro-teg-ge-te
grant it? By some en-chantment
G.
que-sto! più fer-ti-le ta-len-to del mio no non si
chanted! To trick a thousand others I feel quite in the
L.
ste-i, deh pro-teg-ge-te oh
clev-er, No great en-deavor now
sf
p
mf
mf
p
E.
voi la mia cre-du-li-tà, cre-du-li-tà, la
spell-bound, quite fled is my dis-dain, is my dis-dain, quite
G.
dà, più fer-ti-le ta-len-to, no del mio, no, non si dà,
vein, to trick a thousand others, yes, I feel quite in the vein,
L.
De-i, la sua cre-du-li-tà, cre-du-li-tà,
needs it Her sil-ly heart to gain, her heart to gain,
mf
p

(disappears from the window)
E.
mia cre-du-li-tà, la mia cre-du-li-tà!
fled is my dis-dain, quite fled is my dis-dain!
G.
no non si dà, no non si dà!
quite in the vein, quite in the vein.
L.
cre-du-li-tà, cre-du-li-tà!
her heart to gain, her heart to gain.
p
cresc.
p
pp
Recit.
Don Giovanni. (in great spirits.)
Leporello.
Don Giov.
G.
L.
A-mi-co, che ti par? Mi par che abbiate un' a-ni-ma di bronzo. Va
Well, am I not in luck? You may be luck-y, but you've a heart of marble. Come,
(pointing at the window)
G.
là, che sei'l gran gonzo! A-scol-ta be-ne: quan-do co-stei qui vie-ne,
come, you're grow-ing prosy! now learn your part, Sir; when she makes her ap-pear-ance,
G.
tu cor-ri ad ab-brac-ciar-la, fal-le quat-tro ca-rez-ze, fin-gi la vo-ce
run to her and em-brace her, do not spare your caress-es, em-u-late well your
G.
mi-a: poi con bell' ar-te cer-ca te-co con-dur-la in al-tra
mas-ter; next you must find a pre-text that calls you both off to some
Leporello.
Don Giovanni.
Leporello.
G.
L.
par-te. Ma, Si-gno-re Non più re-pli-che! E se poi mi co-no-sce?
distance. But supposing That is settled, then. And should she re-cog-nize me?

Don Giovanni.
(softly)
G.
Non ti co - no - sce - rà, se tu non vuo - i; zit - to: ell' a - pre, ehi, giu - di - zio!
If she should re - cognize you, you're a blockhead. Si - lence, she's coming, now, attention.
He runs off to the side, leaving Leporello alone; Donna Elvira enters from the house, and advances to meet Leporello; Don Giovanni watches their movements from the side.
Donna Elvira. (to Leporello)
Don Giovanni. (aside)
Leporello (aside)
Donna Elvira.
E.
G.
L.
Ec - co mi a vo - i. (Veg - gia - mo che fa - rà.) (Che imbroglio!) Dunque cre - der po -
Once more we meet, then. (I'll stay a while and watch.) (Confound it!) Say, oh dare I be -
E.
trò che i pianti mie - i ab - bian vin - to quel cor? dunque pen - ti - to, l'a - ma - to Don Gio -
lieve that my de - votion has at length touch'd thy heart? And now re - pentant, my dear - ly lov'd Gio -
Leporello.
(imitating D. G's voice.)
Donna Elvira.
E.
L.
vanni, al suo do - ve - re, e all' a - mor mio ri - tor - na? Sì, ca - ri - na! Cru -
vanni, to me return - ing, once more to joy re - stores me? Yes, my treasure! Ah
E.
de - le! se sa - pe - ste quan - te la - gri - me e quan - ti sos - pir voi mi co -
faithless! I'll not tell thee all the mis - er - y, the sighs and the tears that thou hast
Leporello.
Donna Elvira.
Leporello.
E.
L.
sta - te! Io, vi - ta mi - a? Vo - i. Po - ve - ri - na!
cost me! I, love - ly crea - ture? Who else? Oh poor dar - ling!
Donna Elvira.
Leporello.
Donna Elvira.
L.
E.
quanto mi di - spia - ce! Mi fug - gi - re - te più? No, mu - so bel - lo! Sa - re - te sem - pre
'Twas too bad to do so. You'll leave me nev - er - more? No pret - ty creature! And you are mine for
Leporello. (sighing)
Donna Elvira.
Leporello.
(aside)
E.
L.
mi - o? Sempre! Ca - ris - si - mo! Ca - ris - si - ma! (la bur - la mi dà gu - sto.)
ever? Ev - er! How dear you are! How ver - y dear! (this part is not un - pleasant.)

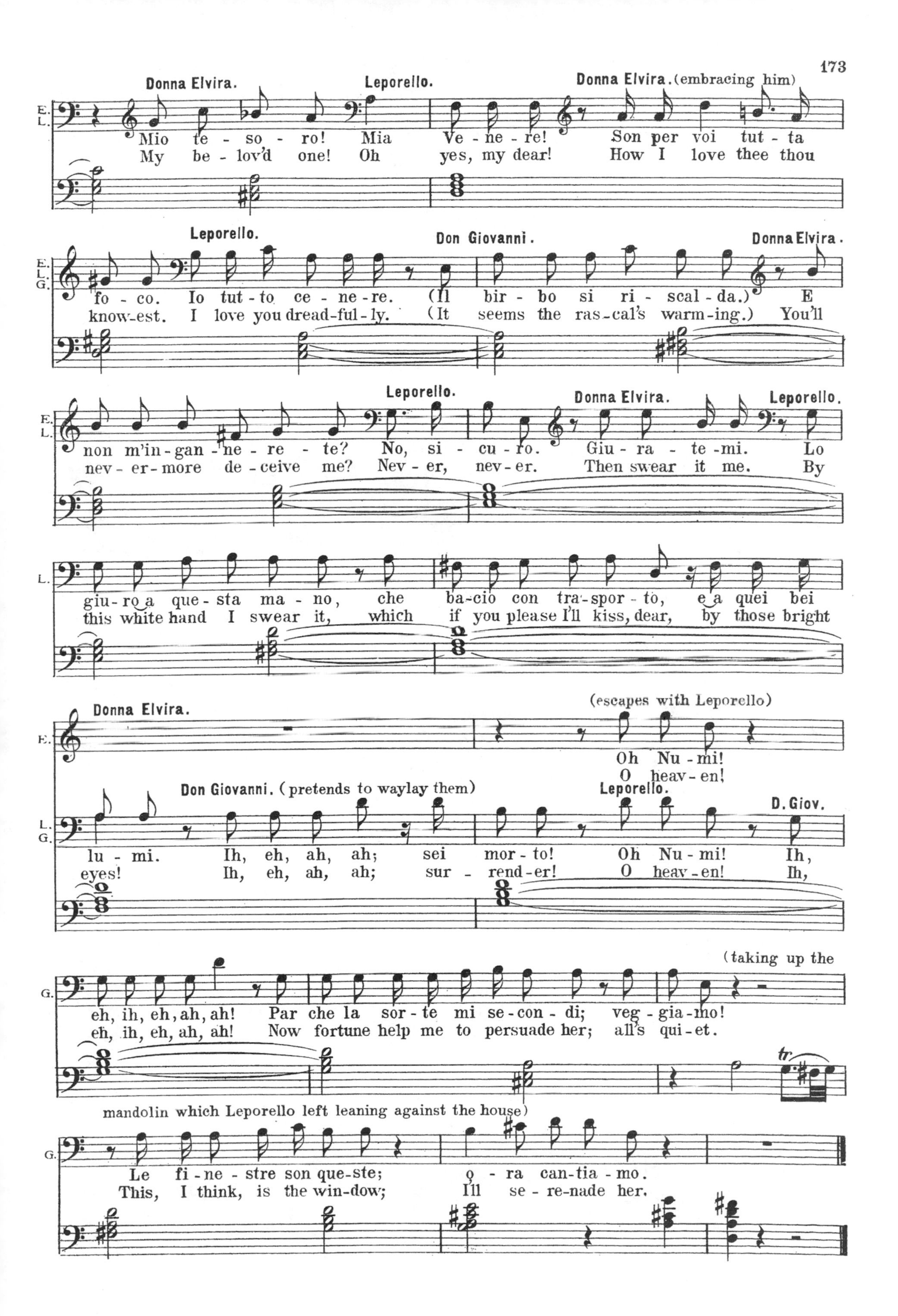
Donna Elvira.
Leporello.
Donna Elvira. (embracing him)
Mio te - so - ro! Mia Ve - ne - re! Son per voi tut - ta
My be - lov'd one! Oh yes, my dear! How I love thee thou
Leporello.
Don Giovanni.
Donna Elvira.
fo - co. Io tut - to ce - ne - re. (Il bir - bo si ri - scal - da.) E
know - est. I love you dread - ful - ly. (It seems the ras - cal's warm - ing.) You'll
Leporello.
Donna Elvira.
Leporello.
non m'in - gan - ne - re - te? No, si - cu - ro. Giu - ra - te - mi. Lo
nev - er - more de - ceive me? Nev - er, nev - er. Then swear it me. By
giu - ro a que - sta ma - no, che ba - cio con tra - spor - to, e a quei bei
this white hand I swear it, which if you please I'll kiss, dear, by those bright
Donna Elvira.
(escapes with Leporello)
Oh Nu - mi!
O heav - en!
Don Giovanni. (pretends to waylay them)
Leporello.
D. Giov.
lu - mi. Ih, eh, ah, ah; sei mor - to! Oh Nu - mi! Ih,
eyes! Ih, eh, ah, ah; sur - rend - er! O heav - en! Ih,
(taking up the
eh, ih, eh, ah, ah! Par che la sor - te mi se - con - di; veg - gia - mo!
eh, ih, eh, ah, ah! Now fortune help me to persuade her; all's qui - et.
tr
mandolin which Leporello left leaning against the house)
Le fi - ne - stre son que - ste; o - ra can - tia - mo.
This, I think, is the win - dow; I'll se - re - nade her.

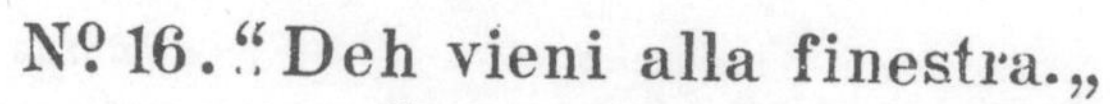
Nº 16. "Deh vieni alla finestra."

Allegretto.
Canzonetta.
Don Giovanni.
G.
staccato
Mandoline
p
Str. pizz.
Deh
From
vie-ni al-la fi-ne-stra, o mio te-so-ro, deh
out thy casement glancing, Oh smile up-on me, With
vie-ni a con-so-lar il pian-to mi-o.
sighs of hap-less love I sing this dit-ty.
Se ne-ghi a me di dar qual-
Thy bo-som I would move, Thou
che ri-sto-ro, da-van-ti agli oc-chi tuoi mo-
hast un-done me, Oh grant the pray'r of love, and

G.
rir– vo- gl'i - o!
shew some pit - y!
Tu
Than
ch'hai la boc-ca dol - ce più — che il mie - le,
ros-es art thou fair - er, Than — ho-ney sweet - er,
tu cheil zuc-che-ro por-ti in mez-zoal co - re!
Bal-mier 'tis when thou sigh-est than west-ern breez - es!
Non es - ser, gio - ja mia, con
Oh, come, my fair, — des-cend, Come,
me cru-de - le!
I en-treat — thee!
la-scia-ti al-men — ve-der, mio
Death shall my torments end, If
bell' — a - mo - re!
death — thee pleas - es.

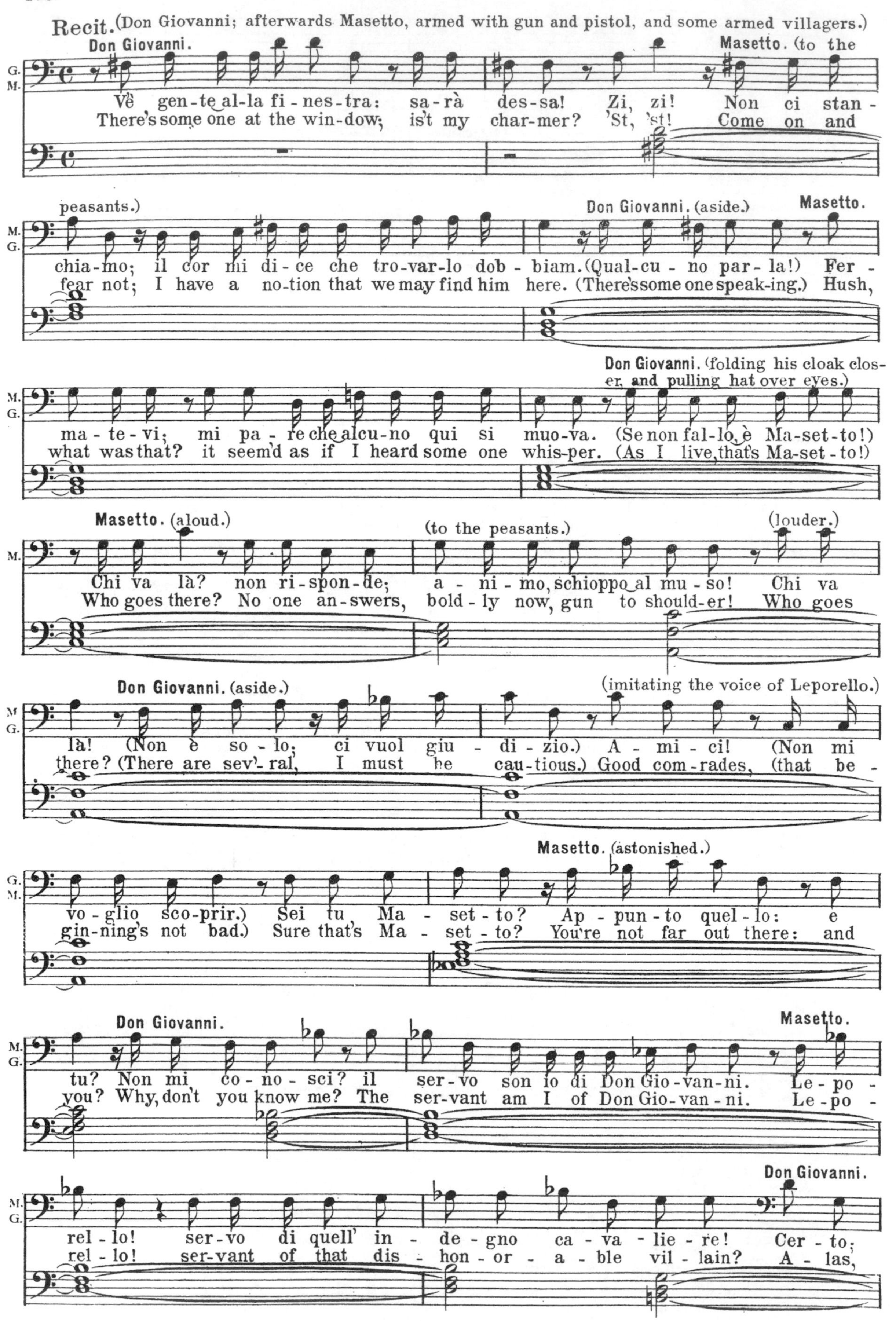
Recit. (Don Giovanni; afterwards Masetto, armed with gun and pistol, and some armed villagers.)
Don Giovanni.
Masetto. (to the peasants.)
G.
M.
Vè gen-te al-la fi-nes-tra: sa-rà des-sa! Zi, zi! Non ci stan-
There's some one at the win-dow; is't my char-mer? 'St, 'st! Come on and
chia-mo; il cor mi di-ce che tro-var-lo dob-biam.(Qual-cu-no par-la!) Fer-
fear not; I have a no-tion that we may find him here. (There's some one speak-ing.) Hush,
Don Giovanni. (aside.)
Masetto.
ma-te-vi; mi pa-re che alcu-no qui si muo-va. (Se non fal-lo, è Ma-set-to!)
what was that? it seem'd as if I heard some one whis-per. (As I live, that's Ma-set-to!)
Don Giovanni. (folding his cloak closer, and pulling hat over eyes.)
Masetto. (aloud.)
(to the peasants.)
(louder.)
Chi va là? non ri-spon-de; a-ni-mo, schioppo al mu-so! Chi va
Who goes there? No one an-swers, bold-ly now, gun to should-er! Who goes
Don Giovanni. (aside.)
(imitating the voice of Leporello.)
là! (Non è so-lo, ci vuol giu-di-zio.) A-mi-ci! (Non mi
there? (There are sev'-ral, I must be cau-tious.) Good com-rades, (that be-
Masetto. (astonished.)
vo-glio sco-prir.) Sei tu Ma-set-to? Ap-pun-to quel-lo: e
gin-ning's not bad.) Sure that's Ma-set-to? You're not far out there: and
Don Giovanni.
Masetto.
tu? Non mi co-no-sci? il ser-vo son io di Don Gio-van-ni. Le-po-
you? Why, don't you know me? The ser-vant am I of Don Gio-van-ni. Le-po-
Don Giovanni.
rel-lo! ser-vo di quell' in-de-gno ca-va-lie-re! Cer-to;
rel-lo! ser-vant of that dis-hon-or-a-ble vil-lain? A-las,

Masetto.
G.
M.
di quel bric-co-ne! Di quell' uom sen-za o-no-re: ah,
of that same ras-cal. Say: that man lost to all hon-our: Ah,
M.
dimmi un po-co, do-ve pos-siam tro-var-lo; lo cer-co con co-stor per tru-ci-dar-lo.
then you just can tell me where we may find him; these friends and I are seek-ing him to kill him.
Don Giovanni. (in centre of group.)
G.
(Ba-ga-tel-le!) bra-vis-si-mo, Ma-set-to! anch' io con voi m'u-ni-sco Per
(Ve-ry pleasant!) You've a good head, Ma-set-to! I'll do my best to help you, and
G.
farglie-la a quel birbo di pa-dro-ne; or senti un po' qual è la mia in-tenzione.
play a trick up-on my grace-less mas-ter; I have a plan will help to take him faster.

Nº 17. "Metà di voi quà vadano."

Aria.

Andante con moto.
Don Giovanni. (to the peasants.)
G.
Me-tà di voi quà va-da-no, e gli altri va-dan là!
Go half to left, and half to right, The road to pi-o-neer,
Corni & Vln.
p
Str.
G.
e pian pia-nin lo cer-chi-no, lon-
And by the way look ev'ry where, He

G.
tan non sia di quà, no! lon - tan, lontan non sia di quà.
can't be far from here, No! he can't, he can't be far from here.
Fl. & Vlns.
p
(going from one to another.)
Se un uom'e una ra - gaz-za pas - seg-giam per la piaz-za, se sot-to a una fi -
If a - ny you catch straying, Some youth and maid de - lay-ing, Or 'neath a window
Fag.
ne-stra fa-re al-l'a-mor sen - ti-te, fe - ri - te pur, fe-ri-te, fe - ri - te pur, fe -
sighing, An am'rous dit-ty ply-ing, Then strike him well and spare not, then strike him well and
Corni sustain.
ri - te, il mio pa-dron sa - rà!
spare not, My mas - ter then is near!
f
tr
Str.
p
In testa egli ha un cap - pel - lo con can-di-di pen-
Up - on his hat a feath-er, A cloak his form con-
tr

G.
nac-chi, ad-dos - so un-gran man-tel - lo, e
ceal-ing, He bears in ev - 'ry weath - er; Ne'er
Tutti.
cresc.
(trying to send the peasants off;
spa - da al fian - co e-gli ha, e spa - da al fian - co e-
knew he doubt or fear, ne'er knew he doubt or
but they act as if they had not understood him.)
gli ha, e spa - da al fian - co e - gli ha, e spa-da al fian-co e-
fear, ne'er knew he doubt or fear, ne'er knew he doubt or
gli ha, e spa-da al fian-co e-gli ha.
fear, ne'er knew he doubt or fear.
(repeating his directions.)
Se un uom' e u-na ra-
If a-ny you catch
cresc.
Fag.
gaz-za pas-seg-giam per la piaz-za,
straying, Some youth and maid de-lay-ing,
Se sot-to a una fi-
Or 'neath a win-dow
Str.

G.
ne-stra fare all' a-mor sen-ti-te, fe-ri-te, fe-ri-te, fe-ri-te, pur fe-
sigh-ing, An am-'rous dit-ty plying, Then strike him, then strike him, then strike him well and
Corni sustain.
cresc.
ri-te, fe-ri-te, pur fe-ri-te, fe-ri-te! Me-tà di voi quà va-da-no,
spare not, Then strike him well and spare not, and spare not! Go half to left and half to right,
f
decresc.
Fl. Ob. & Cor. sustain.
e gli al-tri va-dan là. E
The road to pi-o-neer, And
pian pianin lo cer-chi-no, lon-tan non sia di
by the way look ev-'ry where, He can't be far from
(pushing the peasants
quà, no, lon-tan, lon-tan non sia di quà. An-da-te, fa-te
here, no, he can't, he can't be far from here. A-way as I've di-
tr
f
p

off at either side.)
G.
presto, An-da-te, fa-te pre-sto, fa - te pre-sto, fa-te pre-sto, fa - te presto, fa-te
rected, A-way as I've di-rect-ed, Haste, a-way as I've direct-ed, Haste, a-way as I've di -
tr
f
p
cresc.
(to Masetto.)
presto, Tu sol ver-rai con me, tu sol verrai con me, verrai con me, verrai con
rected, Thou, friend, abide with me, Thou, friend, abide with me, abide with me, abide with
Str.
cresc.
f Tutti.
(putting his arm familiarly around Masetto.)
me, Noi far dobbiam il re-sto, e già ve-drai cos' è, cos' è, cos'
me; Some-what I have re-flect-ed, The end you soon shall see, you soon shall
Wood.
Str.
sfp
è, noi far dobbiam il re-sto, e già ve-drai cos'
see; Some - what I have re - flect-ed, The end you soon shall
(promenading to and fro with Masetto.)
è, cos' è, cos' è, e già vedrai cos' è, cos' è, cos' è, e già ve-drai cos'
see, you soon shall see, the end you soon shall see, you soon shall see, the end you soon shall

(goes off holding Masetto.)
G.
è, e già ve-drai cos' è, e già ve-drai cos' è, e già ve-drai cos' è!
see, the end you soon shall see, the end you soon shall see, the end you soon shall see.
f
Recit.
(Don Giovanni returns, leading Masetto by the hand.)
Don Giovanni.
Zit-to, la-scia ch'io sen-ta! Ot-ti-ma-men-te: dun-que dob-biam uc-
Soft-ly, first let us list-en, that no one's com-ing, So you're re-solv'd on
Masetto.
Don Giovanni.
G.
M.
ci-der-lo? Si-cu-ro! E non ti ba-ste-ria rom-per-gli l'os-sa, fra-cas-sar-gli le
kill-ing him? De-termin'd. 'Twould do if with a blow you were to stun him, or to give him a
Masetto. (hotly.)
Don Giovanni.
Masetto.
spalle? No, no, voglio ammazzar-lo, vo' far-lo in cento brani. Hai buone ar-mi? Co-
hid-ing. No, no, I'll sure-ly kill him, I'll cut him in-to pieces. Shew your weapons! They're
(hands musket and pistol to Don Giovanni.)
Don Giovanni.
Masetto.
M.
spetto! ho pria que-sto mo-schet-to, e poi, que-sta pi-sto-la. E po-i? Non
good ones! Look here, I have a musket, be-sides, there is this pis-tol. Be-sides these? I

Don Giovanni. (beats him with the flat of his sword.)
M.
G.
ba - sta? Oh, ba-sta certo; or pren-di, que-sta per la pi - sto-la, que-sta per il mo -
thought that_They're quite sufficient, we'll try them! There's something for your pistol, there's something for your
Masetto. (crying out and falling.) Don Giovanni.
G.
M.
schetto! Ahi, ahi! la te - sta mi-a! Ta-ci, o sei mor-to! Que-sta per am - maz -
musket! Oh, my poor head is broken! Hush, or you're dead, man! Here's for your prom-is'd
(Throws weapons down before Masetto, and exit hastily behind tavern.)
G.
zar-lo, que-sta per far-lo in bra-ni! Vil - la - no, ma-scal - zon! cef - fo da ca-ni!
kill-ing, know, ere you cut in pieces, You spite-ful bragging knave, Fortune's ca-prices!
Masetto. (crying out.)
Zerlina. (with a lantern.)
M.
Z.
Ahi! ahi! la te - sta mi - a! ahi, ahi, le spal-le, e il pet-to_ Di sen-
Oh, oh, my head is bro-ken, oh, oh, my back-bone, my shoulder. Did I
Masetto.
Z.
M.
ti - re mi par-ve la vo - ce di Ma-set-to! O Dio, Zer - li-na, Zer-li-na,
hear some one speak-ing? I thought it was Ma-set-to! Oh dear, Zer - li-na, Zer-li-na,
Zerlina. Masetto.
M.
Z.
mi-a, soc - cor-so! Co-sa è sta - to? L'i - ni-quo, il scel - le-ra-to mi
dearest, Come help me! What has hap-pen'd? The vil-lain, The base as-sas-sin has
Zerlina. Masetto.
M.
Z.
rup-pe l'os-sa e i ner-vi. Oh po - ve - ret - ta me! chi? Le-po - rel-lo! o qual-che
left no bone un-bro-ken. Oh dear, what can I do! who? Le-po - rel-lo! or else some
Zerlina. (helping him to rise.)
M.
Z.
dia-vol che so-mi-glia a lu - i! Cru-del! non tel diss' i - o che con que-sto tua
fiend, that look'd exactly like him. The wretch! Did I not tell you that your jeal-ous and

Z.
paz-za ge-lo-si-a ti ri-dur-re-sti a qual-che brut-to pas-so?
most un-ru-ly tem-per would sure-ly bring you ere long in-to some trouble?
Masetto. Zerlina. Masetto. Zerlina.
Z. M.
do-ve ti duo-le? Qui. E po-i? Qui, e ancor-a qui! E poi non ti duol
Where does it hurt you? Here. Be-sides, where? Here, and al-so here! Is nothing else the
Masetto.
al-tro? Duol-mi un po-co que-sto piè, que-sto brac-cio, e que-sta
mat-ter? Yes, there's some-thing with this foot, and this el-bow, I can-not
Zerlina.
M. Z.
ma-no. Via, via, non è gran mal, se il re-sto è sa-no.
bend it. Come, come, if that's the worst, there's no great harm done.
Vien-te-ne me-co a ca-sa; pur-chè tu mi pro-met-ta d'es-se-re men ge-
Come with me home to sup-per, and give your faith-ful prom-ise you'll nev-er-more be
lo-so, io, io ti gua-ri-rò, ca-ro il mio spo-so.
jeal-ous; those bruis-es can be cured, where love is zeal-ous.
Nº. 18. "Vedrai, carino."
Grazioso.
Aria.
Str. Corni sustain.
Mezza voce.
Cello.
tr
Wood.
Zerlina.
Ve-drai, ca-ri-no, se sei buo-ni-no, che bel ri-me-di-o
Come, shall I tell thee How what be-fell thee Soon can be cured By
p
Cor.

Z.
ti vo-glio dar!
my po-tent charm?
Vl & Wind
tr
È na-tu-ra-le,
No garden grows it,
str
non dà di-sgu-sto, e lo spe-zia-le non lo sa far, no,
Tho' it a bound-eth, Like furnace glows it, Yet none'twill harm, no,
non lo sa far, no, non lo sa far. È un cer-to bal-sa-mo
none it will harm, no, none it will harm. All guard and cherish it,
che por-to ad-dos-so, da-re t'el pos-so, se il vuoi pro-var.
Gold can-not buy it, Say, wilt thou try it? Soft 'tis, and warm.
Sa-per vor-re-sti
Canst thou not guess it?
do-ve mi sta, do-ve, do-ve, do-ve mi sta?
Has thy wit flown, say has all thy wit then flown?

(lays Masetto's hand on her heart)
Z.
Fl.
Cl.
Fag.
Strs. & Corni
Sen - ti - lo bat - te - re,
Hear how it throbs with-in,
Toc - ca mi quà, sen - ti - lo
'Tis all thy own, Hear how it
mf
bat - te - re, sen ti - lo bat - te - re,
throbs with-in, hear how it throbs within,
toc - ca-mi
'Tis all thine
p
Vl
Wind
tr
Bassi & Violi
quà! sen - ti - lo bat - te - re, sen - ti - lo bat - te - re,
own, hear how it throbs with - in, hear how it throbs with - in,
sen - ti - lo bat - te - re, toc - ca-mi quà! quà! quà!
hear how it throbs with-in, 'Tis all thine own, thine, thine!
sen - ti - lo bat - te - re, toc-ca-mi quà, quà! toc-ca-mi quà, quà!
Hear how it throbs with - in, Ah 'tis thine on-ly, it is thine on-ly,

(Exit with Masetto)
Z.
toc-cami quà, quà, toc-ca-mi quà!
It is thine on-ly, 'Tis all thine own!
cresc.
f
tr
p
pp
Scene. A dark courtyard, with three doors, before the house of Donna Anna. Leporello with Donna Elvira on his arm. He is wearing Don Giovanni's hat and cloak.
Recit. Leporello.
L.
Di mol-te fa-ci il lu-me s'av-vi-ci-na, o mio ben; stia-mo qui a-sco-si,
Lights ev'rywhere surround us, some are com-ing this way; We'll stand a-side here,
Donna Elvira.
L. E.
fin-chè da noi si sco-sta. Ma che te-mi, a-do-ra-to mio spo-so?
where they will not per-ceive us. My a-dor'd one, and why should they not see us?
Leporello.
(aside)
L.
Nul-la, nul-la cer-ti ri-guar-di, io vo've-der se il lu-me è già lon-ta-no. (Ah
Oh, for reasons, certain pre-cautions. Just let me see, I think they are re-treating. (How
Donna Elvira.
(Leporello goes further away)
L. E.
co-me da co-stei li-be-rar-mi?) Riman-ti, a-ni-ma bel-la. Ah! non la-sciar-mi!
shall I fly, and she not per-ceive me?) My dear, wait here a moment. Ah, do not leave me!

No. 19 "Sola, sola in bujo loco."
Sextet.

Andante
Donna Elvira.
Sola, sola in bujo loco palpitar il cor mi
All around so dark and lonely, O'er my heart a fear is
p
sfp
p
Fl. Fag. Strs.
sento, e m'assale un tal spavento, che mi sembra di mo-
stealing, Such a tremor, past all concealing, As if death itself were
mf
p
Leporello.
(groping his way)
rir, che mi sem - bra di morir. Più che
near, as if death itself were near. Deuce is
mf p
cresc.
f
p
Wind
cerco, men ritrovo questa porta, questa porta sciagurata;
in it, where's the doorway? These confounded walls on ev'ry side surround it!
(finds the door)
(misses it again)
piano, piano, l'ho trovata, l'ho tro-
Softly, softly, I have found it, I have
Ob.

L.
va-ta! ec-co il tem-po di fug-gir, ec-co il tem-po di fug-
found it! Stars be-thank'd, the coast is clear, stars be thank'd, the coast is
(Enter Don
gir, ec-co il tem-po, ec-co il tem-po, ec-co il tem-po di fug-gir!
clear, stars be thank'd, the coast is clear, oh stars be thank'd, the coast is clear!
Octavio and Donna Anna in mourning)
Don Octavio.
O.
Fag. Trombe & Tymp.
p
Fl. & Vlns.
Ter-gi il ci-glio, o vi-ta
Cease from griev-ing, oh be-
mi-a, e dà cal-ma al tuo do-
lov'd one, Think thy fa-ther sees from
Cor. sustain
lo-re! l'om-bra o-
heav-en. How sore for
mai del ge-ni-to-re pe-na a-
him thy heart is riv-en, Let a
tr

O.
vrà de' tuoi mar - tir, de'
smile at last ap - pear, at
Donna Anna.
A.
La - scia al - men al - la mia
Ah! be - lieve I know thy
O.
tuoi mar - tir.
last ap - pear.
Tympani 2 measures
A.
pe - na que-sto pic - co - lo ri -
kind - ness, But I can - not cease la -
A.
sto - ro; sol la
ment - ing; Ev - 'ry
A.
mor - te, sol la mor - te, o mio te -
ef - fort, ev - 'ry ef - fort but aug -

A.
so - ro, il mio - pian - to - può fi -
ment - ing grief for him I hold so
A.
nir, il mio - pian - - - - to
dear, grief for him I
Donna Elvira. (unseen by the others)
A.
E.
può fi - nir.
hold so dear.
Ah dov' è lo spo - so
Oh my hus-band, I have
Strs
Leporello. (by the door, unseen by the others)
E.
L.
mi - o? Se mi tro - va, son per -
lost thee! Not for worlds I'd have her
Donna Elvira. (also approaching the door.)
E.
U - na por - ta la vegg' i - o, che - to, che - to io vo' par-
What in-trud - er now has cross'd thee! Speak a word if thou art
L.
du - to! U - na por - ta la vegg'
find me! Sure the door must be be-

E.
tir, che - to, che - to io vo' par - tir!
near, speak a word if thou art near.
L.
i - o, che - to, che - to io vo' par - tir, che - to, che - to, che - to,
hind me. Hark! me-thinks a voice I hear, hark! me-thinks a voice I
Wind
Zerlina.
Z.
Fer - ma, bric-co - ne, do - ve ten
Wretch, now we hold thee, whith-er art
Masetto.
M.
Fer - ma, bric-co - ne, do - ve ten
Wretch, now we hold thee, whith-er art
Leporello. (trying to escape, he is suddenly confronted by Zerlina and Masetto.)
L.
che - to, che - to, che - to io vo' par - tir.
hear; Ha! the door, es-cape is near.
Tutti
Donna Anna. (Leporello, forced into centre, kneels, and hides his face in Don Giovanni's cloak.)
A.
Ec - co il fel - lo - ne, com' e - ra
Naught now can save thee, why art thou
Zerlina.
Z.
va - i?
go - ing?
Don Octavio.
O.
Ec - co il fel - lo - ne, com' e - ra
Naught now can save thee, why art thou
Masetto.
M.
va - i?
go - ing?

A.
quà? Ah, mo-ra il per - fi - do! che m'ha tra -
here? Die, thou per - fid - ious one! death here we
Z.
Ah, mo-ra il per - fi - do! che m'ha tra -
Die, thou per - fid - ious one! death here we
O.
quà? Ah, mo-ra il per - fi - do! che m'ha tra -
here? Die, thou per - fid - ious one! death here we
M.
Ah, mo-ra il per - fi - do! che m'ha tra -
Die, thou per - fid - ious one! death here we
di - to, che m'ha tra - di - to!
swear thee! death here we swear thee!
Strs.
p
Donna Elvira. (discovering herself, and unveiling)
E.
O mio ma - ri - to! pie - tà, pie - tà, pie -
Oh heav'n, for - bear ye! He is my hus - band

Donna Anna.
(sotto voce)
A.
È Donna Elvi-ra? è Don - na El - vi - ra?
'Tis Donna Elvi-ra! 'tis Don - na El - vi - ra!
Donna Elvira.
E.
tà!
dear!
Zerlina.
(sotto voce)
Z.
È Donna El-vi-ra? è Donna El-vi - ra?
'Tis Donna El-vi-ra! 'tis Donna El-vi - ra!
Don Octavio.
(sotto voce)
O.
È Donna Elvi-ra? Donna El-vi - ra?
'Tis Donna Elvi-ra! Donna El-vi - ra!
Masetto.
(sotto voce)
M.
È Donna El-vi - ra?
'Tis Donna El-vi - ra!
Donna Anna.
A.
quel - la ch'io ve - do? ap - pe - na il
She for him plead - ing? Her wrongs all un-
Zerlina.
Z.
quel - la ch'io ve-do? ap-pe - na il cre - do, ap-pe - na il
She for him pleading? Her wrongs all un-heed - ing, her wrongs all un-
Don Octavio.
O.
quel-la ch'io ve - do? ap - pe - na il
She for him plead - ing? Her own wrongs un -
Masetto.
M.
quel - la ch'io ve - do? ap - pe - na il
She for him plead - ing? Her wrongs all un -

A.
cre - do! No, no, no, no! mor-
heed - ing? No, no, no, no! he
Z.
cre - do! No, no, no no! mor-
heed - ing? No, no, no, no! he
O.
cre - do! No, no, no, no! mor-
heed - ing? No, no, no, no! he
M.
cre - do! No, no, no, no! mor-
heed - ing? No, no, no, no! he
Tutti
Vlns
Cor
Bassi
Donna Anna.
A.
rà! No,
dies! No,
Donna Elvira.
E.
Pie - tà! Pie - tà!
Oh hear me! Oh hear me!
Zerlina.
Z.
rà! No,
dies! No,
Don Octavio.
O.
rà! No,
dies! No,
Masetto.
M.
rà! No,
dies! No,

A.
no, no, no, no,
no, no, no, no,
E.
pie - tà, pie - tà,
for - bear, for - bear,
Z.
no, no, no, no, no,
no, no, no, no, no,
O.
no, no, no, no, no,
no, no, no, no, no,
M.
no, no, no, no, no,
no, no, no, no, no,
f p f
Donna Anna.
A.
mor - rà!
he dies!
Zerlina.
Z.
mor - rà!
he dies!
(They seize upon him, Leporello discovers himself and kneels down.)
Don Octavio.
O.
mor - rà!
he dies!
Masetto.
M.
mor - rà!
he dies!
(as though in tears)
Leporello.
L.
Per - don, per - do - no! Si - gno - ri
Good friends, oh spare me! You're quite mis -
Fl. Ob. Fag.
fp cresc p
Leporello.
L.
mie - i! quello io non so - no, sbaglia co -
tak - en! Oh how you scare me! oh how I'm
p cresc p

(Throwing back the cloak. General astonishment; Donna Elvira flies to Donna Anna.)
L.
ste - i, vi - ver la - scia - te - mi per ca - ri -
shak - en! But oh, for pit - y's sake, oh kill me
cresc.
cresc.
f
p
cresc.
L.
tà, vi - ver la - scia - te - mi per ca - ri - tà, per ca - ri -
not! Oh no, for pit - y's sake, oh kill me not, oh kill me
f
p
cresc.
p
p
Donna Anna.
A.
sotto voce
Dei! Le - po - rel - lo? Che ingan - no è
What! Le - po - rel - lo? My eyes de -
f
Donna Elvira.
E.
sotto voce
Dei! Le - po - rel - lo? Che ingan - no è
What! Le - po - rel - lo? My eyes de -
f
Zerlina.
Z.
sotto voce
Dei! Le - po - rel - lo? Che ingan - no è
What! Le - po - rel - lo? My eyes de -
f
Don Octavio.
O.
sotto voce
Dei! Le - po - rel - lo? Che ingan - no è
What! Le - po - rel - lo? My eyes de -
f
Masetto.
M.
sotto voce
Dei! Le - po - rel - lo? Che ingan - no è
What! Le - po - rel - lo? My eyes de -
f
Leporello.
L.
tà, per ca - ri - tà!
not, oh, kill me not!
tr tr tr tr tr tr tr

A.
que - sto!
ceive me!
Le - - po - rel - lo?
Le - - po - rel - lo?
E.
Z.
O.
M.
Che ingan-no è que-sto!
My eyes de-ceive me!
stu - pi - da re - sto!
Who would be-lieve me?
stu - pi - do re - sto!

A.
che mai sar - rà, che mai sar - rà,
This is some plot, this is some plot,
E.
che mai sar - rà, che mai sar - rà, che mai sar -
This is some plot, this is some plot, this is some
Z.
che mai sar - rà, che mai sar - rà, che mai sar -
This is some plot, this is some plot, this is some
O.
che mai sar - rà, che mai sar - rà, che mai sar -
This is some plot, this is some plot, this is some
M.
che mai sar - rà, che mai sar -
This is some plot, this is some
A.
che mai sar - rà, che mai sar - rà!
this is some plot, this is some plot.
E.
-rà, che mai sar - rà, che mai sar - rà!
plot, this is some plot, this is some plot.
Z.
-rà, che mai sar - rà, che mai sar - rà!
plot, this is some plot, this is some plot.
O.
-rà, che mai sar - rà, che mai sar - rà!
plot, this is some plot, this is some plot.
M.
-rà, che mai sar - rà, che mai sar - rà!
plot, this is some plot, this is some plot.

Molto allegro.
Leporello.
Mil - le tor - bi -
Fear and doubt - ing
Donna Anna.
Mil - le tor - bi di pen - sie - ri
Fear and doubt - ing quite dis - tract me,
Donna Elvira.
Mil - le tor - bi - di pen-sie-ri
Fear and doubt - ing quite dis-tract me,
Zerlina.
Mil - le tor - bi - di pen - sie - ri
Fear and doubt - ing quite dis - tract me,
Don Octavio.
Mil - le tor - bi - di pen - sie - ri
Fear and doubt - ing quite dis - tract me,
Masetto.
Mil - le tor - bi - di pen - sie - ri
Fear and doubt - ing quite dis - tract me,
Leporello.
di pen - sie - ri
quite dis - tract me,
Leporello.
mi s'ag - - gi - ran per la
All my head is in con -

Donna Anna.
A.
mi s'ag - gi - ran per la te - sta.
All my head is in con - fu - sion.
Donna Elvira.
E.
mi s'ag - gi - ran per la te - sta.
All my head is in con - fu - sion.
Zerlina.
Z.
mi s'ag - gi - ran per la te - sta.
All my head is in con - fu - sion.
Don Octavio.
O.
mi s'ag - gi - ran per la te - sta.
All my head is in con - fu - sion.
Masetto.
M.
mi s'ag - gi - ran per la te - sta.
All my head is in con - fu - sion.
Leporello.
L.
te - sta. Mil - le tor - bi - di pen -
fu - sion. Fear and doubt - ing quite dis -
f
p
Leporello.
L.
cresc.
sie - ri mi s'ag - gi - ran per la te - sta; se mi sal - vo in tal tem -
tract me, all my head is in con - fu - sion; Would in - deed 'twere a de -
cresc.
f
L.
pe - sta, è un pro - di - gio in ve - ri - tà.
lu - sion, And I safe - ly from this spot.
f

A.
Che gior- na - ta, o stel - le͜ è que-sta, o stel - le͜ è questa!
'Tis a vi - sion, a vile de - lu - sion, a vile de - lu-sion!
E.
Che gior- na - ta, o stel - le͜ è que-sta, o stel - le͜ è questa!
'Tis a vi - sion, a vile de - lu - sion, a vile de - lu-sion!
Z.
Che gior- na - ta, o stel - le͜ è que-sta, o stel - le͜ è questa!
'Tis a vi - sion, a vile de - lu - sion, a vile de - lu-sion!
O.
Che gior- na - ta, o stel - le͜ è que-sta, o stel - le͜ è questa!
'Tis a vi - sion, a vile de - lu - sion, a vile de - lu-sion!
M.
Che gior- na - ta, o stel - le͜ è que-sta, o stel - le͜ è questa!
'Tis a vi - sion, a vile de - lu - sion, a vile de - lu-sion!
L.
è͜ un pro - di - gio in ve - ri - tà, se mi
Were I safe - ly far from this spot, Would in
sf
sf
Wind.
Str.
L.
sal - vo in tal tem-pe-sta, è͜ un pro-di-gio in ve - ri - tà, è͜ un pro-di-gio͜ in ve-ri-
deed 'twere a mere de - lu-sion, And I safe-ly far from this spot, Would indeed 'twere a de-
f
L.
tà, in ve-ri-tà, in ve-ri - tà, è͜ un pro - di - gio in ve - ri -
lu-sion, And I safe-ly from this spot, Were I but safe - ly from this
sf
sf
fp
fp

D. Anna. (sotto voce)
Che im - pen - sa - ta no - vi - tà!
Be this mask - ing ne'er for got,
D. Elv. (sotto voce)
Che im - pen - sa - ta no - vi - tà!
Be this mask - ing ne'er for got,
Zerlina. (sotto voce)
Che im - pen - sa - ta no - vi - tà!
Be this mask - ing ne'er for got,
D. Oct. (sotto voce)
Che im - pen - sa - ta no - vi - tà!
Be this mask - ing ne'er for got,
Mas. (sotto voce)
Che im - pen - sa - ta no - vi - tà!
Be this mask - ing ne'er for got,
Lep.
tà! Mil - le tor - bi - di pen - sie - ri mi s'ag -
spot! Fear and doubting quite dis - tract me, All my
Vln. Wind. Vln.
p
che im - pen - sa - ta, che im - pen - sa - ta no - vi -
Be this mask - ing, be this mask - ing ne'er for -
gi - ran per la te - sta! se mi sal - vo in tal tempe - sta, è un pro - di - gio
head is in con - fu - sion, Would indeed 'twere a mere de - lu - sion, And I safe - ly

A.
tà! no - vi -
got, ne'er for -
E.
tà! che im - pen - sa - ta no - vi -
got, Be this mask - ing ne'er for -
Z.
tà! che impen - sa - ta no - vi -
got, Be this mask-ing ne'er for-
O.
tà! che im - pen - sa - ta no - vi -
got, Be this mask - ing ne'er for -
M.
tà! che im - pen - sa - ta no - vi -
got, Be this mask - ing ne'er for -
L.
in ve - ri - tà! èun pro - di - gio in ve - ri -
far from this spot, Were I safe - ly from this
A.
tà! Mil - le tor - bi - di pen - sie - ri mi s'ag -
got! Fear and doubting quite dis - tract me, All my
E.
tà! Mil - le, mil - le tor - bi - di pen - sie - ri
got! Fear and doubt - ing quite dis - tract me, All my
Z.
tà! mil - le tor - bi - di pen - sie - ri
got! Fear and doubt-ing quite dis - tract me,
O.
tà! Mil - le tor - bi - di pen - sie - ri mi s'ag -
got! Fear and doubting quite dis - tract me, All my
M.
tà! Mil - le tor - bi - di pen - sie - ri
got! Fear and doubt-ing quite dis - tract me,
L.
tà!
spot.

A.
gi - ran per la te - sta.
head is in con - fu - sion.
E.
mi s'ag - gi - ran per la
head, my head is in con -
Z.
mi s'ag - gi - ran per la
All my head is in con -
O.
gi - ran per la te - sta.
head is in con - fu - sion.
M.
mi s'ag - gi - ran per la
All my head is in con -
E.
te - sta.
fu - sion.
Z.
te - sta.
fu - sion.
M.
te - sta.
fu - sion.
Leporello.
L.
cresc.
Mil - le tor - bi - di pen - sie - ri mi s'ag - gi - ran per la
Fear and doubt - ing quite dis - tract me, All my head is in con -
p
L.
f
te - sta, se mi sal - vo in tal tem - pe - sta, è un pro - di - gio in ve - ri -
fu - sion, Would in - deed twere a de - lu - sion, And I safe - ly from this
cresc.
f

D. Anna.
A.
Che giornata, o stelle,è
'Tis a vision, a vile de-
D. Elvira.
E.
Che giornata, o stelle,è
'Tis a vision, a vile de-
Zerlina.
Z.
Che giornata, o stelle,è
'Tis a vision, a vile de-
D. Octavio.
O.
Che giornata, o stelle,è
'Tis a vision, a vile de-
Masetto.
M.
Che giornata, o stelle,è
'Tis a vision, a vile de-
Leporello.
L.
tà, èun prodigio
spot. Were I safely
sf
sf
questa, o stelle,è questa!
lusion, a vile delusion!
questa, o stelle,è questa!
lusion, a vile delusion!
questa, o stelle,è questa!
lusion, a vile delusion!
questa, o stelle,è questa!
lusion, a vile delusion!
questa, o stelle,è questa!
lusion, a vile delusion!
in verità, se mi salvo in tal tem-
far from this spot, Would indeed 'twere a mere de-
Wind
Strings
f

L.
pe-sta èun pro-di-gio in ve-ri-tà, èun pro-di-gio inve-ri-
lu-sion, And I safe-ly far from this spot, Would in-deed 'twere a de-
L.
tà, in ve-ri-tà, in ve-ri-tà, èun pro-di-gio in ve-ri-
lu-sion, And I safe-ly from this spot, Were I but safe-ly from this
sf
sf
fp
fp
D. Anna.
sotto voce
A.
Che im-pen-sa-ta no-vi-tà!
Be this masking ne'er for-got,
D. Elvira.
sotto voce
E.
Che im-pen-sa-ta no-vi-tà!
Be this mask-ing ne'er for-got,
Zerlina.
sotto voce
Z.
Che im-pen-sa-ta no-vi-tà!
Be this mask-ing ne'er for-got,
D. Octavio.
sotto voce
O.
Che im-pen-sa-ta no-vi-tà!
Be this mask-ing ne'er for-got,
Masetto.
sotto voce
M.
Che im-pen-sa-ta no-vi-tà!
Be this mask-ing ne'er for-got,
Leporello.
L.
p
tà! Mil-le tor-bi-di pen-sie-ri mi s'ag-
spot! Fear and doubting quite dis-tract me, All my
Vln.
Wind.
Vln.
p
p

A.
E.
Z.
O.
M.
L.
che im- -pen - sa- -ta, che im - pen-
Be this mask- -ing, be this
gi - ran per la te - sta! se mi sal - vo in tal tem-pe - sta, è un pro-
head is in con - fu - sion, Would in-deed 'twere a mere de - lu - sion, And I
sa - ta no - vi - tà, no -
mask-ing ne'er for - got, ne'er
che im - pen - sa - ta no -
Be this mask-ing ne'er
che impen-
Be this
di - gio in ve - ri - tà! è un pro-
safe-ly far from this spot, Were I
f
p

A.
- vi - tà, che im - pen - sa - ta no - vi - tà,
— for - got, Be this masking ne'er for - got,
E.
vi - tà, che im-pen - sa - ta no -
for - got, be this mask - ing ne'er
Z.
sa - ta no - vi - tà, che im-pen-sa - ta no - vi - tà, che im-pen-
masking ne'er for - got, be this masking ne'er for - got, be this
O.
vi - tà, che im - pen - sa - ta no -
for - got, be this mask - ing ne'er
M.
vi - tà, che im-pen - sa - ta no -
for - got, be this mask - ing ne'er
L.
di-gio in ve - ri - tà, è un pro - di - gio in ve - ri -
safe - ly from this spot, would that I, would that I were
A.
che im-pen-sa - ta no - vi - tà,
be this mask - ing ne'er for - got,
E.
vi - tà, no - vi - tà,
for - got, ne'er for - got,
Z.
sa - ta no - vi - tà,
mask-ing ne'er for - got,
O.
vi - tà, no - vi - tà,
for - got, ne'er for - got,
M.
vi - tà, no - vi - tà,
for - got, ne'er for got,
L.
tà, in ve - ri - tà,
safe - ly from this spot,
staccato

A.
che im - pen - sa - ta no - vi - tà, che im - pen - sa - ta
be this mask - ing ne'er for - got, be this mask - ing
E.
che im - pen - sa - ta no - vi - tà, che im - pen - sa - ta
be this mask - ing ne'er for - got, be this mask - ing
Z.
che im - pen - sa - ta no - vi - tà, che im - pen - sa - ta
be this mask - ing ne'er for - got, be this mask - ing
O.
che im - pen - sa - ta no - vi - tà, che im - pen - sa - ta
be this mask - ing ne'er for - got, be this mask - ing
M.
che im - pen - sa - ta no - vi - tà, che im - pen - sa - ta
be this mask - ing ne'er for - got, be this mask - ing
L.
è un pro - di - gio in ve - ri - tà, è un pro - di - gio in
Were I safe - ly from this spot, were I safe - ly
A.
no - vi - tà, che im - pen - sa - ta, che im - pen - sa -
ne'er for - got, be this mask - ing, be this mask -
E.
no - vi - tà, che im - pen - sa - ta, che im - pen - sa -
ne'er for - got, be this mask - ing, be this mask -
Z.
no - vi - tà, che im - pen - sa - ta, che im - pen - sa -
ne'er for - got, be this mask - ing, be this mask -
O.
no - vi - tà, che im - pen - sa - ta, che im -
ne'er for - got, be this mask - ing, be
M.
no - vi - tà, che im - pen - sa - ta,
ne'er for - got, be this mask - ing,
L.
ve - ri - tà, è un pro - di - gio
from this spot were I safe - ly,

A.
- - - ta no- - -vi - tà, che im - pen -
- - - ing ne'er for - got, be this
E.
- - - - ta no - vi - tà, che im - pen -
- - - - ing ne'er for - got, be this
Z.
- ta no- - - -vi- -tà, che im - pen -
- ing ne'er for- -got, be this
O.
-pen - sa- -ta no- -vi- -tà, che im - pen -
this mask- -ing ne'er for- -got, be this
M.
che im - pen - sa - ta no - vi - tà, che im - pen -
be this mask - ing ne'er for - got, be this
L.
È un pro - di- - -
Were I safe- - -
A.
sa- -ta no- -vi - tà, che im - pen - sa - ta
mask- -ing ne'er for - got, be this mask - ing
E.
sa- -ta no- -vi - tà, che im - pen - sa - ta
mask- -ing ne'er for - got, be this mask - ing
Z.
sa- -ta no- -vi - tà, che im - pen - sa - ta
mask- -ing ne'er for - got, be this mask - ing
O.
sa- -ta no- -vi - tà, che im - pen - sa - ta
mask- -ing ne'er for - got, be this mask - ing
M.
sa - ta no - vi - tà, che im - pen - sa - ta
mask - ing ne'er for - got, be this mask - ing
L.
-gio in ve - ri - tà, è un pro - di- - -gio in
-ly but from this spot, were I safe- - -ly but

A.
no- -vi-tà, che im-pen-sa-ta no- -vi-
ne'er for-got, be this mask-ing ne'er for-
E.
no- -vi-tà, che im-pen-sa- -ta no- -vi-
ne'er for-got, be this mask- -ing ne'er for-
Z.
no- -vi-tà, che im-pen-sa- -ta no- -vi-
ne'er for-got, be this mask- -ing ne'er for-
O.
no- -vi-tà, che im-pen-sa- -ta no- -vi-
ne'er for-got, be this mask- -ing ne'er for-
M.
no-vi-tà, che im-pen-sa- -ta no- -vi-
ne'er for-got, be this mask- -ing ne'er for-
L.
ve-ri-tà, è un pro-di- -gio in ve- -ri-
from this spot, were I safe- -ly but from this
(exit D. Anna)
A. tà! got!
E. tà! got!
Z. tà! got!
O. tà! got!
M. tà! got!
L. tà! spot!

Recit.
Zerlina.(to Leporello)
Dun-que quel-lo sei tu, che il mio Ma-set-to po-co fà cru-del-men-te mal-trat-tasti!
It was you, then who with your cru-el blows, this ve-ry night, near-ly kill'd my poor Ma-set-to!
Donna Elvira.(to Leporello)
Dun-que tu m'in-gan-na-sti, o scel-le-ra-to, spac-cian-do-ti con me da Don Gio-van-ni!
It was you, heart-less ri-bald, who be-guil'd me, who led me forth as though 'twere Don Gio-van-ni!
Don Octavio.(to Leporello)
Dun-que tu in que-sti pan-ni ve-ni-sti qui per qual-che tra-di-men-to!
Why dost thou wear those gar-ments? thou must be here for some un-law-ful pur-pose!
Donna Elvira.
A me toc-ca pu-nir-lo.
'Tis I who will chas-tise him,
Zerlina.
An-zi a me.
So will I.
Don Octavio.
No, no, a me.
No, no, 'tis I.
Masetto.
Ac-cop-pa-te-lo me-co tut-ti tre.
How this vi-per to crush, we all will try.
Allegro assai.
Nº 20. "Ah, pietà! Signori miei!,,
Aria.
Leporello.
Ah, pie-tà! Si-gno-ri miei! ah pie-tà, pie-tà, pie-tà, pie-tà di me, pie-tà
Ah, be not so hard on me, give me leave, good friends, to speak, oh give me leave to speak!
Dò ra-gio-ne a voi, a
Wrongs like yours sure-ly had un-
fp
f
p

L.
le - i, a voi, a le - i. Ma, ma, il de-lit-to, il de-
done me, had sure un- done me, But, but oh be-lieve me, oh be-
Cor. Fag. & Bassi.
lit - to mio non è, mio non è, Il pa - dron con pre - po -
lieve me, I am not he you seek. I will tell you how my
Fl.
Str.
ten - za, l'in-no- cen- za mi ru - bò, l'in- no - cen - za mi ru -
mas-ter Did from bad to worse de-scend, did from bad to worse de -
(to Elvira)
bò. Donna Elvi-ra! compa-ti - te!
scend. Donna Elvi-ra! do you tell them,

L.
com-pa - ti - te! Voi ca-pi - te come an-
do you tell them, By what arts he gains his
Vlns.

(to Masetto)
L.
dò, voi ca-pi-te, voi ca-pi-te, voi ca-pi-te come an-dò! Di Ma-
end, do you tell them, do you tell them by what arts he gains his end. As for
Tutti.
(motioning to Elvira)
set-to non sò nul-la, non sò nul-la, nul-la, nul-la, nul-la, nul-la, vel di-
thee I've not a no-tion what be-fell thee, not a no-tion what be-fell thee, As this
f
p
rà que-sta fan-ciul-la, que-sta fan-ciul-la. È un o-ret-ta
la-dy here can tell thee, Yes, she can tell thee, For I met her
tr
fp
cir-cum-cir-ca, che con lei gi-ran-do vo,
With him phi-lan-d'ring, Well I knew how all would end,
fp
tr
(With embarrassment to Don Octavio)
che con lei gi-ran-do vo. Ah voi, Si-gnore!
Well I knew how all would end. And to your lordship,

L.
non di - co nien - te, cer - to ti - mo - re,
I will ad - mit it, I've act - ed wrongly,
certo acci - den - te, di fuo - ri chiaro, di dentro o - scu - ro, non c'è ri -
not as be - fit - ed I know I've trespass'd I ask your pardon, Lost in the
(pointing at the door)
pa - ro la porta, il mu - ro, io me - ne vo da quel
dark - ness, I entered the gar - den, Nor thought t'of - fend. 'Twas a
la - to, poi qui ce - la - to,
blun - der; Great - - ly I won - der
(slyly edging towards the door)
l'af - far si sa, oh, si
How all was known, all was
mf
p
f
sf
tr

sa! ma
known. Mas-
p
(making for the door)
s'io sa-pe-va, fug-gia per quà, fug-gia per quà, fug-gia per
ters, I would now with speed be gone with speed be gone, yes, I would
pp
mf
p
quà, fug-gia per quà!
now with speed be gone.
(Runs out.)
Recit.
Donna Elvira.
Masetto.
Zerlina.
E.
M.
Z.
Fer-ma, per-fi-do, fer-ma! Il bir-bo ha l'a-li ai pie-di! Con quel ar-te
Hold, thou shalt not es-cape me! He flies like a-ny feath-er! And how neatly,

Don Octavio.
Z.
O.
si sot-tras-se l'i-ni-quo. A-mi-ci mi-ei, do-po ec-ces-si si e-
he e-vad-ed our ques-tion. Friends, this con-firms me, and the crimes we have
O.
normi, du-bi-tar non pos-siam che Don Gio-van-ni non sia l'em-pio uc-ci-
witness'd, we not further can doubt, that Don Gio-van-ni was the vil-lain-ous

so - re del pa - dre di Donn' An - na; in que - sta ca - sa per po -
murd'rer of Don - na An - na's fa - ther. Do me the fa - vor here a -
che o - re ferma - te - vi, un ri - cor - sa vo' far a chi si de - ve, è in poch' i -
while yet to stay with her. I will go now, and seek the law's as - sist - ance. The day of
(Exeunt D. Elvira, Zerlina, and Masetto.)
stanti ven - di - car - vi pro - met - to. Co - sì vuo - le do - ver, pie - ta - de, af - fet - to.
reck'ning is at hand, oh thou traitor, and thy doom is assured, or sooner or lat - er.
Nº 21. "Il mio tesoro intanto."
Aria.
Andante grazioso.
Clar. Fag. and Vln.
Strings con sordini, Bassi pizz.
tr
f
Don Octavio.
Il mio te - so - ro in - tan - to an -
To my be - loved, O _ has - ten, To
p
Strings.
Cl.
Fag.
da - te, an - da - - te a _ con - so - lar! e del bel ci - glio il
com - fort, to com - - fort _ her sad heart! Sweet are the tears that
Corni sustain.
pian - to cer - ca - te _ di a - sciu - gar, _ cer - ca - te, cer - ca - - te, cer -
chas - ten, Yet grieve not those who part, _ that grieve _ not, that grieve _ not, that
3
3

O.
ca- -te- di-a- -sciu-gar, cer-ca- - - - - -
grieve not those who part, That grieve
- - - - - - -te dia- -sciu-gar.
not those who part.
Vln.
f senza sordini
Di-te-le, che i suoi tor-ti a ven-di-car io va-do, a
Tell her, to see her right-ed, Ne'er will I cease pur-su-ing, ne'er
p
vendi-car io va-do. Che sol di stra-gi e mor-ti
will I cease pur-su-ing, My sword and faith I've plighted,
cresc.
f
fp
p
nun- zio vogl'io tor-nar, nun- -zio vogl'io tor-
Naught my re-solve shall thwart, Naught my re-solve shall
fp
f
p

nar, sì, nunzio vogl'io tor - nar!
thwart, Naught, naught my re-solve shall thwart.
cresc.
f
p
Il mio te-so-ro in-
To my be-loved, O
con sordini.
tan - to An-da - te, an-da- - te a con-so-
has - ten, To com - fort, to com- - fort her sad
lar! e del bel ciglio il pian-to cer-ca - te di a - sciu-gar, cer-
heart, Sweet are the tears that chas-ten, Yet grieve not those who part, that
ca- te, cer-ca - te, cer-ca - te di a - sciu - gar, cer-
grieve not, that grieve not, that grieve not those who part, that

ca- - - - - - - - - - - - -te
grieve not
dia - sciu-gar. Di- te-le che i suoi tor - ti
those who part. Tell her, to see her right - ed
senza sord.
a, ven-di-car io va - do, a ven-di-car io
ne'er will I cease pur-su - ing, Ne'er will I cease pur-
cresc.
va- - - - - - - -do, che sol di stra - gi e
su- - - - - - - -ing. My sword and faith I've
mor - ti nun - zio vogl'io tor - nar,
plight - ed, Naught my re - solve shall thwart,
f
p
fp

nun - zio, nun zio vogl' io tor-
naught, no, naught my re - solve shall
nar, Che sol di stra - gie mor- ti
thwart, My sword and faith I've plight - ed,
nun - zio vogl'io tor - nar, sì, nun - zio vogl'io tor-
Naught my re-solve shall thwart, naught, naught my re-solve shall
nar!
thwart! (Exit).

(Zerlina, with a razor in her hand, drags on Leporello by the hair.)
Zerlina.
a tempo
Re - sta-ti quà! Re - sta-ti quà!
Here you shall stay! Here you shall stay!
Leporello.
Per ca - ri - tà!
Oh spare me, pray!
Zerlina.
Re - sta-ti quà! Re - sta-ti quà, quà,
Here you shall stay, Here you shall stay, here
Recit.
Leporello. (trying to free himself).
Zerlina.
quà! Per ca - ri - tà, Zer - li - na! Eh! non c'è ca - ri - tà per pa - ri
stay! For pit - y's sake, Zer - li - na! No, for vil-lains like you there is no
Leporello.
Zerlina.
tuo-i. Dun-que ca - var - mi vuo - i? I ca - pel - li, la te - sta,
pit-y. Sure - ly you would not hurt me? I will first tear your eyes out,
Leporello. (trying to coax her.)
Zerlina. (holding him off.)
il co - re e glioc-chi. Sen - ti, ca - ri - na mi - a! Guai, se mi toc - chi!
and then cut your head off. Non-sense, lis-ten to rea-son! Dare but to touch me!
Ve - drai, schiu - ma de' bir - bi, qual pre - mio n'ha chi le ra - gaz - zein -
I'll teach you, scum of e - vil, with base de - ceit, murd'rous - ly to ill -
Leporello. (aside).
Zerlina. (dragging Le-
giu - ria. (Li - be - ra - te - mi, o Dei, da que - sta fu - ria!) Ma-set-to! O -
use us. (Oh ye gods, how shall I es-cape this fu - ry!) Ma-set-to! ho -
porello about during the whole scene.)
là! Ma - set - to! do - ve dia - vo - lo è i - to? Ser - vi!
la! Ma - set - to! why, Ma - set - to, where are you? neigh-bors!

Leporello. (a peasant enters.)
Z.
L.
gen-te! nes-sun vien, nes-sun sen-te_ Fa pia-no per pie-
ser-vants! no one comes, no one hears me. Pray do not call so
Zerlina.
tà! non strascinarmi a co-da di ca-val-lo! Ve-drai, vedrai co-me fi-ni-sce il
loud! Dragg'd at the horse's tail is some-thing like this. You shall not go till you have been well
Leporello.
Zerlina.
Leporello.
bal-lo! Pre-sto quà quel-la se-dia! Ec-co-la! Sie-di! Stan-co non
pun-ish'd. On that chair now be seat-ed. Here I am. Stay there. I'm not fa-
Zerlina.
son. Sie-di, o con que-ste ma-ni ti strappo il cor, e poi lo get-to a'
tigued. Sit there, or these hands shall tear out thy wick-ed heart. So dare to dis-o-
Leporello. (sits down.)
ca-ni. Sie-do, ma tu, di gra-zia, met-ti giù quel ra-so-jo! mi vuoi
bey me. Well, well, but now in mer-cy, put a-way that vile ra-zor! would you
Zerlina.
for-se sbar-bar? Sì, ma-scal-zo-ne, io sbar-ba-re ti vo' sen-za sa-
help me to shave? Yes, I will shew you how to shave without either soap or
Leporello.
Zerlina.
Leporello. (gives it.)
po-ne. E-ter-ni De-i! Dam-mi la man! La ma-no.
wa-ter. Oh gra-cious good-ness! Give me your hand! There, take it.
Zerlina.
Leporello. (gives the others).
Zerlina.
(ties Leporello's hands with her handkerchief the peasant assists her.)
L'al-tra! Ma che vuoi far-mi? Vog-lio far, vog-lio far quel-lo che par-mi.
That one! What mischief strikes her? You shall see, I will do just as I like, sir.

Nº 21b "Per queste tue manine."

Duet.

Allegro moderato.
Leporello.
L.
Per que-ste tu-e ma-ni - ne, Can-di-de e te-ne-
Come here, oh I con-jure thee, Thy heart, I know, is
f
rel - le, per que - sta fres - ca pel - le, ab-bi pie-tà di
ten - der, Oh let those fin - gers slen - der, Li-ber-ty give to
Zerlina.
L.
Z.
me, ab-bi pie-tà di me! Non v'è pie-tà bric-co-ne, non v'è pie-tà, bric-
me, li-ber-ty give to me! No, no, thou man ungrateful, no, no, thou man un-
p
f
Z.
co-ne, son u-na ti-gre i-ra-ta, un a-spi-de un le-o-ne, no, no, pie-tà non
grateful, All good is lost up-on thee, Thou more than vi-per hateful, No, no, no, no, I
p
Z.
v'è, pie-tà non v'è, no, no, pie-tà non v'è,
will not set thee free, I will not set thee free,
cresc.
f
p

Z.
nò, nò, pie-tà non v'è!
I will not set thee free!
Sei mor - to se ti
Nay, stir not, or thou
Leporello.
L.
Ah, di fug-gir si pro-vi, ah, di fug-gir si pro-vi!
If thou all help de - ni-est, if thou all help de - ni-est!
p
cresc.
mo-vi, sei mor-to se ti mo-vi, se ti movi, se ti movi!
di-est, nay, stir not, or thou di-est, or thou diest, or thou di-est!
tr
Bar -
Mur -
cresc.
Bar - - ba - ro tra - di - to - re,
Well earn'd is thy dis - as - ter!
- ba-ri, ingiu - sti Dei! bar - ba-ri, ingiu - sti
- der, de-ceit and treason! mur-der, de-ceit and
bar-ba - ro tra - di - to - re, del tuo padrone il co-re a - ves-si qui con
well earn'd is thy dis - as-ter, Thou and thy cru-el master, Well pun-ish'd both shall
(She ties him to the chair)
De-i! in ma-no di co-ste-i, chi
treason! She will not list to rea-son, No

Z.
te, del tuo padrone il co - re a-ves-si qui con te!
be, Thou and thy cru-el mas - ter, well punish'd both shall be.
L.
ca-pi - tar mi fe', chi ca - pi-tar mi fe'? Deh
way t'es-cape I see, no way t'es-cape I see! Oh
Z.
Sen
What
L.
non mi stringer tan - to! l'a-ni-ma mia sen va!
bind me not so tight - ly, Or I shall sure - ly faint!
Z.
va-da, sen va - da, o re - sti, in - tan - to non par-ti-rai di
mat-ter? it serves thee but right - ly, May-be thou wilt now learn some re -
L.
Z.
quà!
straint.
L.
Che stret - te, oh Dei, che bot - te! è
Kind for - tune, do thou re - store me, Is't
Ob.

Z.
L.
Di gioja e di di-let-to sen-to brillar mi il
What joy to see him pin-ing, Snar'd, too, by my de-
gior-no, ovver è not-te? Che
light or dark be-fore me? I'm
Vln.
Fag.
p
tr
pet-to! di gioja e di di-let-to sen-to brillar mi il pet-to! co-sì, co-sì cogl'
signing! what joy to see him pin-ing, snar'd, too, by my de-signing! Your arts we know, de-
scos-se di tre-muoto, che
help-less quite, and blinded, My
uo-mi-ni, co-sì, co-sì si fa, co-sì, co-sì cogl' uo-mini, co-sì, co-sì si
ceit-ful men, we'll teach you to re-pent, your arts we know, de-ceit-ful men, we'll teach you to re-
bu-ja o-scu-ri-tà, che bu-ja o-scu-ri-
cour-age all is spent, my cour-age all is
fa!
pent!
Sei mor-to, mor-to, mor-to,
Nay, stir not, stir not or thou
tà. Ah! di fug-gir si pro-vi, ah! di fug-gir si provi!
spent, Thou ne'er all help de-ni-est, thou ne'er all help de-ni-est.
cresc.

Z.
L.
mor-to, se ti mo-vi, se ti mo-vi!
di-est, or thou di-est, or thou di-est!
Deh, non mi_strin-ger_tan-to,
Oh, bind me_not_so_tight-ly,
tr
f
sf
p
Wind.
Sen va-da, sen va-da, o re-sti, in-
What mat-ter? it serves thee but right-ly, May
l'a-ni-ma mia sen va!
Or I shall sure-ly faint!
tan-to non par-ti-rai di quà, non par-ti-rai, non par-ti-rai, non par-ti-rai di
be thou wilt now learn some re-straint, May be thou'lt now learn some re-straint, Now learn thou some re-
cresc.
quà!
straint!
Che stret-te, oh Dei! che bot-te! è
Kind for-tune, do thou re-store me! Is't
Ob.

Z.
Di gio-ja e di di-let-to sen-to bril-lar mi il
What joy to see him pin-ing, Snar'd, too, by my de-
L.
gior-no,ov-ver è not-te? Che
light or dark be-fore me? I'm
tr
Fag.
f
p
pet-to, di gio-ja e di di-let-to sen-to bril-lar mi il pet-to! co-sì, co-sì, cogl'
signing, What joy to see him pin-ing, Snar'd, too, by my de-signing, Your arts we know, de-
scos-se di tre-muo-to, che
help-less quite and blinded, My
uo-mi-ni, co-sì, co-sì si fa, co-sì, co-sì, cogl' uo-mi-ni, co-sì, co-sì si
ceit-ful men, We'll teach you to re-pent, Your arts we know, de-ceit-ful men, we'll teach you to re-
bu-ja o-scu-ri-tà, che bu-ja o-scu-ri-
cour-age all is spent, my cour-age all is
fa, co-sì, co-sì, co-sì si fa, co-sì, co-sì, co-sì si
pent, yes, yes, we'll teach you to re-pent, Yes, yes, we'll teach you to re-
tà! Oh Dei, che strette! oh Dei, che bot-te!
spent! Oh is it light or dark be-fore me?
tr

Z.
fa, co - sì, co - sì, co - sì, co - sì, co - sì, co - sì si
pent, We know, we know, we know, we know, we know your arts, we
L.
è not-te o gior - no, e gior no o not - te? che
Oh say is't light or dark be - fore me? I'm
Z.
fa, co - sì, co - sì, co - sì, co - sì, co - sì si fa, co - sì, co - sì, co - sì, co -
know, we know, we know, we know, we know your arts, we know, we know, we know, we know, we
L.
scos - - - - - - se di
help - - - - - - less quite,
Z.
sì, co - sì si fa, co - sì, co - sì, co - sì, co - sì si
know, we know your arts, de - ceit - ful men, We'll teach you to re -
L.
tre - muo - to, che bu - ja o - scu - ri -
and blind - ded, my cour - age all is
Z.
fa, co - sì, co - sì, co - sì, co - sì si fa, co - sì, co - sì,
pent, de - ceit - ful men, we'll teach you to re - pent, we'll teach, we'll teach
L.
tà, che bu - ja o - scu - ri - tà, che bu - ja,
spent, my cour - age all is spent, Ah me, my
cresc.

Z.
co-sì si fa!
you to re - pent! (exit)
L.
bu - ja o-scu - ri - tà!
cou - rage all is spent!
tr
f
Recit.
Leporello. (to the Peasant)
L.
A-mi-co, per pie-tà un po-co d'a-qua fres-ca, o ch'io mi
Come hith-er, my good friend, oh let me have some wa-ter, I'm near-ly
L.
mo-ro! guar-da un po' co-me stret-to mi le-gò l'as-sas-
per-ish'd! just look here, how I'm strangled, I can-not stir a
(Exit Peasant.)
(struggling)
L.
si-na! Se po-tes-si li-be-rar-mi coi den-ti? Oh ven-ga il
fin-ger! Oh the vix-en! On-ly try to un-loose me, these gor-dian
L.
dia-vo-lo a di-sfar que-sti gruppi! io vo' ve-de-re di rom-pe-re la
knots un-tie, with your teeth you might do it. The cord's so twisted, where is the end? I
L.
cor-da co-me è for-te! pau-ra del-la mor-te!
can not move it, as-sist me, or else I shall die here!
(He pulls hard and the window
L.
E tu, Mercu-rio, pro-tet-tor de' la-dri, pro-teg-gi un ga-lant'uom! co-raggio
Mer-cu-ry aid me! If to thieves thou'rt gracious, as-sist an honest man, Now for it,

falls to which the end of the cord was fastened.)

L.
bra-vo! pria che co-stei ri - tor - ni, Bi - so - gna dar di spro - ne al - la cal -
Well done! Now ere the jade re - turns here, I must be at some dis - tance, Fortune at -

(Escapes, dragging after him the chair and window.)

L.
ca - gna, E stra - sci - nar, se oc - cor - re, u - na mon - ta - gna!
tend me, to ev - 'ry star that's luc - ky I now com - mend me!

Zerlina. (entering with Donna Elvira, Masetto and Peasants).

Z.
An - diam, an - diam, Si - gno - ra! ve - dre - te in qual ma -
This way, 'twas here, Se - no - ra, I'll shew you how I've se -

Donna Elvira.

Z. E.
nie - ra ho con - cio il scel - le - ra - to. Ah, so - pra lu - i si sfoghi il mio fu -
cured him. He can - not move a fin - ger. Ah, let me see him, my an - ger he shall

Zerlina. Donna Elvira.

E. Z.
ror! Stel - le! in qual mo - do si sal - vò quel bric - co - ne? L'avrà sot - trat - to
feel. Oh heav'n! what can this be? he's es - cap'd! who has help'd him? That I will tell you;

Zerlina.

E. Z.
l'em - pio suo pa - dro - ne. Fu des - so sen - za fal - lo: an - che di
'twas his wick - ed mas - ter. It could have been no oth - er, and Don Oc -

(Masetto and Peasants hasten out)

Z.
que - sto in - for - miam Don Ot - ta - vio: a lui si a - spet - ta Far per noi
ta - vio must know of this oc - currence. My mind mis - gives me! Ven - geance ap -

(Exit)

Z.
tut - ti o do - man - dar ven - det - ta!
proaches, that bless - ed hope re - vives me!

Nº 21c "In quali eccessi, o Numi."

Recitative and Aria.

Allegro assai.
E.
Strings throughout Recit.
Donna Elvira. (alone).
In qua-li ecces-si, o Numi, in quai mi-sfat-ti or-ri-bi-li, tre-men-di è av-
In what a-byss-es of er-ror, in-to what dangers, thy reckless path pur-su-ing, have
vol-to il scia-gu-ra-to!
guilt and fol-ly brought thee!
(collecting herself)
Ah no! non
The wrath of
puo-te tar-dar l'i-ra del cie-lo, la giu-sti-zia tar-dar.
heaven will surely over-whelm thee, it is swift to de-stroy.
(with energy)
Sen-tir già par-mi la fa-ta-le sa-et-ta,
The lightning flash of re-tri-bu-tion im-pendeth,
che gli piomba sul ca-po!
it will soon be up-on thee!

E.
A-per-to veg-gio il ba-ra-tro mortal!
E-ter-nal ru-in at last will be thy doom.
tr tr
p
Mi-se-ra Elvi-ra! che con-tra-sto d'af-fet-ti,
Wretched El-vi-ra! What a tem-pest within thee
in sen ti nasce!
thy heart di videth!
Per-chè que-sti so-spi-ri?
Ah wherefore is this longing?
e quest' am-ba-scie?
These pangs of sor-row?
Aria.
Mi tra-dì quell' al-ma in-
Cru-el heart, thou hast be-
gra-ta, quell' al-ma in-gra-ta, in-fe-li-ce, o
tray'd me, thou hast be-tray'd me, Grief un-end-ing up-
Cl.
Fag.
cresc.
p cresc.

E.
Di - o! mi fa, in - fe - li - - ce, o Di - o! mi fa, in - fe -
on me he cast, grief un - end - ing on me he cast, grief, ah
Vlns.
Fag.
Cl.
li - ce, o Di - o! o Dio! mi fa.
grief un-end-ing up-on me he cast.
Fl.
Fag.
Ma tra - di - ta, e ab - ban - do - na - ta,
Pity yet lin-gers, I'll not up-braid thee,
Vlns.
Fl.
pro - vo an - cor per lui pie - tà, pro - vo an - cor per
Ne'er can I for - get the past, ne'er can I for -
Cl.
Fag.
Vlns.
lui pie - tà, pro - - - vo an - cor per lui, per
get the past, ne'er can I, can I for -
Str.
Fag.
Cello

E.
lui, per lui pie - tà. Mi tra - di quell' al - ma in - gra - ta, quell'
get the hap - py past. Cru - el heart, thou hast be - tray'd me, thou
Cl.
Fag.
al - ma in - gra - ta, in - fe - li - ce, o Di - o! mi fa, in - fe - li - ce, o
hast be - tray'd me, Grief un - end - ing up - on me he cast, Grief un - end - ing
cresc.
p cresc.
mfp
sfp
Di - o! mi fa, in - fe - li - ce, o Di - o! o Dio! mi fa!
on me he cast, Grief, ah, grief un - ending on me he cast!
Cor.
Quan - do sento il mio tor - mento, il mio tor - mento, di ven - det - ta il
When my wrongs a - rise be - fore me, a - rise be - fore me, Thoughts of ven - geance
Vln.
Fl.
Cello
cor fa - vel - la, ma se guar - do il suo ci - men - to,
stir my bo - som, But the love that at first he bore me
Str.

E.
pal - pi - tan - do il cor mi va, pal - pi - tan -
Binds my heart to him at last, Binds my heart
Fl.
Fag.
E.
- do il cor, il cor mi va, il
to him, to him at last, binds
Fag. & Cello.
E.
cor mi va. Mi tra - dì quell'al - ma ingra - ta, quell' al - ma in -
it to him! Cru - el heart, thou hast be - tray'd me, thou hast be -
Fl.
Fl.
Cl.
E.
gra - ta, in - fe - li - ce, o Di - o! mi fa, in - fe - li - ce, o Di - o! mi
tray'd me, Grief un - end - ing up - on me he cast, Grief un - end - ing on me he
cresc.
p cresc.
mfp
sfp
E.
fa, in - fe - li - ce, o Di - o, o Dio! mi fa!
cast, Grief, ah grief un - ending up - on me he cast.
mfp
sfp
Vlns
Cello & Wood.
sf
sf
sf
sf
sf

E.
Ma tra-di-ta, e ab-ban-do-na-ta, pro-vo an-
Pi-ty yet lin-gers, I'll not up-braid thee, Ne'er can
p
sf
cor per lui pie-ta, per lu-i
I for-get the past, ah, nev-er
Fl.
Cl.
Fag.
Cello
Str.
pie-tà, pro-vo an-cor per lui pie-tà,
for-get, ne'er can I for-get the past,
pro-vo an-cor per lui pie-tà, per lui pie-tà, per
ne'er can I for-get the past, ah, ne'er can I for-
cresc.
lui pie-tà!
get the past. (Exit.)
f

Scene.— An enclosed churchyard, several equestrian statues; statue of the Commandant; with inscription in golden lettering.
Recit.
Don Giovanni. (leaps over the wall, laughing; is still wearing Leporello's hat and cloak.)
Ah, ah, ah, ah, questa è buona, or la-scia-la cer-car; che bel-la not-te! è più chia-ra del gior-no, sembra fat-ta per gir a zon-zo a cac-cia di ra-gaz-ze.
Ha, ha, ha, ha! most a-musing, They will not seek me here. What splendid moonlight! 'tis as light as in day-time; this is just such a night as suits for the chase of pret-ty damsels.
(looking at his watch.)
È tar-di? Oh, ancor non so-no due del-la not-te; a-vrei voglia un po' di sa-per come è fi-ni-to l'af-far tra Le-porello e Donn' El-vi-ra: s'egli ha a-vu-to giu-di-zio!
What time is't? ah, not yet two o'clock in the morning; I wish now I-knew how the droll encounter ended between that poor Elvira and Le-po-rello. Let me hope he was prudent!
Leporello. (behind the wall.)
Al-fin vuo-le ch'io fac-cia un pre-ci-pi-zio.
'Faith' I think he's de-ter-min'd on my ru-in.
Don Giovanni.
È des-so; oh Le-po-rel-lo!
I hear him. Well, Le-po-rel-lo?
Leporello. (from the wall)
Chi mi chia-ma?
Some one call'd me?
Don Giovanni.
Non co-no-sci il pa-dron?
Don't you yet know my voice?
Leporello.
Co-sì nol co-nosces-si!
I don't know it at all, sir.
Don Giov.
Co-me, bir-bo?
Don't you? scoundrel.
Leporello.
Ah, sie-te voi? scu-sa-te!
Oh, is it you? ex-cuse me.
Don Giovanni.
Co-sa è sta-to?
What has hap-pen'd?
Leporello.
Per ca-gion
On your ac-

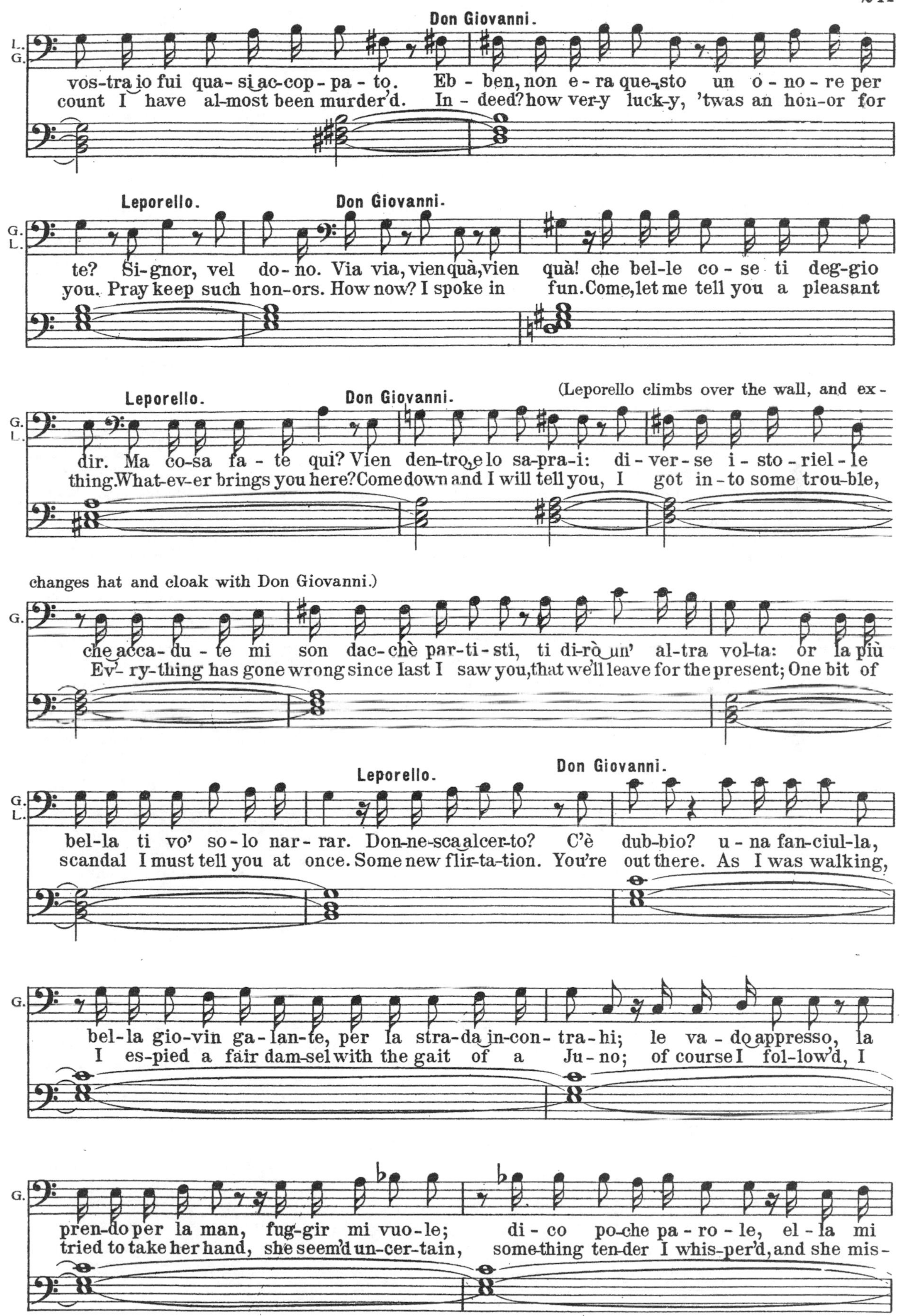
Don Giovanni.
L.
G.
vos-tra io fui qua-si ac-cop-pa-to. Eb-ben, non e-ra que-sto un o-no-re per
count I have al-most been murder'd. In-deed? how ver-y luck-y, 'twas an hon-or for
Leporello.
Don Giovanni.
G.
L.
te? Si-gnor, vel do-no. Via via, vien quà, vien quà! che bel-le co-se ti deg-gio
you. Pray keep such hon-ors. How now? I spoke in fun. Come, let me tell you a pleasant
Leporello.
Don Giovanni.
(Leporello climbs over the wall, and ex-
G.
L.
dir. Ma co-sa fa-te qui? Vien den-tro, e lo sa-pra-i: di-ver-se i-sto-riel-le
thing. What-ev-er brings you here? Come down and I will tell you, I got in-to some trou-ble,
changes hat and cloak with Don Giovanni.)
G.
che acca-du-te mi son dac-chè par-ti-sti, ti di-rò un' al-tra vol-ta: or la più
Ev'-ry-thing has gone wrong since last I saw you, that we'll leave for the present; One bit of
Leporello.
Don Giovanni.
G.
L.
bel-la ti vo' so-lo nar-rar. Don-ne-sca alcer-to? C'è dub-bio? u-na fan-ciul-la,
scandal I must tell you at once. Some new flir-ta-tion. You're out there. As I was walking,
G.
bel-la gio-vin ga-lan-te, per la stra-da in-con-tra-hi; le va-do appresso, la
I es-pied a fair dam-sel with the gait of a Ju-no; of course I fol-low'd, I
G.
pren-do per la man, fug-gir mi vuo-le; di-co po-che pa-ro-le, el-la mi
tried to take her hand, she seem'd un-cer-tain, some-thing ten-der I whis-per'd, and she mis-

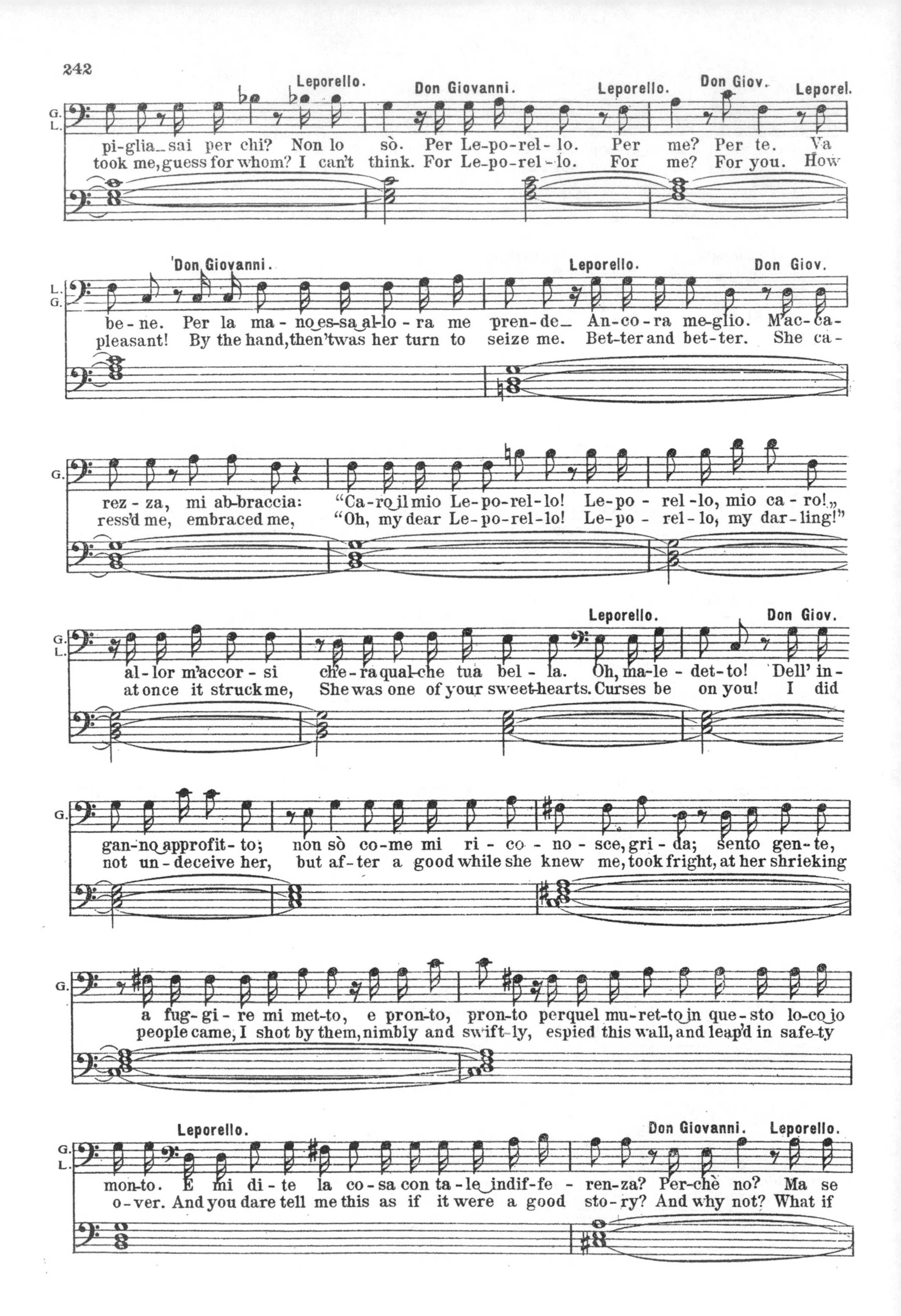
Leporello. Don Giovanni. Leporello. Don Giov. Leporel.
G. L.
pi-glia_sai per chi? Non lo sò. Per Le-po-rel-lo. Per me? Per te. Va
took me, guess for whom? I can't think. For Le-po-rel-lo. For me? For you. How
Don Giovanni. Leporello. Don Giov.
L. G.
be-ne. Per la ma-no es-sa al-lo-ra me pren-de_ An-co-ra me-glio. M'ac-ca-
pleasant! By the hand, then 'twas her turn to seize me. Bet-ter and bet-ter. She ca-
G.
rez-za, mi ab-braccia: "Ca-ro il mio Le-po-rel-lo! Le-po-rel-lo, mio ca-ro!„
ress'd me, embraced me, "Oh, my dear Le-po-rel-lo! Le-po-rel-lo, my dar-ling!"
Leporello. Don Giov.
G. L.
al-lor m'accor-si ch'e-ra qual-che tua bel-la. Oh, ma-le-det-to! Dell' in-
at once it struck me, She was one of your sweet-hearts. Curses be on you! I did
G.
gan-no approfit-to; non sò co-me mi ri-co-no-sce, gri-da; sento gen-te,
not un-deceive her, but af-ter a good while she knew me, took fright, at her shrieking
G.
a fug-gi-re mi met-to, e pron-to, pron-to per quel mu-ret-to in que-sto lo-co io
people came, I shot by them, nimbly and swift-ly, espied this wall, and leap'd in safe-ty
Leporello. Don Giovanni. Leporello.
G. L.
mon-to. E mi di-te la co-sa con ta-le indif-fe-ren-za? Per-chè no? Ma se
o-ver. And you dare tell me this as if it were a good sto-ry? And why not? What if

(The moon breaks through the clouds, and floods the statue of the Commandant with ghostly light.)
Don Giovanni (laughs loudly)
L.
G.
fos - se co - stei sta - ta mia mo - glie? Me - glio an - co - ra!
she were my wife, then would you laugh, sir? All the loud - er.
Adagio.
The Statue.
C.
Di ri - der fi - ni - rai pria dell au - ro - - ra!
Your jest will turn to woe ere it is morn - ing!
Ob. Cl. Fag. 3 Trombones & Bassi
Don Giovanni.
Leporello.
G.
L.
Chi ha par - la - to? Ah, qual-che a - ni - ma sa - rà dell' al - tro mon - do,
Who was speak - ing? Oh, some soul tor - ment - ed, from the land of spir - its,
Don Giovanni. (puts his hand to his sword, looks about among the tombs and strikes at some of the statues.)
L.
G.
che vi co - no - sce a fon - do. Ta - ci, sciocco! chi va là? chi va là?
pays homage to your mer - its. Si - lence, ras - cal. Who goes there? Who goes there?
Adagio.
The Statue.
C.
Ri - bal - do au - da - ce! La - scia a' mor - ti la pa -
Mis - guid - ed, per - vert - ed, An - ger not the de - part -
Leporello.
Don Giovanni.
C.
L.
G.
ce! Ve l'ho det - to! Sa - rà qual - cun di fuo - ri che si bur - la di no - i!
ed! As I told you! It must be some one hid - ing by yon wall, laugh - ing at us.
(With indifference and disdain)
G.
Ehi, del Commenda - to - re non è que - sta la sta - tua? leg - gi un po - co quel - la iscri -
Say can that hideous structure be the Comman - dant's sta - tue? That inscription I'd like to

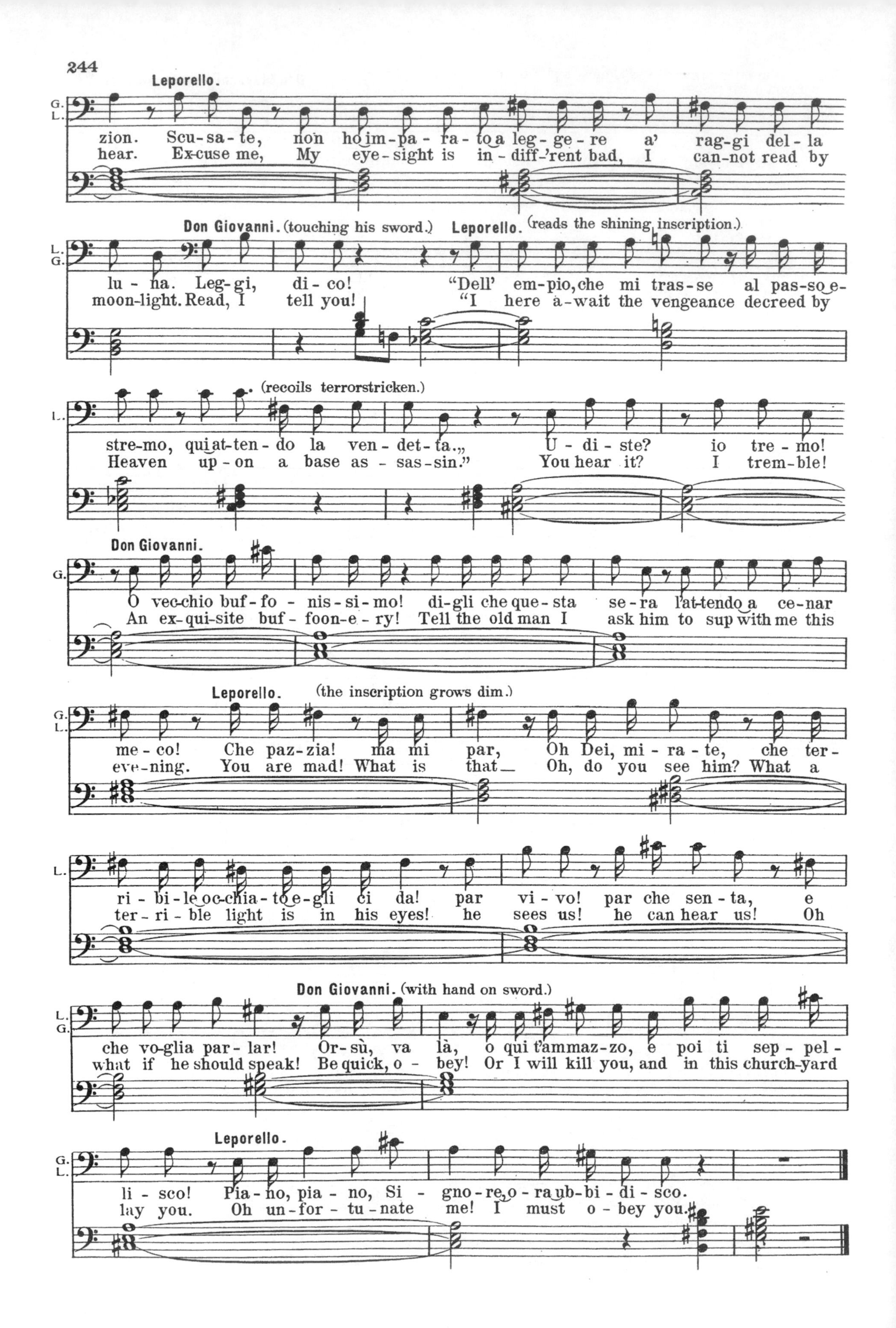
Leporello.
G.
L.
zion. Scu-sa-te, non ho im-pa-ra-to a leg-ge-re a' rag-gi del-la
hear. Excuse me, My eye-sight is in-diff-'rent bad, I can-not read by
Don Giovanni. (touching his sword.) Leporello. (reads the shining inscription.)
L.
G.
lu-na. Leg-gi, di-co! "Dell' em-pio, che mi tras-se al pas-so e-
moon-light. Read, I tell you! "I here a-wait the vengeance decreed by
(recoils terrorstricken.)
L.
stre-mo, qui at-ten-do la ven-det-ta." U-di-ste? io tre-mo!
Heaven up-on a base as-sas-sin." You hear it? I trem-ble!
Don Giovanni.
G.
O vecchio buf-fo-nis-si-mo! di-gli che que-sta se-ra l'at-tendo a ce-nar
An ex-qui-site buf-foon-e-ry! Tell the old man I ask him to sup with me this
Leporello. (the inscription grows dim.)
G.
L.
me-co! Che paz-zia! ma mi par, Oh Dei, mi-ra-te, che ter-
eve-ning. You are mad! What is that_ Oh, do you see him? What a
L.
ri-bi-le oc-chia-to e-gli ci da! par vi-vo! par che sen-ta, e
ter-ri-ble light is in his eyes! he sees us! he can hear us! Oh
Don Giovanni. (with hand on sword.)
L.
G.
che vo-glia par-lar! Or-sù, va là, o qui t'ammaz-zo, e poi ti sep-pel-
what if he should speak! Be quick, o-bey! Or I will kill you, and in this church-yard
Leporello.
G.
L.
li-sco! Pia-no, pia-no, Si-gno-re, o-ra ub-bi-di-sco.
lay you. Oh un-for-tu-nate me! I must o-bey you.

Nº 22. "O statua gentilissima."

Duet.

Allegro.
Leporello. (to the Commandant.)
Tutti.
O sta-tua gen-ti-lis-sima del gran Commenda-
Oh thou most no-ble monument, Our Commandant re-
(to Don G.)
to-re_ Padron! mi trema il co-re, non pos-so, non posso terminar!
sembling, Oh, sir, see how I'm trembling, I can-not, I can no further go.
Don Giov.
Wind.
Fi-
Pro-
Cor.
ni-scila, o nel pet-to ti met-to questo acciar, ti met-to questo ac-
ceed at once, or I'll spear thee, I'll kill thee at a blow, I'll kill thee at a
cresc.
Leporello. (aside.)
Don Giovanni. (aside.)
Leporello.
ciar! Che im-piccio, che ca-priccio! Che gusto! che spas-set-to! Io sento mi ge-
blow! He's madder now than ev-er! His cowardice di-verts me. If I could on-ly
Don Giovanni.
Lo voglio far tremar, lo voglio far tremar!
How can one tremble so? how can one tremble so?
(to the statue)
lar, io sen-to mi ge-lar! O sta-tua gen-ti-
go, If I could on-ly go! Oh thou most no-ble

(starting back)
L.
lis - sima_ benchè di mar - mo siate_ Ah Padron! Padron mi - o! mira - te! mi -
mon - ument, I speak with fear and wonder, Master, look! Oh look yonder, oh master, look
f
tr
p
tr
Don Giovanni. (advancing menacingly)
L.
G.
ra - te! che se-guita a guar-dar, che seguita a guar-dar! Mo - ri,
yonder, See how his eye-balls glow, see how his eye-balls glow! Die then,
cresc.
f
Leporello.
G.
L.
mori! No, no, no, no, atten-dete, at - ten - de - te!
die then. No, no, oh wait a moment, wait a moment!
Str.
p
(going back)
L.
Si - gnor, il padron mi - o_
My mas - ter here in - vites thee,
Wind.
Str.
p

L.
ba - da - te ben, non i - o_
Not I, great sir, it frights me,
Wind.

(The statue nods its head)
L.
vor - ria con voi ce - nar! Ah! ah! ah! — che scena è
To — sup with him this night. Ah, ah, ah, — I'm not in -
L.
questa! ah, ah, ah, — che sce-na è que - sta! o ciel! chi - nò la
venting, Ah. ah, ah, — I'm not in - vent - ing, He nods, he nods con -
Don Giovanni. (not looking at him)
G.
Va là, che sei un buf - fo - ne, va là, che sei un buf - fo - ne, un buf -
Thou fool, what's there to scare thee? thou fool, what's there to scare thee, what is
L.
te - sta!
sent - ing!
cresc.
Leporello.
G.
L.
fo - ne, un buf - fo - ne! Guar-da-te, guar - da-te, guar-da-te an-cor, pa -
there, what's there to scare thee? Oh master, oh master, oh look your-self and
f
p
Don Giovanni.
L.
G.
dro - ne! E che deg-gio guar-dar, deggio guardar, deg-gio guar-dar?
spare me! What is this wondrous sight, what is this wondrous, wondrous sight?
cresc.
f

Leporello.
(imitates the statue)
(the statue bends its head)
L.
Col - la mar-mo - rea testa ei fa co - sì, co - sì.
See, with his head of marble, He nods, just so, just so.
p
mf
p
p
D. Giov.
(sees the statue)
G.
Col - la mar-mo - rea testa ei fa co - sì, co - sì.
See with his head of marble, He nods just so, just so.
L.
Col - la mar-mo - rea testa ei fa co - sì, co - sì.
See with his head of marble, He nods just so, just so.
f
p
Don Giovanni. (to the statue)
G.
Par - la - te! se po - te - te.
Give an - swer, if thou hear'st me,
cresc.
f
Ver - re-te a ce-na? ver - re-te a ce-na?
Wilt come to supper? wilt come to supper?

The Statue. (inclining its head.)
Don Giovanni.
mezza voce
Sì!
Yea!
Bi - zar-ra è in ver la
A strange ad - ven - ture,
Leporello.
Mo - - - ver mi pos - so ap - pe - na, mi
Now we are ru - in'd tru - ly, He
sf
fp
Cor.
sce - na, ver - rà il buon vecchio, il buon vec - chio a
tru - ly, He hath ac - cept - ed, ac - cept - ed
man - ca, o Dei, la le - na! mi man - ca, o Dei, la
takes it all so cool - ly, he takes it all so
ce - na. A pre-pa-rar - la an - dia - mo, a pre-pararla an-
du - ly; Come, let us go, make read - y, Come, come, let us make
lena! Per cari - tà, par - tiamo, per ca - ri - tà, par-tiamo, an - diamo via di
coolly, oh let us go, oh master, my limbs I cannot steady, To run away is
dia - mo, par - tia - mo via di quà! Bi - zar - ra è in ver la
read - y To meet this ston-y guest! A strange ad - ven - ture,
quà! an-diamo, andia-mo via di quà! per ca - ri - tà, par - tiamo, andiamo via di
best, oh come, to run a-way is best! My limbs I cannot steady, To run away is

G.
sce - na, ver - rà il buon vec-chio a ce - na; A
tru - ly, He hath ac - cept - ed du - ly, Come,
L.
quà, per ca - ri - tà, par - tiamo, andiamo via di quà, andiamo via di
best, my limbs I can not steady, to run a-way is best, to run a-way is
pre - parar - la an-diamo, partia - mo via di quà, par -
let us go, make ready, to meet this stony guest, To
quà! andiamo via di quà, andiamo, andiamo via di quà, an-diamo, andiamo via di
best, to run away is best, oh come, to run a-way is best, oh come, to run away is
tia - mo via di quà.
meet this ston - y guest.
(Exeunt.)
quà, via di quà, via di quà, di quà, di quà, di quà!
best, come away, come a - way, to run a - way is best!
pp
Recit.
Scene. – A darkened chamber.
Don Octavio.
O.
Calma-tevi, i-dol mi - o! di quel ri - baldo vedrem puni-ti in bre-ve i gra-vi eccessi,
Yes, all now re - assures us; the hand of justice will soon arrest his course of guilt and fol-ly,
Donna Anna.
Don Octavio.
O.
A.
ven-di-ca - ti sarem. Ma il padre, o Di - o! Con - vien chi-na-re il ci-glio al vo-
and we shall be aveng'd. My father, I've lost him! What is decreed by heaven, we must

le - re del ciel. Re - spi - ra, o ca - ra! di tua per - dita a - ma - ra fia do -
pa - tiently bear. Oh rouse thee, my dearest, from the sad re - col - lection; brighter
ma - ni, se vuoi, dol - ce com - pen - so que - sto cor, questa ma - no, che il mio te - nero a -
days are before thee. Say to - morrow thou wilt bless my af - fection, let thy hand be the
Donna Anna.
Don Octavio.
mor. O Dei! che di - te in si tri - sti mo - men - ti. E che? vor -
pledge. Ah no, how can'st thou speak of joy when I'm weeping? Ah then, since
re - sti con in - du - gi no - vel - li ac - cre - scer le mie pe - ne? cru -
faith - ful love or pray'rs can - not move thee, too well I see that thou dost not

Nº 23. "Crudele?"

Recitative and Aria.

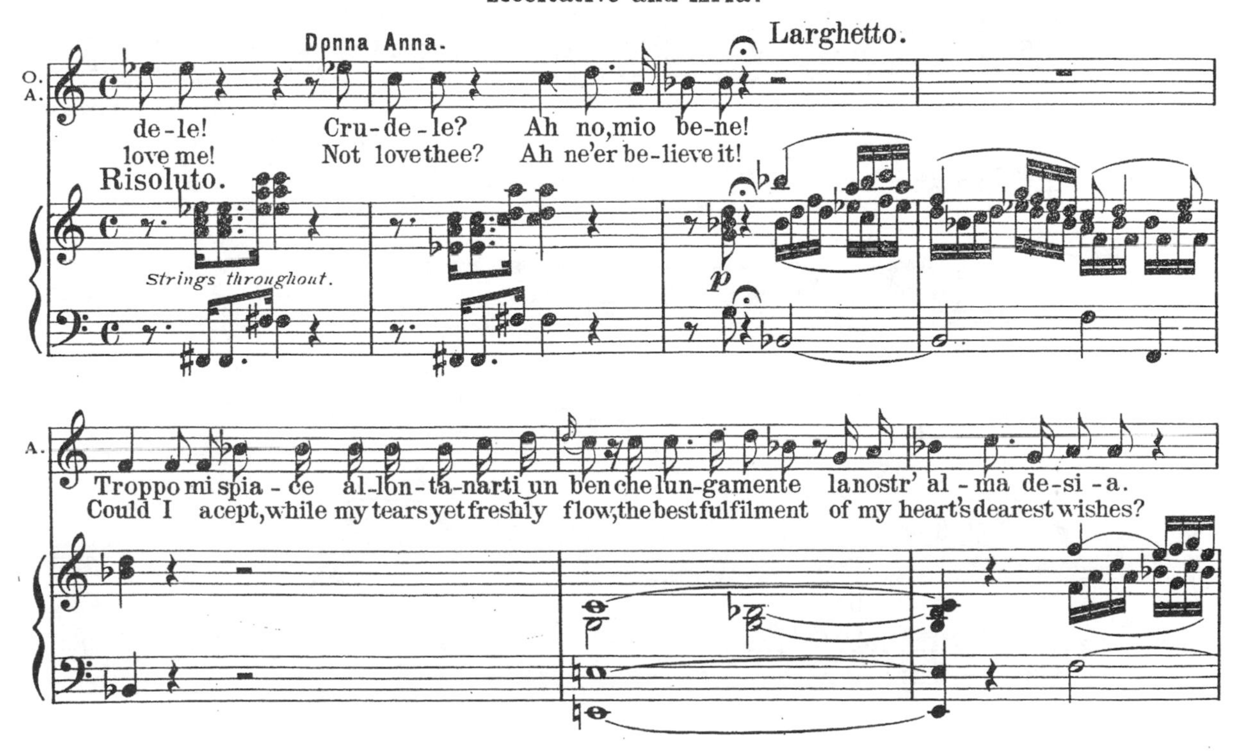
Donna Anna.
Larghetto.
de - le! Cru - de - le? Ah no, mio be - ne!
love me! Not love thee? Ah ne'er be - lieve it!
Risoluto.
Strings throughout.
Troppo mi spia - ce al - lon - ta - narti un ben che lun - gamente la nostr' al - ma de - si - a.
Could I acept, while my tears yet freshly flow, the best fulfilment of my heart's dearest wishes?

A.
Mai il mondo, oh Di - o! non se -
I cannot, I dare not, Ah, nor
f
p
dur la co-stan-za del sen-si - bil mio core; ab-ba-stan-za per te mi parla a -
seek to persuade me, till my grief is assuaged. All my heart is thine own, of that be
sf
p
Larghetto.
mo-re! Non mi
certain. Tell me
Cl.
Fag.
Vln.
sotto voce
Fl.
p
dir, bell' i - dol mi - o, che son i - o cru-del con
not, Oh thou be - lov'd one, That thou'rt constant to me in
mf
mfp
te, tu ben sa - i quant' io t'a -
vain, That I love thee, ah well thou
Str.
Fag.
Cor.
p

A.
ma - i, tu co-no-sci la mia fè, tu co -
know'st it, That I'll ev-er thine re-main, That I'll
Fag.
Cl.
Fl.
no - sci la mia fè.
ev - er thine re-main.
Cal - ma,
Stay, oh
Cl.
Fag.
Fl. Fag.
calma il tuo tor-mento,
stay thy fond mis-giving,
Se di duol non vuoi ch'io
Doubt me not, oh I con-
mo - ra, se - di duol non vuoi ch'io mo-ra, non vuoi ch'io mo-ra.
jure thee, doubt me not, oh I conjure thee, oh I con-jure thee!
Fag.
Violin
cresc.
f
Non mi dir, bell' i - dol mi - o, che son
Tell me not, oh thou be - lov'd one, That thou'rt
p

A.
i - o cru - del con te; cal - ma, cal - ma il tuo tor -
constant to me in vain; Stay, oh stay then thy fond mis-
mf
sf
p
Cor. sustain
men - to, se di duol non vuoi ch'io
giv - ing, Doubt me not, oh I con -
mo - ra, non vuoi ch'io mo - ra!
jure thee, oh I con - jure thee!
Allegretto moderato.
f
p
mfp
Vlns.
p
tr
Wind.
For - se, forse un giorno il cie - lo an -
Love and hope do both, do both as -
tr

A.
co - ra sen - ti - rà, sen-ti - rà pie - tà di me! forse un
sure me, That kind heav'n yet will smile, will smile a - gain, Love and
A.
giorno il cielo an-co-ra sen-ti - rà
hope do both assure me, That kind Heav'n
p
A.
A.
pie - tà di me, sen - ti - rà pie -
will smile a - gain, smile a-gain, that
A.
tà, pie - tà di me, sen - ti -
heav'n will smile a - gain, that kind
cresc.
sfp
p

rà pie-tà di me, for-se, for-se il cie-lo un
heav'n will smile a-gain, Love and hope as-sure me, as-
Vln.
Wind
sf
p
gior-no sen-ti-rà pie-tà di
sure me, That kind heav'n will smile a-
fp
tr
me, sen-ti-rà pie-tà di me, pie-tà di
gain, that kind heav'n will smile a-gain, will smile a-
fp
p
cresc.
me.
gain. (Exit.)
f
Recit.
Don Octavio. (alone)
Ah, si se-gua il suo pas-so: Io vo' con le-i di-vi-de-re i mar-
Ah, her foot-steps I fol-low. To me 'tis dear to par-take her ev-'ry
ti-ri: Sa-ran me-co men gra-vi i suoi so-spi-ri.
sor-row; Give me pa-tience, oh love, to wait some blest mor-row. (Exit.)
A.
O.

Nº 24. "Già la mensa e preparata.„
Finale.

A lighted hall. The table prepared for a banquet.

Allegro vivace.
Don Giovanni.
G.
Già la mensa è prepa - ra-ta.
Ah, I see the ta-ble's ready.
(to the musicians of his private band.)
Voi suo - na-te, ami-ci cari!
Play a gay and festive measure!
Giacchè
Cost - ly
spen-do i miei da - na - ri, io mi vo - glio di - ver - tir.
is my cup of pleasure; And I'll drain it to the end.
cresc.

(to Leporello)
Leporello.
Leporel-lo, presto in ta-vola! Son prontis - simo a ser - vir, son pron-
Lepo-rel-lo, serve the sup-per. All is read - y to com mand, all is
Don Giovanni. (to Lep.)
tis - simo a ser-vir. Giac - chè spen-do i miei da - na-ri, io mi
read - y to command. Cost - ly is my cup of pleasure, And I'll
cresc.
vo - glio di - ver - tir. Voi suo-na - te, a-mi - ci ca-ri! Giacchè
drain it to the end. Play a gay and fes - tive measure, Costly
(to the musicians)
cresc.
spen-do i miei da - na-ri, io mi vo-glio di - ver-tir, io mi voglio di-ver-
is my cup of pleasure, And I'll drain it to the end, Yes, I'll drain it to the
cresc.
Allegretto.
Leporello.
tir. (The private band begins the first piece,
end. melody from Martin's Una cosa rara.)
Bravi! "Cosa rara!,,
Bravi! "Cosa rara!"
(Music on stage: 2 Ob., Clar., Bassoons, Horns.)
Ob.

259

Don Giov.
G.
Che ti
Is this
f
(eating; to Lep.)
G.
L.
Leporello.
par del bel con-cer - to? È ___ con-for - me, è con - for-me al vo - stro
mu - sic to thy lik - ing? I ___ must own I have heard some things more
Don Giovanni.
L.
G.
merto. Ah che piatto sa-po - ri-to! ah che piatto sa-po - ri-to! ah che piatto sa-po-
striking. Here's a dish to be commended, here's a dish to be commended, here's a dish to be com-
p
Leporello. (aside)
G.
L.
ri - to! Ah che bar-baro appe - ti - to!
mended! Would this meal were safely end - ed!
p
L.
Che boc-co - ni da gi-gan-te! mi par proprio di sve-nir, mi par proprio di sve-
While I watch his giant mouth-fuls, I his courage compre-hend, I his courage compre-

Don Giovanni. (aside)
G.
nir. Nel ve-der i miei boc-co-ni, gli par proprio di sve-nir, gli par proprio di sve-
hend. While he watches ev-'ry mouthful, Who on me is to at-tend, who on me is to at-
pp
sf
p
sf
p
G.
L.
Leporello
Don Giov.
nir. ___ Ah che bar-baro appe-ti-to! che boc-co-ni da gi-gante! Nel ve-
tend? ___ While I watch his giant mouthfuls, I his courage compre-hend. While he
cresc.
f
p
p
sf
p
sf
p
sf
G.
L.
Leporello.
der i miei boc-co-ni, gli par proprio di svenir, di sve-nir! Ah che bar-baro appe-
watches ev-'ry mouthful, Who on me, who on me is to at-tend? Would this meal were safely
p
f
L.
G.
Don Giovanni.
Leporello.
Don Giovanni.
ti-to! Gli par proprio di sve-nir. Che boc-co-ni da gi-gan-te! Gli par proprio di sve-
end-ed. Who on me is to at-tend? While I watch his giant mouthfuls. Who on me is to at-
p
f
p
G.
nir, gli par proprio di sve-nir, gli par proprio di sve-nir.
tend? who on me is to at-tend? who on me is to at-tend?
L.
Leporello. mi par proprio di sve-nir, mi par proprio di sve-nir.
I his courage compre-hend, I his courage compre-hend.
(The private band finishes the first piece.)
p Strings in Orch.

Don Giovanni.
Leporello.
(The private band begins the 2d. piece from Paisiello's
Fra i due litiganti il terzo gode.)
G.
L.
Piat-to!
Wine here!
Ser-vo!
Ready!
Allegretto.
f
Leporello.
Don Giovanni.
L.
G.
Ev - vi-va-no i li-ti - ganti. Ver - sa il vi-no!
Long life to "i li-ti-ganti!" Fill my goblet!
G.
Ec - cel - len - te
Choice a - ro - ma,
p
(Leporello changes Giovanni's plate)
Leporello (aside)
G.
L.
mar-zi - mino! Que - sto pez-zo
good-ly vintage! I'll de - vour this
f
p
f
L.
G.
Don Giovanni.
di fa - giano, pia - no, piano,piano,piano, pia-no vo'inghiot - tir. Sta man-
piece of pheasant, Soft - ly softly,softly,softly, while I down-wards bend. None to
p

(aside)
G.
giando quel mar-rano! fin-ge-rò di non ca-pir.
serve me, this is pleasant, Ras-cal, say, wilt thou at-tend?
(Private band finishes the second piece.)
f
p Strings in Orch.
L.
Leporello.
(Private band begins the 3d. piece, from Mozart's Figaro.)
Moderato.
Questo
That's a
Cl.
f
p
L.
poi la co-no-sco pur troppo.
song I have heard but too oft-en.
mf
p
Don Giovanni (without looking at him)
Leporello. (with his mouth full)
G.
L.
Le-po-rel-lo! Pa-dron mi-o!
Le-po-rel-lo! Yes, sir, com-ing!
tr
f
p
Don Giovanni.
Leporello. (clearing his throat.)
Par-la schietto, par-la schietto, mascal-zo-ne. Non mi la-scia una flus-
Well, speak out, man, well speak out, what art thou mumbling? I beseech you, stay from
Cl.

Don Giov.
L.
G.
sio-ne le pa-ro - le pro - fe-rir, le pa-ro-le pro-ferir. Mentre io
grumbling, I've a cold that will not mend, I've a cold that will not mend. I ex-
tr
cresc.
f
p
Leporello.
Don Giov. (looking towards him)
man - gio fischia un po - co. Non sò far. Cos' è?
pect thee to a - muse me. Sir, I can't! Why not?
cresc.
Leporello.
Scusa - te! scu - sa - te! sì ec-cel-len-te è'l vo-stro cuo - co, sì ec-cel -
Excuse me! ex-cuse me! When such vi - ands dainty in - vite me, when such
lente, sì eccellen-te è'l vo-stro cuo-co, che lo volli anch'io pro-var, che lo volli anch'io pro-
viands, when such dainty viands invite me Wonder not, if I par-take, wonder not if I par-
mf p
Don Giovanni.
Sì eccel-lente è il cuo-co mi-o, che lo volle anch' ei pro-
It is clear thou must par - take, it is clear thou must par-
var, sì eccellen - te, che lo volli anch'io pro-
take. Wonder not, then, wonder not if I par-
3/4

Allegro assai.
Donna Elvira. (rushes in distractedly)
E.
L'ul - ti - ma pro - va dell' a - mor mi - o an - cor vogl'
Love bids me ven - ture One more en deav - or, Ere we for
G.
var.
take.
(Exeunt all servants but Leporello.)
L.
var.
take.
(The private band finishes the 3d piece.)
Allegro assai.
f Tutti
p
f
p
f
p
i - o fa - re con te. Più non ram - men - to gl'in - gan - ni
ev - er A - sun - der fly. Though you may scorn me, I'll not re -
f
p
tr
tuo - i, gl'in - gan - ni tuo - i, pie - ta - - de io
sent it, I'll not re - sent it, I come to
cresc.
p
sen - to!
warn thee!
Don Giovanni. (rising and dismissing the players with a sign.)
(kneeling)
Da te non
With love I've
Cos' è? Cos' è?
Pray why? pray why?
Leporello.
Cos' è? Cos' è?
Pray why? pray why?
cresc.
f

(distant thunder of an approaching storm.)
E.
chie - de quest' alma op - pres - sa del - la sua fe - de qual - che mer -
end - ed, Joy long hath left me, Lone and un - friend - ed, I long to
sf
sf
p
Don Giovanni. (trying to raise her.)
E.
G.
cè. Mi ma - ra - vi - glio! co - sa vo - le - te? co - sa vo -
die. You quite sur - prise me! Your wish re - veal then! your wish re -
f
p
p
f
p
G.
(kneels)
le - te? Se non sor - ge - te non re - sto in piè, non re - sto in
veal then! If you must kneel then, Why so must I, Why so must
cresc.
f
Donna Elvira.
G.
E.
piè! Ah non de - ri - de - re gli af - fan - ni mie - i!
I! Cru - el, de - ride me not, For thee I'm su - ing!
Leporello.
L.
Qua - si da
Her wrongs are
p
p
E.
Don Giovanni. (He gets up and raises her)
Ah, non de - ri - de - re!
Cru - el, de - ride me not,
G.
Io ti de - ri - de - re!
Come, sweet one, chide me not!
L.
pian - ge - re mi fa co - ste - i, qua -
all for - got, For him she's su - ing, Her
tr
tr

E.
G.
L.
(With affected tenderness)
Ah non de - ri - de-re!
Cru-el, de - ride me not!
Io te de - ri - de-re?
Nay sweet one, chide me not!
Cie-lo! per - chè?
Why wilt thou cry?
si da pian - ge - re mi fa co - ste-i.
wrongs are all for - got, For him she's su - ing!
tr
cresc.
Don Giovanni.
Che vi - - ta can-gi!
Thy life - a - mend thou!
Che vuoi, mio be - ne?
For what dost ask me?
p
Bra - va!
Not bad!
Cor per - fi - do!
Mis - guid - ed one!
fp
Cor per - fi - do!
mis - guid - ed one!
cor per - - - -
mis - guid - - -
Leporello.
Bra - va!
Not bad!
Cor per - - - -
mis - guid - - -
f

E.
fi-do!
ed one!
Don Giovanni. (turning toward the table).
L.
G.
fi-do!
ed one!
La - - scia ch'io man-gi,
This fool - ing end now,
tr
p
G.
(seats himself again at the table, and begins to eat)
la - - scia ch'io man-gi,
this fool - ing end now.
Vlns.
mf
Donna Elvira. (with disdain).
Res - ta - ti, bar-ba-ro!
Wretch, I a - ban-don thee,
Leporello.
G.
L.
e se ti pia - ce, man-gia con me!
When thou hast supp'd well, No more thou'lt sigh!
Se — non si -
If — he re -
f
nel lez-zo im - mon-do e - sem - pio or - ri - bi - le d'i - ni - qui -
More and more hate - ful, Ev - er de - test - ed be, Thee I dis -
muo - ve del suo do - lo - re, di sasso ha il co - re, o cor non
lents not to — see her griev - ing, His heart de - ceiv - ing hard as
cresc.

tà!
own!
Don Giovanni. (recklessly raising his glass).
ha!
stone.
Vi-van le femmi-ne, vi-va il buon vi-no!
Maidens both fair and young, Good wine, and plen-ty,
so-stegno e glo-ri-a d'u-ma-ni-tà, so-stegno e glo-ri-a
To these are prais-es due, To these a-lone, to these are prais-es due,
cresc.
Donna Elvira.
Re-sta-ti, bar-ba-ro! nel
Wretch, I a-bandon thee! more,
d'u-ma-ni-tà!
to these a-lone!
Vi-van le fem-mi-ne,
Maidens both fair and young,
Leporello.
Se non si muo-ve
If he re-lent not
lez-zo im-mon-do, re-sta-ti, bar-ba-ro!
more than hate-ful, Wretch, I a ban-don thee!
vi-va il buon vi-no! vi-van le
good wine and plen-ty, Maid-ens both
del suo do-lo-re, di sas-so
to see her griev-ing, His heart is

E.
nel lez-zo im mon-do! e - - sem-pio or - ri - bi-le
More and more hate-ful, Ev - - er de - test - ed be,
G.
fe - mi - ne vi-va il buon vi - no! so - ste-gno e glo - ri-a
fair and young, good wine, and plen-ty, To these are prais - es due,
L.
ha il co - re, di sas-so ha il co - re o
de - ceit - ful, and hard, his heart is
fp
fp
p
tr
cresc.
E.
d'i-ni- qui - tà!
Thee I dis - own!
G.
d'u-ma-ni - tà,
To these a lone,
so-ste-gno e glo-ri-a d'u-ma-ni-
To these are prais-es due, To these a-
L.
cor non ha
hard as stone.
f
p
E.
e - sem-pio or - ri - bi - le d'i - ni - qui - tà, di - ni - qui-
Ev - er de - test-ed be, Thee I dis - own, thee I dis-
G.
tà, so-steg-no e glo - ri - a d'u - ma - ni - tà, d'u - ma - ni-
lone, to these are prais - es due, to these a - lone, to these a -
L.
Di sasso ha il co - re, o cor non ha! o cor non
His heart's de - ceit - ful, and hard as stone, and hard as
mf
p
f
p

(going out of mid-
tà, dì - ni - qui - tà, e-sem-pio or - ri - bi - le d'i - ni - qui - tà!
own, thee I dis - own, ev - er de - test - ed be, thee I dis - own!
tà, d'u - ma - ni - tà, so - ste - gno e glo - ri - a d'u - ma - ni - tà!
lone, to these a - lone, to these are prais - es due, to these a - lone!
ha, o cor non ha, di sasso ha il co - re, o cor non ha!
stone, and hard as stone, his heart's de - ceit - ful, hard as stone.
tr
p
cresc.
f
fp
dle door, recoils terrified)
D. Elvira. (rushes out at the opposite side)
Don Giovanni.
Ah!
Ah!
Che gri - do è que - sto
A scream, what can have
Leporello.
Che
A
fp
sfp
p
(to Lep.)
ma - i? che gri - do, che gri - do è que - sto ma - i? va a ve-
happen'd? What means it? a scream, what - ev - er means it? Go and
gri - do è que - sto ma - i! che gri - do è que - sto ma - i?
scream, what can have hap - pen'd! A scream, what can have hap - pen'd?
f
p
(Leporello goes, and when off the stage cries out)
der, va a ve - der che cosa è sta - to.
see, go and see what is the matter.
fp
fp
fp
fp

Don Giovanni.
G.
Leporello.
Che gri - do in - dia - vo - la - to! che gri - do in - dia - vo -
What - ev - er means this clatter? what - ev - er means this
L.
Ah!
Ah!
sfp
p
cresc.
la - to! Lepo - rel - lo, che cos' è? che cos' è? che cos'
clatter? Lepo - rel - lo, art thou mad? art thou mad? art thou
f
p
Leporello. Allegro molto
è? Ah! Si - gnor! per ca - ri - tà! non an -
mad? Oh, good Sir! for heav - en's sake Not a
(Leporello returns dismayed and shuts the door.)
da - te fuor di quà! L'uom di sas - so, l'uo - mo
step do that way take. White and ston - y, he's be
bian - co, ah! pa - dro - ne! io ge - lo, io man - co. Se ve -
hind me, Oh, good mas - ter, I'm fainting, don't mind me, If you

Don Giov.
L.
G.
de-ste che fi-gu-ra se sen-ti-ste, co-me fa, ta, ta, ta, ta! Non ca-
saw his mar-ble features, If you heard him near-er draw, ta, ta, ta, ta! I be-
cresc.
pi-sco niente af-fat-to. Tu sei mat-to in ve-ri-tà, in ve-ri-
lieve thou art de-mented. One could scare thee with a straw, yes, one could
Leporello.
Ta, ta, ta, ta!
Ta, ta, ta, ta!
f
p
cresc.
tà, in ve-ri-tà!
scare thee with a straw!
Leporello.
Don Giovanni.
Ah! sen-ti-te! Qualcun bat-te!
Hark! he's coming! Some one's knocking!
(knocking heard at the door.)
tr
sf
p
f
Don Giov.
Leporello. (trembling)
Don Giov.
Leporello.
(kneeling)
Apri! Io tre-mo! A-pri, di-co! Ah!
Open! I dare not! Go this instant! Ah!
Vl.
Don Giov.
Leporello.
Don Giovanni.
Apri! Ah! Matto! Per to-gliermi d'in-tri-co ad a-prir io stesso an-
Open! Ah! Coward! if I would be en-lightened, I must go myself and

(takes a light and goes to open the door)
Leporello. (trembling, aside)
G.
L.
drò, io stes-so an-drò. Non vo' più veder la-mi-co, pian pia-nin m'a-scon-de-
see, I'll go and see. Oh, to death I sure am frightened, Here I'll hide where none can
cresc.
f
Strs.
p
(Don G. opens)
Andante.
(The ghost of the Commandant appears as a marble statue.)
The Commandant.
L.
C.
rò, m'a-scon-de-rò! (Leporello hides under the table)
see, where none can see.
Don Gio-
Don Gio-
(clap of thunder)
Tutti.
f
ff Tutti Tromboni Tympani &c
C.
van-ni a ce-nar te-co m'in-vi-ta-sti! e son ve-nu-to!
van-ni! by thee in-vit-ed, Here be-hold me As thou'st di-rect-ed.
Strs.
p
p Wind
Don Giovanni (striving to collect himself)
G.
Non l'avrei giammai cre-du-to; ma fa-rò quel che po-trò. Leporel-lo! un altra
Tru-ly I did not ex-pect it, But a-new I'll sup with thee. Leporel-lo, serve the
f
p
f
G.
ce-na! fa che su-bi-to si por-ti!
ta-ble, For my guest an-oth-er cov-er!
Leporello (puts his head from under the table)
L.
Ah padron, ah pa-dron! Ah padron! siam tutti
Sir, be still, say no more! With us both now all is
p
f
p
f
p

Don Giovanni.
(He rises as if to obey)
The Commandant.
(Don Giov. starts; Leporello retreats to back.)
L.
G.
C.
mor-ti. Van-ne, di-co! Fer-ma un po'! Non si pa-sce di ci-bo mor-
o-ver. Go, di-rect-ly! No need of that! Earth-ly food he no lon-ger de-
Timp.
fp
Tutti
ta - - - - le, chi si pa-sce di ci-bo ce-le-ste!
sir - - - - eth, who of heav-en-ly food hath par-tak-en!
Al - tre cu - re, più gra - vi di
Cast a - - way from thee now all such
cresc.
p
que - ste, al - tra bra - ma quag-
tri - fling, Heed the sen - tence I
giù mi gui - dò. Par - la
hith - - - - er have brought. Well, what
Don Giovanni.
Leporello.
La ter-za-na d'a-ve-re mi
Sure a fit of the a-gue hath

G.
dun - que! che chie - di? che
would'st thou? I list - en, well,
C.
L.
sem-bra, e le mem-bra fer-mar più non sò, la ter-za-na d'a-ve-re mi
seiz'd me, Of all mo-tion be-reft, I'm dis-traught! Sure a fit of the a-gue hath
vuo - i?
tell me!
The Commandant.
Par - lo; a-scol - ta! più tem-po non
Si - lence, and mark me, this hour thou hast
sem-bra, e le mem-bra fer-mar più non sò.
seiz'd me, Of all mo-tion be-reft, I'm dis-traught!
Wind sustain.
(angrily and defiantly; he is quite cool again).
Par-la, par- la, a-scoltan - do ti sto.
Speak then, tell me, of fear know I naught.
ho.
sought.
Par - lo; a -
Si - lence, an
Ah le membra fermar più non sò; la ter-za-na d'a-ve-re mi
Ah, of mo-tion bereft, I'm distraught, Sure a fit of the a-gue has
cresc.
p

C.
scol - - ta! più tem - - po non
make me, this hour thou hast
L.
sem-bra, la ter-za-na d'a-ve-re mi sem-bra, e le membra fer-mar più non
seiz'd me, sure a fit of the a-gue has seiz'd me, of all mo-tion be-reft, I'm dis-
cresc.
p
Don Giovanni.
C.
G.
ho. Par-la, par-la, a - scol - tan - do ti sto.
sought. Speak then, tell me, of fear know I naught.
L.
sò!
traught.
The Commandant.
C.
Tu m'in - vi - ta - sti a ce - na,
Thou didst thy - self in - vite me,
f
cresc.
il tuo do - ver or sa - i, ri - spon - di -
For that I must re - quite thee; Then an - swer
fp
f
p
mi, ri - spon - di - mi, ver - ra - i tu a ce - nar
me, then an - swer me, As my guest, when shall I
f
p
cresc.
p

Don Giovanni. (calmly and coldly.)
me-co?
claim thee?
A tor-to di vil-
Of fear none shall ac-
Leporello. (standing far off, trembling)
Oi-bò, oi-bò; tempo non ha, scu-sa-te.
Say no, say no. he is en-gag'd, excuse him.
(impatiently)
ta-te taccia-to mia sa-rò!
cuse me, To none will I succumb!
The Commandant.
Ho già ri-sol-to.
I have de-termined.
Ri-sol-vi! Ver-
De-ter-mine! Thou'lt
The Commandant.
Don Giovanni.
ra-i?
come then?
Ho fer-mo il co-re in pet-to, Non ho ti-
My heart is firm with-in me, I have no
Leporello.
Di-te di no, di-te di no!
Say that you can't, say that you can't!
Vlns.
(giving his right hand)
mor- ver-rò!
fear, I'll come.
The Commandant. (offering his left hand)
Ec-co-la!
Take it, then!
Dam-mi la ma-no in pe-gno!
Give me thy hand in tok-en!
Wind.

(with a cry of horror)
G.
Ohimè! che ge-lo è que-sto mai?
Ah me! What deadly chill is this?
C.
Cos'hai? pen - ti-ti, can-gia vi - ta, è
What is't? Turn thee, ere heav'n hath doom'd thee, There's
cresc.
l'ul-ti-mo mo-men-to!
time yet for re-pentance.
(vainly tries to free himself)
No, no, ch'io non mi pen-to, van - ne lon-tan da me!
For me there's no re-pentance, Va - nish thou from my sight!
Pen-ti-ti, scel - le - ra-to!
Dread then the wrath e - ter-nal!
No, vec-chio in-fa - tu-a to!
A-way, thou spectre in-fer-nal!
No! No!
Pen-ti-ti! Yet repent!
Pen-ti-ti! Yet repent!

G.
C.
No! no!
No! no!
Sì! sì!
Yes! yes!
(wresting his hand away, with a terrible cry.)
No! no! no!
No! no! no!
Sì! sì! Ah! tem -
Yes! yes! Now must
Allegro. Don Giovanni. (in desperation.)
Da qual tremo - re in-
Terrors unknown are
(Flames appear in all directions,
po più non vè! (Exit.)
my soul take flight!
Allegro.
the earth trembles)
so - li - to sento assa - lir gli spi - ri - ti! don -
freez-ing me, Demons of doom are seiz - ing me, Is

G.
d'e-sco-no quei vor-ti-ci di fo - co pien d'or-ror?
hell let loose to tor-ture me? Or does it mock my sight?
Chorus (from below with hollow voices)
Tut-to a tue
Torments e -
p
f
p cresc.
sf
G.
Chi
My
col-pe è po - co! vie - ni! c'è un mal peg -
ter - nal wait thee! Burn-ing in end-less
f
G.
l'a-nima mi la-cera? Chi m'a-gi-ta le vi-scere? Che
soul is rent with ag-o-ny! Condemn'd to end-less mis-ery, Oh
Leporello.
L.
Che cef - fo di - spe-ra-to! Che ge-sti da dan -
The fire of doom surrounds him, Its fier-y glare con -
gior!
night!
f
G.
stra-zio, ohimè, che sma - nia! Che in - fer - no, che ter -
doom of wrath and ter - ror, No more to see the
L.
na - to! che gri - di! che la - men-ti!
founds him, What sounds, what sights of ter - ror!

G.
ror!
light!
Chi
My
L.
co - me mi fa ter - ror, mi fa ter - ror!
Oh I shall die, oh I shall die of fright!
Chorus of Spirits.
Tut - to a tue col - pe è
Torments e - ter - nal
sf
l'a - nima mi la - cera?
soul is rent with ag - ony,
Chi m'a - gi - ta le
Condemn'd to end - less
Che eef - fo - di - spe - ra - to!
The fire of doom sur - rounds him.
Che
Its
po - co!
wait thee!
Vie - ni! c'è un mal peg - gior!
Burn - ing and end - less night!
f
vi - scere?
mis - ery,
che stra - zio, ohimè, che sma - nia!
Oh doom of wrath and ter - ror!
Ah!
Ah!
ge - sti da dan - na - to! che gri - di! che la - men - ti! che
fier - y glare confounds him, What sounds, what sights of ter - ror, what

G.
che in - fer - no! che ter - ror!
Oh dread - ful, end - less night!
L.
gri - di! che la - menti! co - me mi fa ter - ror!
sounds, what sights of terror! Oh I shall die of fright!
Vie - ni! vie - ni! vie - ni! c'è un mal peg -
end - less, end - less, Burning and end-less
D. Giov.
(The flames increase and engulf Don Giovanni)
Leporello.
G.
L.
Ah!
Ah!
Ah!
Ah!
gior!
night.
sf
p
f
p
cresc.
Allegro assai.
Donna Elvira and Zerlina.
E.
Z.
Ah! dov' è il
Where is the
Don Octavio.
O.
(All enter, accompanied by ministers of justice.)
Ah! dov' è il
Where is the
Masetto.
M.
Ah! dov' è il
Where is the
Allegro assai.
f
f

per - fi - do? dov' è l'in - degno? tut-to il mio sdegno
mis - cre-ant? Where is the traitor? By fate o'er - taken,
sfo-gar io vo', sfo-gar io vo'!
Now fall-en low, now fall - en low!
Donna Anna.
So - lo mi - ran - dolo. stret - to in ca - te - ne, al - le mie pe - ne cal - ma da - rò.
Seize him, im - pris - on him, Who ne'er re - lent - ed, Who ne'er re - pent - ed! No mer - cy shew.
Leporello (appears, pale and trembling.)
Più non spe - ra - te di ritro - varlo, più non cerca - te_
Not here you'll find him, For ev - er vanish'd, Flames went behind him,

Donna Anna, Elvira and Zerlina.
A. E. Z.
Cos' è? fa - vel-la! cos' è? fa -
Say what be - fell him? say what be -
Don Octavio.
O.
Cos' è? fa - vel-la! cos' è? fa -
Say what be - fell him? say what be -
Masetto.
M.
Cos' è? fa - vel-la! cos' è? fa -
Say what be - fell him? say what be -
L.
Lon-tano an - dò, lon - tano an - dò. Ven - ne un co - los - so,
He's gone be - low, he's gone be - low. That man gi - gantic,
f p f
vel-la! Via pre - sto, sbriga-ti! via presto, sbriga - ti!
fell him? Quick, tell us all you know, quick, tell us all you know.
venne un co - losso — Ma se non pos-so, ma se non
that man gi - gantic, He's driv'n me frantic, he's driv'n me
p f p f p

A.
E.
Z.
Pre-sto fa-
Tell us, and
O.
Pre-sto fa-
Tell us, and
M.
Pre-sto fa-
Tell us, and
L.
pos-so, ma se non pos-so, ma se non pos-so, ma se non pos-so—
frantic, he's driv'n me frantic, he's driv'n me frantic, he's driv'n me frantic!
f
vel-la, sbri-ga-ti!
quickly, tell us all.
vel-la, sbri-ga-ti!
quickly, tell us all.
vel-la, sbri-ga-ti!
quickly, tell us all.
Leporello.
Tra fumo e fuoco— ba-da-te un po-co—
Noth-ing I'll garble, That man of marble,
p
l'uo-mo di sas-so— fer-ma-te il pas-so— giu-sto là sot-to—
Grim and tre-mendous, Oh heav'n de-fend us— Came here and warn'd him
sf
p

L.
die-de il gran bot - to - giu - sto là il dia - vo - lo se'l tran - gu -
He mad - ly scorn'd him, 'Mid flamings sul - phurous He went be -
cresc.
f
A.
E.
Z.
Stel - - le! che sen-to!
Tru - - ly a wonder!
O.
Stel - - le! che sen-to!
Tru - - ly a wonder!
M.
Stel - - le! che sen-to!
Tru - - ly a wonder!
L.
giò! Ve-ro è l'e - ven-to.
low. In fire and thunder.
p
f
p
cresc.
f
Donna Anna.
A.
Ah, cer - to è l'om - bra che l'incon -
I saw him too, with mien of
Donna Elvira.
E.
Ah, cer - to è l'om - - bra che m'in - con -
I saw the spec - - tre with mien of
Zerlina.
Z.
Ah, cer - to è
I saw the
Don Octavio.
O.
Ah, cer - to è
I saw the
p

A.
trò,
woe,
Ah!
I
cer - to è l'om - - bra
saw the spec - - tre
E.
trò,
woe,
Ah!
I
cer - to è l'om - - bra
saw the spec - - tre
Z.
l'ombra,
spectre,
Ah!
I
cer - to è l'om - - bra
saw the spec - - tre
O.
l'ombra,
spectre,
Ah!
I
cer - to è l'om - - bra
saw the spec - - tre
Masetto.
M.
Ah! cer - to è l'om - - bra, è l'om - - bra
I saw the spec - - tre, the spec - - tre
A.
che l'in - con - trò, ah! cer-to è l'om-bra,
with mien of woe, I saw him, I saw him,
E.
che m'in - con - trò, ah! cer-to è l'om-bra,
with mien of woe, I saw him, I saw him,
Z.
che m'in - con - trò, ah! cer-to è l'om-bra,
with mien of woe, I saw him, I saw him,
O.
che m'in - con - trò, ah! cer-to è l'om-bra,
with mien of woe, I saw him, I saw him,
M.
che m'in - con - trò, ah! cer-to è l'om-bra,
with mien of woe, I saw him, I saw him,

A.
ah! cer - to, cer - to e l'om - - - - bra che
I saw, I saw the spec - - - - tre with
E.
ah! cer-to, ah cer - to è l'om-bra che
I saw him, I saw the spec-tre with
Z.
ah! cer - to, cer - to è l'om - - bra che m'in - -
I saw, I saw the spec - - - tre with mien
O.
ah! cer-to e l'om - bra che m'in - -
I saw him, I saw him with mien
M.
ah! cer - - - to e l'om - - bra che m'in - -
I saw the spec - - tre with mien
A.
l'in - con - trò.
mien of woe.
E.
m'in - con - trò.
mien of woe.
Z.
con - trò.
of woe.
O.
con trò.
of woe.
M.
con - trò.
of woe.
cresc.
f

Larghetto.
Don Octavio.
(to Donna Anna.)
O.
Or che tut-ti, o_ mio te-so-ro! ven-di-ca-ti_siam dal
Heav'n it-self then our cause has righted! Days of peace now_dawn be-
Str.
p
cie-lo, por-gi, por-gi, a me un ri-sto-ro, non mi_
fore us, Grant, oh grant then the vows we plight-ed, Now at_
Wind sustain
Fag.
Donna Anna.
O.
A.
far_ lan-guire an-cor. Lascia, o ca-ro! un an-no an-
last_ may be_ ful-fill'd. I but ask_ thee, oh my be-
Vlns.
co-ra, al-lo sfo-go del mio cor.
lov'd one, To de-lay_ but one short year,
cresc.
Al de-sio di chi t'a-do-ra,
Lov-ers' pleadings are commandments,
D. Octavio.
Al de-sio di chi m'a-do-ra, ce-der deve un fi-do a-
Lov-ers' pleadings are commandments, On thy faithful love I_
p

 (giving Don O. her hand.)

A.
ce- der deve un fi- do a-mor, ce-der de-ve, ce- der de- ve un fi- do a-
On thy faithful love I build, on thy faithful love, thy faith- ful love I
O.
mor, ce-der de-ve, ce- der de- ve un fi- do a-
build, on thy faithful love, thy faith- ful love I
A.
mor. Al de- sio di chi t'a- do- ra,
build, Lov- ers' pleadings are commandments,
O.
mor. Al de- sio di- chi m'a-
build, Lov- ers' pleadings are com-
A.
ce der deve un fi- do a-mor, ce-der de-ve, ce- der
on thy faithful love I build, lovers' pleadings are com-
O.
do- ra, ce- der deve un fi- do amor, ce-der de-ve, ce- der
mandments, on thy faithful love I build, lovers' pleadings are com-
A.
de- ve un fi- do a- mor, un-
mandments, up- on thy faith- ful
O.
de- ve un fi- do a- mor, un
mandments, up- on thy faith- ful

A.
fi - do un fi - do a - mor.
love, thy love I build.
(to Donna A. and Don O.)
Donna Elvira.
E.
Io men vado in un ri - ti - ro, a fi - nir la vi - ta
To a convent I be - take me, There to end my troubled
O.
fi - do un fi - do a - mor.
love, thy love I build.
mi - a!
life.
Zerlina.
Z.
Noi, Ma - setto, a casa an - diamo! a cenar in compa - gni - a.
Now Ma - set - to, wait no longer, Till we two are man and wife.
Masetto.
M.
Noi, Zer - lina, a casa an - diamo! a cenar in compa - gni - a.
Now Zer - li - na, wait no longer, Till we two are man and wife.
Leporello.
L.
Ed io vado all' o - ste -
And I'll seek another
Zerlina.
Re - sti dunque quel birbon, con Pro - ser - pina e Plu -
And let him in flames a - tone, Who no mer - cy e'er has
Masetto.
Re - sti dunque quel birbon, con Pro - ser - pina e Plu -
And let him in flames a - tone, Who no mer - cy e'er has
ri - a a tro - var padron miglior. Re - sti dunque quel birbon, con Pro - ser - pina e Plu -
master, and be - gin anoth - er life. And let him in flames a - tone, Who no mer - cy e'er has
f

Z.
ton, con Pro-ser-pi-na e Plu-ton. E noi
shewn, Who no mer-cy e'er has shewn. And now
M.
ton, con Pro-ser-pi-na e Plu-ton. E noi
shewn, Who no mer-cy e'er has shewn. And now
L.
ton, con Pro-ser-pi-na e Plu-ton. E noi
shewn, Who no mer-cy e'er has shewn. And now
Fl. Vln.
tr
p
Z.
tut-ti o buo-na-gen-te, ri-pe-tiam al-le-gra-mente l'an-ti-
let us all_ u-nit-ed Sing the verse of old in-dit-ed, Join in
M.
tut-ti o buo-na gen-te, ri-pe-tiam al-le-gra-men-te l'an-ti-
let us all u-nit-ed Sing the verse of old in-dit-ed, Join in
L.
tut-ti o buo-na gen-te, ri-pe-tiam al-le-gra-men-te l'an-ti-
let us all u-nit-ed Sing the verse of old in-dit-ed, Join in
tr
tr
Z.
chis-si-ma can-zon, l'an-ti-chis-si-ma can-zon, l'an-ti-chis-si-ma can-zon:
cho-rus ev-'ry_ one, join in cho-rus ev-'ry one, join in cho-rus ev-'ry one.
M.
chis-si-ma can-zon, l'an-ti-chis-si-ma can-zon, l'an-ti-chis-si-ma can-zon:
cho-rus ev-'ry one, join in cho-rus ev-'ry one, join in cho-rus ev-'ry one.
L.
chis-si-ma can-zon, l'an-ti-chis-si-ma can-zon, l'an-ti-chis-si-ma can-zon:
cho-rus ev-'ry one, join in cho-rus ev-'ry one, join in cho-rus ev-'ry one.

Presto.
Donna Anna.
sotto voce
Que - sto è il fin di chi fa mal, di
Lib - er - tines, ye thus shall end, ye
Str.
chi fa mal, Questo è il fin,
thus shall end, Lib - er - tines,
Donna Elvira.
Que - sto è il fin,
Lib - er - tines,
Zerlina.
sotto voce
Que - sto è il
Lib - er -
Don Octavio.
Que - sto è il fin,
Lib - er - tines,
Masetto.
Que - sto è il fin,
Lib - er - tines,
Leporello.
Que - sto è il fin,
Lib - er - tines,
Wind.
Zerlina.
fin di chi fa mal, di chi fa mal.
tines, ye thus shall end, ye thus shall end.

Donna Anna and Donna Elvira.
(unis.)
A.
E.
Que - sto è il fin, que - sto è il fin di chi fa mal, di
Lib - er - tines, lib - er - tines, ye thus shall end, ye
Z.
Que- sto è il fin, que - sto è il fin di chi fa mal, di
Lib - er - tines, lib - er - tines, ye thus shall end, ye
O.
Que- sto è il fin, que - sto è il fin di chi fa mal, di
Lib - er - tines, lib - er - tines, ye thus shall end, ye
M.
Que - sto è il fin di chi fa mal, di
Lib- -er- -tines, ye thus shall end, ye
L.
Que - sto è il fin di chi fa mal, di
Lib- -er- -tines, ye thus shall end, ye
tr
A.
E.
chi fa mal, di chi fa mal, que- sto è il fin di
thus shall end, ye thus shall end. Lib - er - tines, ye
Z.
chi fa mal, di chi fa mal, que- sto è il fin di
thus shall end, ye thus shall end. Lib - er - tines, ye
O.
chi fa mal, di chi fa mal, que- sto è il fin di
thus shall end, ye thus shall end. Lib - er - tines, ye
M.
chi fa mal, di chi fa mal, que- sto è il fin di
thus shall end, ye thus shall end. Lib - er - tines, ye
L.
chi fa mal, di chi fa mal, que- sto è il fin di
thus shall end, ye thus shall end. Lib - er - tines, ye
tr
tr

A.
E.
chi fa mal, di chi fa mal. E de'
thus shall end, ye thus shall end. He who
Z.
chi fa mal, di chi fa mal. E de'
thus shall end, ye thus shall end. He who
O.
chi fa mal, di chi fa mal. E de'
thus shall end, ye thus shall end. He who
M.
chi fa mal, di chi fa mal. E de'
thus shall end, ye thus shall end. He who
L.
chi fa mal, di chi fa mal. E de'
thus shall end, ye thus shall end. He who
Vlns.
Tutti
A.
E.
per - - fi - di la mor - - -
wrought for sel- - fish plea - - -
Z.
per - - fi - di la mor - - -
wrought for sel- - fish plea - - -
O.
per - - fi - di la mor - - -
wrought for sel- - fish plea - - -
M.
per - - fi - di la mor - - -
wrought for sel- - fish plea - - -
L.
per - - fi - di la mor - - -
wrought for sel- - fish plea - - -

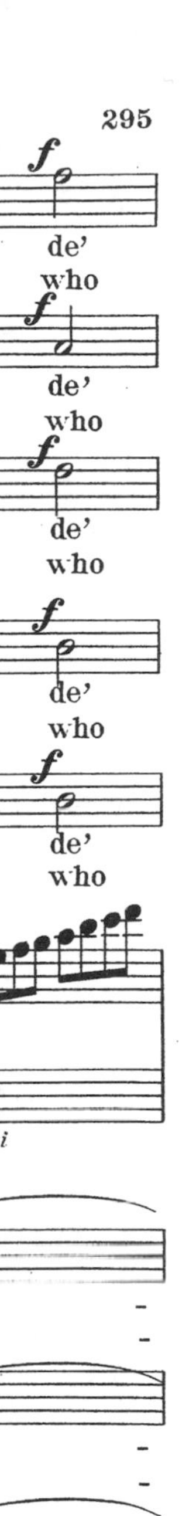

A.
E.
- - te al - la vi - ta _ è _
- - sure, Shall de - part with -
Z.
- - te al - la _ vi - ta _ è _
- - sure, Shall de - part with -
O.
- - te al - la vi - ta è
- - sure, Shall _ de - part _ with -
M.
- - te al - la vi - ta è
- - sure, Shall _ de - part _ with -
L.
- - te al - la
- - sure, Shall de -
Wind
Cello
A.
E.
sem - pre, è sem - pre u - gual, _ è sempre u - gual.
out, yes, with - out _ a friend, _ with - out a friend.
Z.
sem - pre è sem - pre u - gual, _ è sempre u - gual.
out, _ with - out _ a friend, _ with - out a friend.
O.
sem - pre, è sem - pre u - gual, _ è sempre u - gual.
out, _ yes, with - out a friend, _ with - out a friend.
M.
sem - pre, è sem - pre u - gual, _ è sempre u - gual.
out, yes, with - out a friend, _ with - out a friend.
L.
vi - ta è sem - pre u - gual, _ è sempre u - gual.
part, and with - out a friend, _ with - out a friend.

A.
E.
E de' per- -fi - di la
He who wrought for sel- -fish
Z.
E' de' per- -fi - di la
He who wrought for sel- -fish
O.
E de' per- -fi - di la
He who wrought for sel- -fish
M.
E de' per- -fi - di la
He who wrought for sel- -fish
L.
E de' per- -fi - di la
He who wrought for sel- -fish
A.
E.
mor - - - - te al -
plea - - - - sure Shall
Z.
mor - - - - te al -
plea - - - - sure Shall
O.
mor - - - - te al -
plea - - - - sure Shall
M.
mor - - - - te al -
plea - - - - sure Shall
L.
mor - - - - te
plea - - - - sure

A.
E.
la vi - ta è sem - - pre è sem -
de - part with - out, yes, with - out,
Z.
la vi - ta è sem - pre u - gual,
de - part with - out, a friend,
O.
la vi - ta è sem - pre, è sem - - -
de - part, shall de - part, and with - out
M.
la vi - ta è sem - pre, è sem - - -
de - part shall de - part, and with - out
L.
p
al - la vi - ta è sem - - -
Shall de - part, and with - out
tr
p
tr
A.
E.
- - pre, è sem - - - - -
with - out
Z.
è sem - - - -
with - out
O.
- - pre, è sem -
a friend, with - out
M.
L.
tr
tr
tr
tr
tr

A.
E.
Z.
O.
M.
L.
f
- pre u-gual, al - la vi - ta è sem - pre u - gual,
a friend, Shall de - part with - out a friend,
- pre u - gual, al - la vi - ta è sem - pre u - gual,
a friend, Shall de - part with - out a friend,
pre u - gual, al - la vi - ta è sem - pre u - gual,
a friend, Shall de - part with - out a friend,
pre u - gual, al - la vi - ta è sem - pre u - gual,
a friend, Shall de - part with - out a friend,
pre u - gual, al - la vi - ta è sem - pre u - gual,
a friend, Shall de - part with - out a friend,
al - la vi - ta è sem - pre u - gual, è sem - pre u -
shall de - part with - out a friend, with - out a

A.
E.
gual, è sem - pre u - gual, sem - pre u -
friend, with - out a friend. Thus they
Z.
gual, è sem - pre u - gual, sem - pre u -
friend, with - out a friend. Thus they
O.
gual, è sem - pre u - gual, sem - pre u -
friend, with - out a friend. Thus they
M.
gual, è sem - pre u - gual, sem - pre u -
friend, with - out a friend. Thus they
L.
gual, è sem - pre u - gual, sem - pre u -
friend, with - out a friend. Thus they
A.
E.
gual.
end.
Z.
gual.
end.
O.
gual.
end.
M.
gual.
end.
L.
gual.
end.
Strs.
p
tr
tr
Wind
tr
Tutti
f
End of the Opera.

Dover Opera, Choral and Lieder Scores

Bach, Johann Sebastian, ELEVEN GREAT CANTATAS. Full vocal-instrumental score from Bach-Gesellschaft edition. *Christ lag in Todesbanden, Ich hatte viel Bekümmerniss, Jauchhzet Gott in allen Landen,* eight others. Study score. 350pp. 9 x 12. 23268-9

Bach, Johann Sebastian, MASS IN B MINOR IN FULL SCORE. The crowning glory of Bach's lifework in the field of sacred music and a universal statement of Christian faith, reprinted from the authoritative Bach-Gesellschaft edition. Translation of texts. 320pp. 9 x 12. 25992-7

Bach, Johann Sebastian, SEVEN GREAT SACRED CANTATAS IN FULL SCORE. Seven favorite sacred cantatas. Printed from a clear, modern engraving and sturdily bound; new literal line-for-line translations. Reliable Bach-Gesellschaft edition. Complete German texts. 256pp. 9 x 12. 24950-6

Bach, Johann Sebastian, SIX GREAT SECULAR CANTATAS IN FULL SCORE. Bach's nearest approach to comic opera. *Hunting Cantata, Wedding Cantata, Aeolus Appeased, Phoebus and Pan, Coffee Cantata,* and *Peasant Cantata.* 286pp. 9 x 12. 23934-9

Beethoven, Ludwig van, FIDELIO IN FULL SCORE. Beethoven's only opera, complete in one affordable volume, including all spoken German dialogue. Republication of C. F. Peters, Leipzig edition. 272pp. 9 x 12. 24740-6

Beethoven, Ludwig van, SONGS FOR SOLO VOICE AND PIANO. 71 lieder, including "Adelaide," "Wonne der Wehmuth," "Die ehre Gottes aus der Natur," and famous cycle *An die ferne Geliebta.* Breitkopf & Härtel edition. 192pp. 9 x 12. 25125-X

Bizet, Georges, CARMEN IN FULL SCORE. Complete, authoritative score of perhaps the world's most popular opera, in the version most commonly performed today, with recitatives by Ernest Guiraud. 574pp. 9 x 12. 25820-3

Brahms, Johannes, COMPLETE SONGS FOR SOLO VOICE AND PIANO (two volumes). A total of 113 songs in complete score by greatest lieder writer since Schubert. Series I contains 15-song cycle *Die Schone Magelone*; Series II includes famous "Lullaby." Total of 448pp. 9⅜ x 12¼.
Series I: 23820-2
Series II: 23821-0

Brahms, Johannes, COMPLETE SONGS FOR SOLO VOICE AND PIANO: Series III. 64 songs, published from 1877 to 1886, include such favorites as "Geheimnis," "Alte Liebe," and "Vergebliches Standchen." 224pp. 9 x 12. 23822-9

Brahms, Johannes, COMPLETE SONGS FOR SOLO VOICE AND PIANO: Series IV. 120 songs that complete the Brahms song oeuvre, with sensitive arrangements of 91 folk and traditional songs. 240pp. 9 x 12. 23823-7

Brahms, Johannes, GERMAN REQUIEM IN FULL SCORE. Definitive Breitkopf & Härtel edition of Brahms's greatest vocal work, fully scored for solo voices, mixed chorus and orchestra. 208pp. 9⅜ x 12¼. 25486-0

Debussy, Claude, PELLÉAS ET MÉLISANDE IN FULL SCORE. Reprinted from the E. Fromont (1904) edition, this volume faithfully reproduces the full orchestral-vocal score of Debussy's sole and enduring opera masterpiece. 416pp. 9 x 12. (Available in U.S. only) 24825-9

Debussy, Claude, SONGS, 1880–1904. Rich selection of 36 songs set to texts by Verlaine, Baudelaire, Pierre Louÿs, Charles d'Orleans, others. 175pp. 9 x 12. 24131-9

Fauré, Gabriel, SIXTY SONGS. "Clair de lune," "Apres un reve," "Chanson du pecheur," "Automne," and other great songs set for medium voice. Reprinted from French editions. 288pp. 8⅜ x 11. (Not available in France or Germany) 26534-X

Gilbert, W. S. and Sullivan, Sir Arthur, THE AUTHENTIC GILBERT & SULLIVAN SONGBOOK, 92 songs, uncut, original keys, in piano renderings approved by Sullivan. 399pp. 9 x 12. 23482-7

Gilbert, W. S. and Sullivan, Sir Arthur, HMS PINAFORE IN FULL SCORE. New edition by Carl Simpson and Ephraim Hammett Jones. Some of Gilbert's most clever flashes of wit and a number of Sullivan's most charming melodies in a handsome, authoritative new edition based on original manuscripts and early sources. 256pp. 9 x 12. 42201-1

Gilbert, W. S. and Sullivan, Sir Arthur (Carl Simpson and Ephraim Hammett Jones, eds.), THE PIRATES OF PENZANCE IN FULL SCORE. New performing edition corrects numerous errors, offers performers the choice of two versions of the Act II finale, and gives the first accurate full score of the "Climbing over Rocky Mountain" section. 288pp. 9 x 12. 41891-X

Hale, Philip (ed.), FRENCH ART SONGS OF THE NINETEENTH CENTURY: 39 Works from Berlioz to Debussy. 39 songs from romantic period by 18 composers: Berlioz, Chausson, Debussy (six songs), Gounod, Massenet, Thomas, etc. French text, English singing translation for high voice. 182pp. 9 x 12. (Not available in France or Germany) 23680-3

Handel, George Frideric, GIULIO CESARE IN FULL SCORE. Great Baroque masterpiece reproduced directly from authoritative Deutsche Handelgesellschaft edition. Gorgeous melodies, inspired orchestration. Complete and unabridged. 160pp. 9⅜ x 12¼. 25056-3

Handel, George Frideric, MESSIAH IN FULL SCORE. An authoritative full-score edition of the oratorio that is the best-known, most-beloved, most-performed large-scale musical work in the English-speaking world. 240pp. 9 x 12. 26067-4

Lehar, Franz, THE MERRY WIDOW: Complete Score for Piano and Voice in English. Complete score for piano and voice, reprinted directly from the first English translation (1907) published by Chappell & Co., London. 224pp. 8⅜ x 11¼. (Available in U.S. only) 24514-4

Liszt, Franz, THIRTY SONGS. Selection of extremely worthwhile though not widely-known songs. Texts in French, German, and Italian, all with English translations. Piano, high voice. 144pp. 9 x 12. 23197-6

Monteverdi, Claudio, MADRIGALS: BOOK IV & V. 39 finest madrigals with new line-for-line literal English translations of the poems facing the Italian text. 256pp. 8⅛ x 11. (Available in U.S. only) 25102-0

Moussorgsky, Modest Petrovich, BORIS GODUNOV IN FULL SCORE (Rimsky-Korsakov Version). Russian operatic masterwork in most-recorded, most-performed version. Authoritative Moscow edition. 784pp. 8⅜ x 11¼. 25321-X

Mozart, Wolfgang Amadeus, THE ABDUCTION FROM THE SERAGLIO IN FULL SCORE. Mozart's early comic masterpiece, exactingly reproduced from the authoritative Breitkopf & Härtel edition. 320pp. 9 x 12. 26004-6

Mozart, Wolfgang Amadeus, COSI FAN TUTTE IN FULL SCORE. Scholarly edition of one of Mozart's greatest operas. Da Ponte libretto. Commentary. Preface. Translated Front Matter. 448pp. 9⅜ x 12¼. (Available in U.S. only) 24528-4

Dover Orchestral Scores

Bach, Johann Sebastian, COMPLETE CONCERTI FOR SOLO KEYBOARD AND ORCHESTRA IN FULL SCORE. Bach's seven complete concerti for solo keyboard and orchestra in full score from the authoritative Bach-Gesellschaft edition. 206pp. 9 x 12. 24929-8

Bach, Johann Sebastian, THE SIX BRANDENBURG CONCERTOS AND THE FOUR ORCHESTRAL SUITES IN FULL SCORE. Complete standard Bach-Gesellschaft editions in large, clear format. Study score. 273pp. 9 x 12. 23376-6

Bach, Johann Sebastian, THE THREE VIOLIN CONCERTI IN FULL SCORE. Concerto in A Minor, BWV 1041; Concerto in E Major, BWV 1042; and Concerto for Two Violins in D Minor, BWV 1043. Bach-Gesellschaft editions. 64pp. 9⅜ x 12¼. 25124-1

Beethoven, Ludwig van, COMPLETE PIANO CONCERTOS IN FULL SCORE. Complete scores of five great Beethoven piano concertos, with all cadenzas as he wrote them, reproduced from authoritative Breitkopf & Härtel edition. New Table of Contents. 384pp. 9⅜ x 12¼. 24563-2

Beethoven, Ludwig van, SIX GREAT OVERTURES IN FULL SCORE. Six staples of the orchestral repertoire from authoritative Breitkopf & Härtel edition. *Leonore Overtures,* Nos. 1–3; Overtures to *Coriolanus, Egmont, Fidelio.* 288pp. 9 x 12. 24789-9

Beethoven, Ludwig van, SYMPHONIES NOS. 1, 2, 3, AND 4 IN FULL SCORE. Republication of H. Litolff edition. 272pp. 9 x 12. 26033-X

Beethoven, Ludwig van, SYMPHONIES NOS. 5, 6 AND 7 IN FULL SCORE, Ludwig van Beethoven. Republication of H. Litolff edition. 272pp. 9 x 12. 26034-8

Beethoven, Ludwig van, SYMPHONIES NOS. 8 AND 9 IN FULL SCORE. Republication of H. Litolff edition. 256pp. 9 x 12. 26035-6

Beethoven, Ludwig van; Mendelssohn, Felix; and Tchaikovsky, Peter Ilyitch, GREAT ROMANTIC VIOLIN CONCERTI IN FULL SCORE. The Beethoven Op. 61, Mendelssohn Op. 64 and Tchaikovsky Op. 35 concertos reprinted from Breitkopf & Härtel editions. 224pp. 9 x 12. 24989-1

Brahms, Johannes, COMPLETE CONCERTI IN FULL SCORE. Piano Concertos Nos. 1 and 2; Violin Concerto, Op. 77; Concerto for Violin and Cello, Op. 102. Definitive Breitkopf & Härtel edition. 352pp. 9⅜ x 12¼. 24170-X

Brahms, Johannes, COMPLETE SYMPHONIES. Full orchestral scores in one volume. No. 1 in C Minor, Op. 68; No. 2 in D Major, Op. 73; No. 3 in F Major, Op. 90; and No. 4 in E Minor, Op. 98. Reproduced from definitive Vienna Gesellschaft der Musikfreunde edition. Study score. 344pp. 9 x 12. 23053-8

Brahms, Johannes, THREE ORCHESTRAL WORKS IN FULL SCORE: Academic Festival Overture, Tragic Overture and Variations on a Theme by Joseph Haydn. Reproduced from the authoritative Breitkopf & Härtel edition three of Brahms's great orchestral favorites. Editor's commentary in German and English. 112pp. 9⅜ x 12¼. 24637-X

Chopin, Frédéric, THE PIANO CONCERTOS IN FULL SCORE. The authoritative Breitkopf & Härtel full-score edition in one volume; Piano Concertos No. 1 in E Minor and No. 2 in F Minor. 176pp. 9 x 12. 25835-1

Corelli, Arcangelo, COMPLETE CONCERTI GROSSI IN FULL SCORE. All 12 concerti in the famous late nineteenth-century edition prepared by violinist Joseph Joachim and musicologist Friedrich Chrysander. 240pp. 8⅜ x 11¼. 25606-5

Debussy, Claude, THREE GREAT ORCHESTRAL WORKS IN FULL SCORE. Three of the Impressionist's most-recorded, most-performed favorites: *Prélude à l'Après-midi d'un Faune, Nocturnes,* and *La Mer.* Reprinted from early French editions. 279pp. 9 x 12. 24441-5

Dvořák, Antonín, SERENADE NO. 1, OP. 22, AND SERENADE NO. 2, OP. 44, IN FULL SCORE. Two works typified by elegance of form, intense harmony, rhythmic variety, and uninhibited emotionalism. 96pp. 9 x 12. 41895-2

Dvořák, Antonín, SYMPHONY NO. 8 IN G MAJOR, OP. 88, SYMPHONY NO. 9 IN E MINOR, OP. 95 ("NEW WORLD") IN FULL SCORE. Two celebrated symphonies by the great Czech composer, the Eighth and the immensely popular Ninth, "From the New World," in one volume. 272pp. 9 x 12. 24749-X

Elgar, Edward, CELLO CONCERTO IN E MINOR, OP. 85, IN FULL SCORE. A tour de force for any cellist, this frequently performed work is widely regarded as an elegy for a lost world. Melodic and evocative, it exhibits a remarkable scope, ranging from tragic passion to buoyant optimism. Reproduced from an authoritative source. 112pp. 8⅜ x 11. 41896-0

Franck, César, SYMPHONY IN D MINOR IN FULL SCORE. Superb, authoritative edition of Franck's only symphony, an often-performed and recorded masterwork of late French romantic style. 160pp. 9 x 12. 25373-2

Handel, George Frideric, COMPLETE CONCERTI GROSSI IN FULL SCORE. Monumental Opus 6 Concerti Grossi, Opus 3 and "Alexander's Feast" Concerti Grossi–19 in all–reproduced from the most authoritative edition. 258pp. 9⅜ x 12¼. 24187-4

Handel, George Frideric, GREAT ORGAN CONCERTI, OPP. 4 & 7, IN FULL SCORE. 12 organ concerti composed by the great Baroque master are reproduced in full score from the Deutsche Handelgesellschaft edition. 138pp. 9⅜ x 12¼. 24462-8

Handel, George Frideric, WATER MUSIC AND MUSIC FOR THE ROYAL FIREWORKS IN FULL SCORE. Full scores of two of the most popular Baroque orchestral works performed today–reprinted from the definitive Deutsche Handelgesellschaft edition. Total of 96pp. 8⅝ x 11. 25070-9

Haydn, Joseph, SYMPHONIES 88–92 IN FULL SCORE: The Haydn Society Edition. Full score of symphonies Nos. 88 through 92. Large, readable noteheads, ample margins for fingerings, etc., and extensive Editor's Commentary. 304pp. 9 x 12. (Available in U.S. only) 24445-8

Liszt, Franz, THE PIANO CONCERTI IN FULL SCORE. Here in one volume are Piano Concerto No. 1 in E-flat Major and Piano Concerto No. 2 in A Major–among the most studied, recorded, and performed of all works for piano and orchestra. 144pp. 9 x 12. 25221-3

Mahler, Gustav, DAS LIED VON DER ERDE IN FULL SCORE. Mahler's masterpiece, a fusion of song and symphony, reprinted from the original 1912 Universal Edition. English translations of song texts. 160pp. 9 x 12. 25657-X

Mahler, Gustav, SYMPHONIES NOS. 1 AND 2 IN FULL SCORE. Unabridged, authoritative Austrian editions of Symphony No. 1 in D Major ("Titan") and Symphony No. 2 in C Minor ("Resurrection"). 384pp. 8⅛ x 11. 25473-9

Mahler, Gustav, SYMPHONIES NOS. 3 AND 4 IN FULL SCORE. Two brilliantly contrasting masterworks–one scored for a massive ensemble, the other for small orchestra and soloist–reprinted from authoritative Viennese editions. 368pp. 9⅜ x 12¼. 26166-2

Dover Orchestral Scores

Mahler, Gustav, SYMPHONY NO. 8 IN FULL SCORE. Authoritative edition of massive, complex "Symphony of a Thousand." Scored for orchestra, eight solo voices, double chorus, boys' choir and organ. Reprint of Izdatel'stvo "Muzyka," Moscow, edition. Translation of texts. 272pp. 9⅜ x 12¼. 26022-4

Mendelssohn, Felix, MAJOR ORCHESTRAL WORKS IN FULL SCORE. Considered to be Mendelssohn's finest orchestral works, here in one volume are the complete *Midsummer Night's Dream; Hebrides Overture; Calm Sea and Prosperous Voyage Overture;* Symphony No. 3 in A ("Scottish"); and Symphony No. 4 in A ("Italian"). Breitkopf & Härtel edition. Study score. 406pp. 9 x 12. 23184-4

Mozart, Wolfgang Amadeus, CONCERTI FOR WIND INSTRUMENTS IN FULL SCORE. Exceptional volume contains ten pieces for orchestra and wind instruments and includes some of Mozart's finest, most popular music. 272pp. 9⅜ x 12¼. 25228-0

Mozart, Wolfgang Amadeus, LATER SYMPHONIES. Full orchestral scores to last symphonies (Nos. 35–41) reproduced from definitive Breitkopf & Härtel Complete Works edition. Study score. 285pp. 9 x 12. 23052-X

Mozart, Wolfgang Amadeus, PIANO CONCERTOS NOS. 11–16 IN FULL SCORE. Authoritative Breitkopf & Härtel edition of six staples of the concerto repertoire, including Mozart's cadenzas for Nos. 12–16. 256pp. 9⅜ x 12¼. 25468-2

Mozart, Wolfgang Amadeus, PIANO CONCERTOS NOS. 17–22 IN FULL SCORE. Six complete piano concertos in full score, with Mozart's own cadenzas for Nos. 17–19. Breitkopf & Härtel edition. Study score. 370pp. 9⅜ x 12¼. 23599-8

Mozart, Wolfgang Amadeus, PIANO CONCERTOS NOS. 23–27 IN FULL SCORE. Mozart's last five piano concertos in full score, plus cadenzas for Nos. 23 and 27, and the Concert Rondo in D Major, K.382. Breitkopf & Härtel edition. Study score. 310pp. 9⅜ x 12¼. 23600-5

Mozart, Wolfgang Amadeus, 17 DIVERTIMENTI FOR VARIOUS INSTRUMENTS. Sparkling pieces of great vitality and brilliance from 1771 to 1779; consecutively numbered from 1 to 17. Reproduced from definitive Breitkopf & Härtel Complete Works edition. Study score. 241pp. 9⅜ x 12¼. 23862-8

Mozart, Wolfgang Amadeus, THE VIOLIN CONCERTI AND THE SINFONIA CONCERTANTE, K.364, IN FULL SCORE. All five violin concerti and famed double concerto reproduced from authoritative Breitkopf & Härtel Complete Works Edition. 208pp. 9⅜ x 12¼. 25169-1

Ravel, Maurice, DAPHNIS AND CHLOE IN FULL SCORE. Definitive full-score edition of Ravel's rich musical setting of a Greek fable by Longus is reprinted here from the original French edition. 320pp. 9⅜ x 12¼. (Not available in France or Germany) 25826-2

Ravel, Maurice, LE TOMBEAU DE COUPERIN and VALSES NOBLES ET SENTIMENTALES IN FULL SCORE. *Le Tombeau de Couperin* consists of "Prelude," "Forlane," "Menuet," and "Rigaudon"; the uninterrupted 8 waltzes of *Valses Nobles et Sentimentales* abound with lilting rhythms and unexpected harmonic subtleties. 144pp. 9⅜ x 12¼. (Not available in France or Germany) 41898-7

Ravel, Maurice, RAPSODIE ESPAGNOLE, MOTHER GOOSE and PAVANE FOR A DEAD PRINCESS IN FULL SCORE. Full authoritative scores of 3 enormously popular works by the great French composer, each rich in orchestral settings. 160pp. 9⅜ x 12¼. 41899-5

Schubert, Franz, FOUR SYMPHONIES IN FULL SCORE. Schubert's four most popular symphonies: No. 4 in C Minor ("Tragic"); No. 5 in B-flat Major; No. 8 in B Minor ("Unfinished"); and No. 9 in C Major ("Great"). Breitkopf & Härtel edition. Study score. 261pp. 9⅜ x 12¼. 23681-1

Schubert, Franz, SYMPHONY NO. 3 IN D MAJOR AND SYMPHONY NO. 6 IN C MAJOR IN FULL SCORE. The former is scored for 12 wind instruments and timpani; the latter is known as "The Little Symphony in C" to distinguish it from Symphony No. 9, "The Great Symphony in C." Authoritative editions. 128pp. 9⅜ x 12¼. 42134-1

Schumann, Robert, COMPLETE SYMPHONIES IN FULL SCORE. No. 1 in B-flat Major, Op. 38 ("Spring"); No. 2 in C Major, Op. 61; No. 3 in E-flat Major, Op. 97 ("Rhenish"); and No. 4 in D Minor, Op. 120. Breitkopf & Härtel editions. Study score. 416pp. 9⅜ x 12¼. 24013-4

Schumann, Robert, GREAT WORKS FOR PIANO AND ORCHESTRA IN FULL SCORE. Collection of three superb pieces for piano and orchestra, including the popular Piano Concerto in A Minor. Breitkopf & Härtel edition. 183pp. 9⅜ x 12¼. 24340-0

Strauss, Johann, Jr., THE GREAT WALTZES IN FULL SCORE. Complete scores of eight melodic masterpieces: "The Beautiful Blue Danube," "Emperor Waltz," "Tales of the Vienna Woods," "Wiener Blut," and four more. Authoritative editions. 336pp. 8⅞ x 11¼. 26009-7

Strauss, Richard, TONE POEMS, SERIES I: DON JUAN, TOD UND VERKLARUNG, and DON QUIXOTE IN FULL SCORE. Three of the most often performed and recorded works in entire orchestral repertoire, reproduced in full score from original editions. 286pp. 9⅜ x 12¼. (Available in U.S. only) 23754-0

Strauss, Richard, TONE POEMS, SERIES II: TILL EULENSPIEGELS LUSTIGE STREICHE, "ALSO SPRACH ZARATHUSTRA," and EIN HELDENLEBEN IN FULL SCORE. Three important orchestral works, including very popular *Till Eulenspiegel's Merry Pranks*, reproduced in full score from original editions. Study score. 315pp. 9⅜ x 12¼. (Available in U.S. only) 23755-9

Stravinsky, Igor, THE FIREBIRD IN FULL SCORE (Original 1910 Version). Inexpensive edition of modern masterpiece, renowned for brilliant orchestration, glowing color. Authoritative Russian edition. 176pp. 9⅜ x 12¼. (Available in U.S. only) 25535-2

Stravinsky, Igor, PETRUSHKA IN FULL SCORE: Original Version. Full-score edition of Stravinsky's masterful score for the great Ballets Russes 1911 production of *Petrushka*. 160pp. 9⅜ x 12¼. (Available in U.S. only) 25680-4

Stravinsky, Igor, THE RITE OF SPRING IN FULL SCORE. Full-score edition of most famous musical work of the 20th century, created as a ballet score for Diaghilev's Ballets Russes. 176pp. 9⅜ x 12¼. (Available in U.S. only) 25857-2

Tchaikovsky, Peter Ilyitch, FOURTH, FIFTH AND SIXTH SYMPHONIES IN FULL SCORE. Complete orchestral scores of Symphony No. 4 in F Minor, Op. 36; Symphony No. 5 in E Minor, Op. 64; Symphony No. 6 in B Minor, "Pathetique," Op. 74. Study score. Breitkopf & Härtel editions. 480pp. 9⅜ x 12¼. 23861-X

Tchaikovsky, Peter Ilyitch, NUTCRACKER SUITE IN FULL SCORE. Among the most popular ballet pieces ever created; available in a complete, inexpensive, high-quality score to study and enjoy. 128pp. 9 x 12. 25379-1

Tchaikovsky, Peter Ilyitch, ROMEO AND JULIET OVERTURE AND CAPRICCIO ITALIEN IN FULL SCORE. Two of Russian master's most popular compositions. From authoritative Russian edition; new translation of Russian footnotes. 208pp. 8⅜ x 11½. 25217-5

von Weber, Carl Maria, GREAT OVERTURES IN FULL SCORE. Overtures to *Oberon, Der Freischutz, Euryanthe* and *Preciosa* reprinted from authoritative Breitkopf & Härtel editions. 112pp. 9 x 12. 25225-6

Dover Chamber Music Scores

Bach, Johann Sebastian, COMPLETE SUITES FOR UNACCOMPANIED CELLO AND SONATAS FOR VIOLA DA GAMBA. Bach-Gesellschaft edition of the six cello suites (BWV 1007–1012) and three sonatas (BWV 1027–1029), commonly played today on the cello. 112pp. 9⅜ x 12¼. 25641-3

Bach, Johann Sebastian, WORKS FOR VIOLIN. Complete Sonatas and Partitas for Unaccompanied Violin; Six Sonatas for Violin and Clavier. Bach-Gesellschaft edition. 158pp. 9⅜ x 12¼. 23683-8

Beethoven, Ludwig van. COMPLETE SONATAS AND VARIATIONS FOR CELLO AND PIANO. All five sonatas and three sets of variations. Breitkopf & Härtel edition. 176pp. 9⅜ x 12¼. 26441-6

Beethoven, Ludwig van. COMPLETE STRING QUARTETS, Breitkopf & Härtel edition. Six quartets of Opus 18; three quartets of Opus 59; Opera 74, 95, 127, 130, 131, 132, 135 and Grosse Fuge. Study score. 434pp. 9⅜ x 12¼. 22361-2

Beethoven, Ludwig van. COMPLETE VIOLIN SONATAS. All ten sonatas including the "Kreutzer" and "Spring" sonatas in the definitive Breitkopf & Härtel edition. 256pp. 9 x 12. 26277-4

Beethoven, Ludwig van. SIX GREAT PIANO TRIOS IN FULL SCORE. Definitive Breitkopf & Härtel edition of Beethoven's Piano Trios Nos. 1–6 including the "Ghost" and the "Archduke." 224pp. 9⅜ x 12¼. 25398-8

Brahms, Johannes, COMPLETE CHAMBER MUSIC FOR STRINGS AND CLARINET QUINTET. Vienna Gesellschaft der Musikfreunde edition of all quartets, quintets, and sextets without piano. Study edition. 262pp. 8⅞ x 11¼. 21914-3

Brahms, Johannes, COMPLETE PIANO TRIOS. All five piano trios in the definitive Breitkopf & Härtel edition. 288pp. 9 x 12. 25769-X

Brahms, Johannes, COMPLETE SONATAS FOR SOLO INSTRUMENT AND PIANO. All seven sonatas–three for violin, two for cello and two for clarinet (or viola)–reprinted from the authoritative Breitkopf & Härtel edition. 208pp. 9 x 12. 26091-7

Brahms, Johannes, QUINTET AND QUARTETS FOR PIANO AND STRINGS. Full scores of *Quintet in F Minor,* Op. 34; *Quartet in G Minor,* Op. 25; *Quartet in A Major,* Op. 26; *Quartet in C Minor,* Op. 60. Breitkopf & Härtel edition. 298pp. 9 x 12. 24900-X

Debussy, Claude and Ravel, Maurice, STRING QUARTETS BY DEBUSSY AND RAVEL/Claude Debussy: Quartet in G Minor, Op. 10/Maurice Ravel: Quartet in F Major. Authoritative one-volume edition of two influential masterpieces noted for individuality, delicate and subtle beauties. 112pp. 8⅛ x 11. (Not available in France or Germany) 25231-0

Dvořák, Antonín, CHAMBER WORKS FOR PIANO AND STRINGS. Society editions of the F Minor and Dumky piano trios, D Major and E-flat Major piano quartets and A Major piano quintet. 352pp. 8⅜ x 11¼. (Not available in Europe or the United Kingdom) 25663-4

Dvořák, Antonín, FIVE LATE STRING QUARTETS. Treasury of Czech master's finest chamber works: Nos. 10, 11, 12, 13, 14. Reliable Simrock editions. 282pp. 8⅛ x 11. 25135-7

Franck, César, GREAT CHAMBER WORKS. Four great works: Violin Sonata in A Major, Piano Trio in F-sharp Minor, String Quartet in D Major and Piano Quintet in F Minor. From J. Hamelle, Paris and C. F. Peters, Leipzig editions. 248pp. 9⅜ x 12¼. 26546-3

Haydn, Joseph, ELEVEN LATE STRING QUARTETS. Complete reproductions of Op. 74, Nos. 1–3; Op. 76, Nos. 1–6; and Op. 77, Nos. 1 and 2. Definitive Eulenburg edition. Full-size study score. 320pp. 8⅜ x 11¼. 23753-2

Haydn, Joseph, STRING QUARTETS, OPP. 20 and 33, COMPLETE. Complete reproductions of the 12 masterful quartets (six each) of Opp. 20 and 33–in the reliable Eulenburg edition. 272pp. 8⅜ x 11¼. 24852-6

Haydn, Joseph, STRING QUARTETS, OPP. 42, 50 and 54. Complete reproductions of Op. 42 in D Minor; Op. 50, Nos. 1–6 ("Prussian Quartets") and Op. 54, Nos. 1–3. Reliable Eulenburg edition. 224pp. 8⅜ x 11¼. 24262-5

Haydn, Joseph, TWELVE STRING QUARTETS. 12 often-performed works: Op. 55, Nos. 1–3 (including *Razor*); Op. 64, Nos. 1–6; Op. 71, Nos. 1–3. Definitive Eulenburg edition. 288pp. 8⅜ x 11¼. 23933-0

Kreisler, Fritz, CAPRICE VIENNOIS AND OTHER FAVORITE PIECES FOR VIOLIN AND PIANO: With Separate Violin Part, *Liebesfreud, Liebesleid, Schön Rosmarin, Sicilienne and Rigaudon,* more. 64pp. plus slip-in violin part. 9 x 12. (Available in U.S. only) 28489-1

Mendelssohn, Felix, COMPLETE CHAMBER MUSIC FOR STRINGS. All of Mendelssohn's chamber music: Octet, Two Quintets, Six Quartets, and Four Pieces for String Quartet. (Nothing with piano is included.) Complete works edition (1874–7). Study score. 283pp. 9⅜ x 12¼. 23679-X

Mozart, Wolfgang Amadeus, COMPLETE STRING QUARTETS. Breitkopf & Härtel edition. All 23 string quartets plus alternate slow movement to K.156. Study score. 277pp. 9⅜ x 12¼. 22372-8

Mozart, Wolfgang Amadeus, COMPLETE STRING QUINTETS, Wolfgang Amadeus Mozart. All the standard-instrumentation string quintets, plus String Quintet in C Minor, K.406; Quintet with Horn or Second Cello, K.407; and Clarinet Quintet, K.581. Breitkopf & Härtel edition. Study score. 181pp. 9⅜ x 12¼. 23603-X

Schoenberg, Arnold, CHAMBER SYMPHONY NO. 1 FOR 15 SOLO INSTRUMENTS, OP. 9. One of Schoenberg's most pleasing and accessible works, this 1906 piece concentrates all the elements of a symphony into a single movement. 160 pp. 8⅜ x 11. (Available in U.S. only) 41900-2

Schubert, Franz, COMPLETE CHAMBER MUSIC FOR PIANOFORTE AND STRINGS. Breitkopf & Härtel edition. *Trout,* Quartet in F Major, and trios for piano, violin, cello. Study score. 192pp. 9 x 12. 21527-X

Schubert, Franz, COMPLETE CHAMBER MUSIC FOR STRINGS. Reproduced from famous Breitkopf & Härtel edition: Quintet in C Major (1828), 15 quartets and two trios for violin(s), viola, and violincello. Study score. 348pp. 9 x 12. 21463-X

Schumann, Clara (ed.), CHAMBER MUSIC OF ROBERT SCHUMANN, Superb collection of three trios, four quartets, and piano quintet. Breitkopf & Härtel edition. 288pp. 9⅜ x 12¼. 24101-7

Tchaikovsky, Peter Ilyitch, PIANO TRIO IN A MINOR, OP. 50. Charming homage to pianist Nicholas Rubinstein. Distinctively Russian in character, with overtones of regional folk music and dance. Authoritative edition. 120pp. 8⅜ x 11. 42136-8

Tchaikovsky, Peter Ilyitch and Borodin, Alexander, COMPLETE STRING QUARTETS. Tchaikovsky's Quartets Nos. 1–3 and Borodin's Quartets Nos. 1 and 2, reproduced from authoritative editions. 240pp. 8⅜ x 11¼. 28333-X

*Available from your music dealer or write for **free** Music Catalog to*
Dover Publications, Inc., Dept. MUBI, 31 East 2nd Street, Mineola, NY 11501
*Visit us online at **www.doverpublications.com***

Dover Opera, Choral and Lieder Scores

Mozart, Wolfgang Amadeus, DON GIOVANNI: COMPLETE ORCHESTRAL SCORE. Full score that contains everything from the original version, along with later arias, recitatives, and duets added to original score for Vienna performance. Peters edition. Study score. 468pp. 9⅜ x 12¼. (Available in U.S. only) 23026-0

Mozart, Wolfgang Amadeus, THE MAGIC FLUTE (DIE ZAUBERFLÖTE) IN FULL SCORE. Authoritative C. F. Peters edition of Mozart's brilliant last opera still widely popular. Includes all the spoken dialogue. 226pp. 9 x 12. 24783-X

Mozart, Wolfgang Amadeus, THE MARRIAGE OF FIGARO: COMPLETE SCORE. Finest comic opera ever written. Full score, beautifully engraved, includes passages often cut in other editions. Peters edition. Study score. 448pp. 9⅜ x 12¼. (Available in U.S. only) 23751-6

Mozart, Wolfgang Amadeus, REQUIEM IN FULL SCORE. Masterpiece of vocal composition, among the most recorded and performed works in the repertoire. Authoritative edition published by Breitkopf & Härtel, Wiesbaden. 203pp. 8⅜ x 11¼. 25311-2

Offenbach, Jacques, OFFENBACH'S SONGS FROM THE GREAT OPERETTAS. Piano, vocal (French text) for 38 most popular songs: *Orphée, Belle Hélène, Vie Parisienne, Duchesse de Gérolstein,* others. 21 illustrations. 195pp. 9 x 12. 23341-3

Puccini, Giacomo, LA BOHÈME IN FULL SCORE. Authoritative Italian edition of one of the world's most beloved operas. English translations of list of characters and instruments. 416pp. 8⅜ x 11¼. (Not available in United Kingdom, France, Germany or Italy) 25477-1

Rossini, Gioacchino, THE BARBER OF SEVILLE IN FULL SCORE. One of the greatest comic operas ever written, reproduced here directly from the authoritative score published by Ricordi. 464pp. 8⅜ x 11¼. 26019-4

Schubert, Franz, COMPLETE SONG CYCLES. Complete piano, vocal music of *Die Schöne Müllerin, Die Winterreise, Schwanengesang.* Also Drinker English singing translations. Breitkopf & Härtel edition. 217pp. 9⅜ x 12¼. 22649-2

Schubert, Franz, SCHUBERT'S SONGS TO TEXTS BY GOETHE. Only one-volume edition of Schubert's Goethe songs from authoritative Breitkopf & Härtel edition, plus all revised versions. New prose translation of poems. 84 songs. 256pp. 9⅜ x 12¼. 23752-4

Schubert, Franz, 59 FAVORITE SONGS. "Der Wanderer," "Ave Maria," "Hark, Hark, the Lark," and 56 other masterpieces of lieder reproduced from the Breitkopf & Härtel edition. 256pp. 9⅜ x 12¼. 24849-6

Schumann, Robert, SELECTED SONGS FOR SOLO VOICE AND PIANO. Over 100 of Schumann's greatest lieder, set to poems by Heine, Goethe, Byron, others. Breitkopf & Härtel edition. 248pp. 9⅜ x 12¼. 24202-1

Strauss, Richard, DER ROSENKAVALIER IN FULL SCORE. First inexpensive edition of great operatic masterpiece, reprinted complete and unabridged from rare, limited Fürstner edition (1910) approved by Strauss. 528pp. 9⅜ x 12¼. (Available in U.S. only) 25498-4

Strauss, Richard, DER ROSENKAVALIER: VOCAL SCORE. Inexpensive edition reprinted directly from original Fürstner (1911) edition of vocal score. Verbal text, vocal line and piano "reduction." 448pp. 8⅜ x 11¼. (Not available in Europe or the United Kingdom) 25501-8

Strauss, Richard, SALOME IN FULL SCORE. Atmospheric color predominates in composer's first great operatic success. Definitive Fürstner score, now extremely rare. 352pp. 9⅜ x 12¼. (Available in U.S. only) 24208-0

Verdi, Giuseppe, AÏDA IN FULL SCORE. Verdi's glorious, most popular opera, reprinted from an authoritative edition published by G. Ricordi, Milan. 448pp. 9 x 12. 26172-7

Verdi, Giuseppe, FALSTAFF. Verdi's last great work, his first and only comedy. Complete unabridged score from original Ricordi edition. 480pp. 8⅜ x 11¼. 24017-7

Verdi, Giuseppe, OTELLO IN FULL SCORE. The penultimate Verdi opera, his tragic masterpiece. Complete unabridged score from authoritative Ricordi edition, with Front Matter translated. 576pp. 8¼ x 11. 25040-7

Verdi, Giuseppe, REQUIEM IN FULL SCORE. Immensely popular with choral groups and music lovers. Republication of edition published by C. F. Peters, Leipzig. Study score. 204pp. 9⅜ x 12¼. (Available in U.S. only) 23682-X

Wagner, Richard, DAS RHEINGOLD IN FULL SCORE. Complete score, clearly reproduced from B. Schott's authoritative edition. New translation of German Front Matter. 328pp. 9 x 12. 24925-5

Wagner, Richard, DIE MEISTERSINGER VON NÜRNBERG. Landmark in history of opera, in complete vocal and orchestral score of one of the greatest comic operas. C. F. Peters edition, Leipzig. Study score. 823pp. 8¼ x 11. 23276-X

Wagner, Richard, DIE WALKÜRE. Complete orchestral score of the most popular of the operas in the Ring Cycle. Reprint of the edition published in Leipzig by C. F. Peters, ca. 1910. Study score. 710pp. 8⅜ x 11¼. 23566-1

Wagner, Richard, THE FLYING DUTCHMAN IN FULL SCORE. Great early masterpiece reproduced directly from limited Weingartner edition (1896), incorporating Wagner's revisions. Text, stage directions in English, German, Italian. 432pp. 9⅜ x 12¼. 25629-4

Wagner, Richard, GÖTTERDÄMMERUNG. Full operatic score, first time available in U.S. Reprinted directly from rare 1877 first edition. 615pp. 9⅜ x 12¼. 24250-1

Wagner, Richard, LOHENGRIN IN FULL SCORE. Wagner's most accessible opera. Reproduced from first engraved edition (Breitkopf & Härtel, 1887). 295pp. 9⅜ x 12¼. 24335-4

Wagner, Richard, PARSIFAL IN FULL SCORE. Composer's deeply personal treatment of the legend of the Holy Grail, renowned for splendid music, glowing orchestration. C. F. Peters edition. 592pp. 8¼ x 11. 25175-6

Wagner, Richard, SIEGFRIED IN FULL SCORE. *Siegfried,* third opera of Wagner's famous Ring Cycle, is reproduced from first edition (1876). 439pp. 9⅜ x 12¼. 24456-3

Wagner, Richard, TANNHAUSER IN FULL SCORE. Reproduces the original 1845 full orchestral and vocal score as slightly amended in 1847. Included is the ballet music for Act I written for the 1861 Paris production. 576pp. 8⅜ x 11¼. 24649-3

Wagner, Richard, TRISTAN UND ISOLDE. Full orchestral score with complete instrumentation. Study score. 655pp. 8¼ x 11. 22915-7

von Weber, Carl Maria, DER FREISCHÜTZ. Full orchestral score to first Romantic opera, forerunner to Wagner and later developments. Still very popular. Study score, including full spoken text. 203pp. 9 x 12. 23449-5

Wolf, Hugo, THE COMPLETE MÖRIKE SONGS. Splendid settings to music of 53 German poems by Eduard Mörike, including "Der Tambour," "Elfenlied," and "Verborganheit." New prose translations. 208pp. 9⅜ x 12¼. 24380-X

Wolf, Hugo, SPANISH AND ITALIAN SONGBOOKS. Total of 90 songs by great 19th-century master of the genre. Reprint of authoritative C. F. Peters edition. New Translations of German texts. 256pp. 9⅜ x 12¼. 26156-5